W9-CEG-757

Winston-Salem
A HISTORY

Winston-Salem
A HISTORY
by Frank V. Tursi

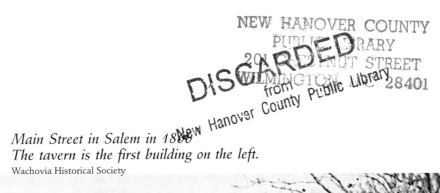

Main Street in Salem in 1866
The tavern is the first building on the left.
Wachovia Historical Society

JOHN F. BLAIR, PUBLISHER
Winston-Salem, North Carolina

MANUFACTURED BY R. R. DONNELLEY & SONS
DESIGNED BY DEBRA LONG HAMPTON

Library of Congress Cataloging-in-Publication Data
Tursi, Frank.
    Winston-Salem : a history / Frank V. Tursi.
        p.   cm.
    Includes bibliographical references (p.   ) and index.
    ISBN 0-89587-115-7 (acid-free)
    1. Winston-Salem (N.C.)—History.   I. Title.
F264.W8T87   1994
975.6'67—dc20   94-14333

To Doris and Diana

Horses and wagons still lumbered down the streets when this picture of Courthouse Square was taken about 1910. The Romanesque courthouse, Forsyth County's second, dominates the picture. The Phoenix Hotel, right, was on the corner of Liberty and Fourth streets.

The Photograph Collection,
Winston-Salem/Forsyth County Public Library

*The staff of
John F. Blair, Publisher
would like to
dedicate this book
to the memories of
John Fries Blair
and
Margaret Blair McCuiston*

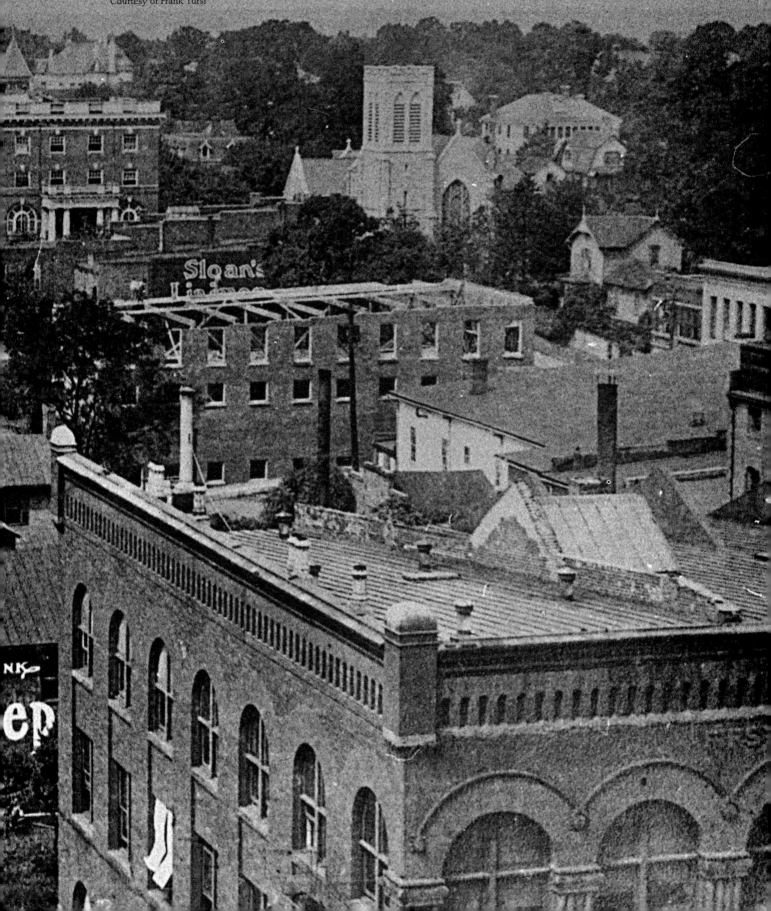

Third Street, between Liberty and Cherry, was tree-lined and peaceful looking when this picture was taken sometime during the 1940s. The original First Presbyterian Church is at the head of Third Street. Winston High School, which burned down in 1923, is next door on the right. The YMCA building is next door on Cherry and Fourth streets.
Courtesy of Frank Tursi

Contents

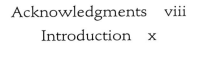

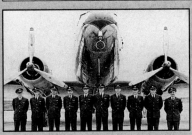

SPRING ST

Looking east on Fourth Street, about 1970
The Photograph Collection,
Winston-Salem/Forsyth County Public Library

CAROLINA HOTEL

WACHOVIA
BANK & TRUST

WINSTON

Now.
Highest interest
the law allows.

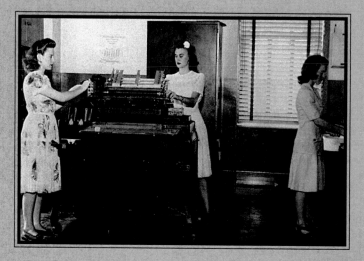

Clockwise, beginning top, left:
Inside a tobacco auction house
North Carolina Division of Archives and History

Bales of cotton head to the Fries mill in Salem
Old Salem, Inc.

Josephine Walker, left, Ruth Barker, and Jacqueline Spainhour
work in the tabulating division at Wachovia Bank and Trust Company
First Wachovia Corporation

The Arista Cotton Mill, which opened in 1890, now part of the Brookstown Mill complex
The Photograph Collection, Winston-Salem/Forsyth County Public Library

Trade Street in 1905 with construction crews erecting the white granite columns of the
Masonic Temple on the corner of Fourth and Trade
The Photograph Collection, Winston-Salem/Forsyth County Public Library

Clockwise, beginning top, left:

The Twin-City Concert Band, 1900
The Moravian Archives of the Southern
Province, Winston-Salem

*Winston had 18 general stores like this one
in the 1890s.*
Collection of Old Salem

*Forsyth Dairy on Second and Liberty streets was
owned by Charles E. Landreth.*
Courtesy of Frank Tursi

Iceman delivering ice
Collection of Old Salem

Acknowledgments

I have Archie Davis to blame for this book. I was a reporter for the *Winston-Salem Journal* when I first met Mr. Davis 10 years ago. We sat in his office at Old Salem, surrounded by paintings of Robert E. Lee and Stonewall Jackson. He spoke passionately about his hometown, describing its rich industrial heritage and its long tradition as a caring, giving place. We've talked many times since, and I've come away from each of our meetings excited about my adopted home and its vibrant history.

Mr. Davis may have provided the first spark of inspiration, but many people I bumped into during my wanderings around town as a reporter unknowingly fanned it. Chester Davis, a *Journal* reporter for more than 30 years, wrote with style and grace about the city's history and people. His stories are the yardstick by which I judge my own. The late Bill East, another *Journal* reporter and editor, left behind a treasure trove of historical stories about the city and was never too busy to answer my dumb questions. The late Joe Bradshaw knew more about the history of Winston-Salem's black residents than anyone. He taught me just how important blacks were to the city's development. Rod Meyer, the director of Historic Bethabara Park, and Michael O. "Mo" Hartley, an archaeologist in Bethania, gave me an appreciation for the importance of the Great Wagon Road to settlement of the area.

This book probably would not have been possible without the understanding of my bosses at the *Journal*. Joe Goodman, the paper's managing editor, and Floyd Rogers, the city editor, allowed me to take some time off to work on it.

Richard Starbuck at the Moravian Archives guided me through the volumes of material there. His sage advice and precise editing of the chapters dealing with Moravian history improved them immeasurably.

Jerry R. Carroll and his staff at the North Carolina Room of the Winston-Salem/Forsyth County Public Library were always there when I needed them. Molly Rawls, the library's photo archivist, helped me cull through the thousands of photographs in the library's collection.

I thank Carolyn Sakowski, the president at John F. Blair, Publisher, for taking a chance on an unpublished book author and then being patient when I missed my deadlines. Steve Kirk, who edited the manuscript, is one of the best editors I've ever worked with in my 20 years as a journalist.

Others who helped along the way include William Rice, president of the Society for the Study of Afro-American History in Winston-Salem and Forsyth County; Nicholas Bragg and Richard Murdoch at the Reynolda House Museum of American Art; J. Ned Woodall, an archaeologist at Wake Forest University; John Woodard, Julia Bradford, and Francis Haber at the North Carolina Baptist Collection at Wake Forest University; Brad Rauschenberg, director of research at the Museum of Early Southern Decorative Arts; Nancy Lovelace, media relations manager at Wachovia Corporation; Steve Morrisey, photo archivist at the North Carolina Division of Archives and History; Jerry Cotton, photo archivist of the North Carolina Collection at the University of North Carolina at Chapel Hill; and David Hauser of Clemmons, who made prints of many of the photographs that appear in this book.

Introduction

Part of Winston-Salem's story comes to life in Old Salem. Guides in 18th-century dress usher visitors through the lovingly restored buildings, where people are busily making bread, dipping candles, and fashioning exquisite silverware. The Moravians' contributions to Winston-Salem are familiar to every child who has taken the spring school tour. Their story has been retold in countless books and portrayed in soft colors by countless artists, who never seem to tire of painting Salem in the spring or Salem in the snow or Salem in the twilight.

It is, indeed, a wonderful story, an inspiring story, a solemn story about the indomitable will of a dignified people. But it is just the opening chapter.

The rest of Winston-Salem's story begins a mile up Main Street from Salem, where the narrow lanes and old buildings give way to wide avenues and hulking red factories. The

Winston part of the city's history tends to be overlooked. Children don't go on pilgrimages to the factories, and artists don't paint pictures of them in the snow. But the factories tell the story of industrial America. They are the legacies left by the twin monarchs—King Tobacco and King Cotton—that transformed a sleepy village into the largest city in the state and one of the most important industrial centers of the New South that emerged from the Civil War.

This book tells both stories. It will take you back to the Moravians' congregational village, a haven in the wilderness where everyone contributed to the common good. You'll also tour the Camel City of the 1920s, a brash place where skyscrapers sprouted almost overnight and visitors were viewed suspiciously if they didn't smoke certain cigarette brands. From the blending of those two heritages—what one writer described as the Salem conscience and the Winston purse—Winston-Salem emerged.

A city is also its people. You'll meet many of them in the following pages: the well-traveled Bishop Spangenberg, who got lost looking for suitable land for a Moravian settlement; R. J. Reynolds and his wife, Katharine, who urged her husband to give back to the community; Simon Green Atkins, who knew that educating the black workers who poured into the city at the turn of the century meant more than just getting them in school; James A. Gray, Jr., who first ran Wachovia Bank and Trust Company and then R. J. Reynolds Tobacco Company and thus shaped the city in his image; and the colorful P. Huber Hanes, Jr., who didn't want to own all the land in Forsyth County, just the land that adjoined his.

They built a thriving city that made it through the Depression and two world wars. The post–World War II boom brought new industry and new people to town, but the city's basic character remained unchanged. A city that had begun as a village run by the Moravian Church became a provincial town ruled by a handful of old families and companies. This oligarchy of businessmen and bankers, led by the men in the boardroom of R. J. Reynolds Tobacco Company, held public office, built hospitals and schools, and made most of the major civic decisions.

Then came the 1980s, a decade of unfettered free enterprise that reshaped Winston-Salem. The buyout of RJR Nabisco, Inc., in 1988 was a watershed event in Winston-Salem's history. The great turning points usually have little to do with philosophy or ideas. They revolve around something more crass: money. The colonists, for instance, weren't so upset with the British that they were willing to go to war over such abstractions as freedom. Taxes lit the

fire that ignited the Revolution. Southern aristocrats almost a century later knew that the abolition of slavery meant an end to cheap farm labor. Thus, the slavery issue helped fuel the Civil War.

So it was in Winston-Salem in the 1980s. Money—or more precisely, greed—fueled the largest business deal in history. People sensed that something fundamental had changed after the RJR Nabisco buyout. Earning money the old-fashioned way—building a company that employed people who made something— was no longer enough. The buyout symbolized a far deeper change, one that reached to the very fiber of the community's fabric.

It was the largest in a series of economic explosions that rocked the city during the 1980s: the buyouts of Hanes Corporation and Piedmont Airlines, the bankruptcy of the city's big trucking companies, the closure of the AT&T plants. Most were homegrown companies whose boardrooms were filled with hometown men. They ruled with a gentle hand and a deeply felt sense of public responsibility.

At least, that's how it's remembered. Whether that's the way it was is of little importance now because it's gone. The economic changes of the 1980s, of which the Reynolds buyout was the largest and most visible, saw to that. The boardrooms now are filled with professional managers whose idea of home is where the Lear jet happens to be parked. The city survived the social and economic turmoil of the 1980s and emerged a changed, but better, place. The third chapter of Winston-Salem's story opens with the city at the end of an old century, looking with hope toward the dawning of a new millennium.

Winston-Salem

A HISTORY

A River and its People

Before the Indians and the settlers and the city, there was a nameless river coursing through a nameless land. Born among the clouds, it bubbled up from springs on the Blue Ridge's high eastern slopes. The crystal-clear brooklet tumbled down the mountains, chattering over rocks and clamoring over falls. Gathering strength and girth, it swept through the foothills, picking up the hues of the land.

For its first 83 miles, the river was forced to the northeast, constrained by rocks that were thrust upward when the continents collided in the ancient past. But at the Sauratown Mountains, near what is now Forsyth County, the river found a gap and turned abruptly south at a place called the Great Bend. It continued through the gentle swells of the Piedmont on a slow and meandering journey to the coast. After 400 miles, the old river finally emptied its water into the sea.

Before we hemmed it in with dams and cleared its banks for corn and tobacco, the river was an alluring jewel sparkling through a land of forests and grasses that stretched to the horizon. It attracted great herds of buffalo and elk that fed on the thick stands of cane and the tender shoots of balsam and spruce buds that grew along the river's banks. Bear and panther stalked the woods, and flocks of pigeons blotted out the sun.

People followed the animals. The first to arrive at the Great Bend were nomadic hunters, tied to the whims of their prey. Later, the Indians learned to plant corn and beans, and they built their small villages along the river's fertile flood plain.

There is still a great deal of mystery surrounding the Indians who lived along the Great Bend and in what is now Forsyth County. We know they were here for about 10,000 years, but we don't know where they came from or who they really were. By the time the first white settlers arrived in the mid-18th century, they were gone.

But before departing, the Indians gave the river a name, the Atkin—"where the many cottonwoods grow."

A Home by the River

Dark rain clouds scudded across the sky as the sun faded below the treetops, and dusk softened the day. The Indians quickened their pace. They were intent on making the cave before nightfall.

There were no more than 25 people in the family. The men led the way, single-file down the path that buffalo and elk herds had trampled through the lush growth at the river's edge. The women followed, then the children. They moved silently, stopping occasionally to pick persimmons or dig sassafras roots.

In the white pines, oaks, and sycamores that towered above the river, the cicadas droned their unending summer symphony. Their melancholy song contrasted with the music of the river, which bubbled and gurgled around rocks and over small rapids.

The Indian family didn't stop to listen to the sounds of the woods. They lived in constant motion, following the animal herds or the ripening blackberries and acorns. They stayed in one place only as long as the herds did, or as long as the berries and nuts held out.

In the dim light, the Indians could barely make out the smaller path that swung away from the river toward the hills in the distance. They climbed through the thick stands of laurel and up the steep jumble of rocks to the mouth of the cave 40 feet above the river's flood plain. It was really nothing more than a ledge of granite in the middle of a hill about 1,200 feet long, but its cavity was deep and high and afforded shelter from the wind and rain. It would be their home for a little while.

Tired from the journey, the family drifted into sleep just as the first, faint flash of lightning streaked across the sky, followed by the low grumble of distant thunder. Tomorrow, the men would hunt for bear, deer, buffalo, and the abundant small game that lived along the river. The women would spend their day collecting berries, nuts, and fruits.

But then the time would come to move on. It was as their forefathers had always done.

Sit in what remains of the old rock shelter above the Yadkin River, surrounded by ancient, crumbling granite, and such musings come as suddenly as a late-summer shower. For here, thousands of years before the pyra-

Opposite page:

The Yadkin River: An alluring jewel coursing through the wilderness.

The Winston-Salem Journal

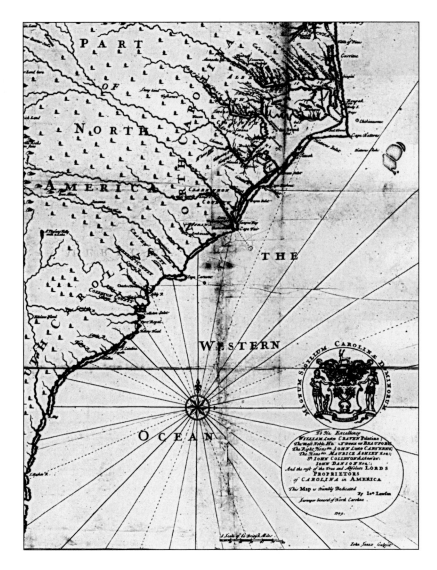

John Lawson's 1709 map of the Carolinas

North Carolina Collection, UNC Library at Chapel Hill

mids were built, lived the first inhabitants of the North Carolina Piedmont.

The little we know of the Indians who lived in what is now Forsyth County comes from places like this rock shelter. More than 500 Indian sites have been found in the county, and from them shine glimmers of the past—the weathered remnants of a rock tool, a jagged piece of a broken bowl, the charred remains of an animal bone. They form a hazy picture of a 10,000-year-old culture that began with nomadic hunters who migrated through the Yadkin basin with the animal herds as the last ice sheets retreated across the continent.

Some stopped here, at this cavern near the Great Bend, 13 miles northwest of Winston-

Salem. They wouldn't recognize their old home today. The rock roof has partially caved in, and floods over the millenniums have deposited tons of debris that almost fill the once-spacious cavern. Rows of corn and tobacco line the flood plain in place of the forest where the first Indians hunted.

In 1972, scientists dug through 11 feet of accumulated debris in the cave and discovered evidence of human occupation starting about 6600 B.C. A piece of charcoal came from a fire that burned more than 8,000 years ago, and successive layers of dirt yielded evidence of continued use for almost 8,500 years.

The first arrivals apparently used the cave periodically while following game or collecting nuts and fruits. They dressed in deer, bear, and buffalo hides and fashioned tools and weapons from rocks, bones, and shells. Judging from some of the projectile points they left in the cave, the atlatl was the favored weapon of these aboriginal hunters. Technically, it was a spear thrower, an extension of the thrower's arm. About 20 inches long, the stick had a peg or socket at one end to hold the butt end of a spear. A man with an atlatl could throw a spear two or three times farther than a man without one.

If his arm was strong and his aim good, the hunter dragged the game he killed back to the cave for skinning. He used rock scrapers honed to razor sharpness. Scientists have found the remnants of such tools in the cave.

Later, the Indians graduated to bows and arrows and learned to fashion crude bowls and pipes from soapstone, or steatite, an easily carved stone common in the Piedmont. Later still, they discovered seeds, and their lives changed forever.

Once they started farming, the Indians found that they didn't have to wander so much to get food. As the climate warmed between 600 and 900 A.D., they abandoned their temporary upland shelters for widely scattered permanent villages along the Yadkin. They grew corn, gourds, and beans on the flood plain. The river provided fish, shellfish, and turtles, and the surrounding woods teemed with game, nuts, and fruits. By the time of Columbus's arrival in America, the people of the Great Bend had built a series of villages along the river.

Families lived together in the villages, with sons leaving the clan to find wives and then returning. The Indians lived in a fluid web of social relations that extended impressive distances, without clear boundaries. The whole notion of a "tribe" probably didn't apply.

That wouldn't do for the Europeans, whose sense of order demanded structure. So when they arrived in the North Carolina Piedmont, the first white explorers organized Indians into tidy groupings. Those who lived along the upper Yadkin were said to belong to the Saponi and Tutelo tribes.

They were Eastern Sioux, cousins of the Indians who moved west before the discovery of America and who later became immortalized in the movies. The two tribes were related and first were recorded as living close to one another—the Saponi near Lynchburg, Virginia, and the Tutelo around Salem, Virginia. It's possible that some lived as far south as the Yadkin River, but no one knows for sure.

We do know that, beginning in the late 17th century, the tribes moved around the Piedmont of Virginia and North Carolina quite a bit, staying in one place 50 or so years and then moving on. They were trying to escape raiding Iroquois and bothersome white trappers and traders. The Saponi, a Siouan word for "flowing" or "gentle," may have stopped for a time at the Great Bend before settling farther downstream on the Yadkin, around the Trading Ford near present-day Salisbury. The Tutelo, an Iroquoian word for all Sioux of the south Atlantic coast, followed the Saponi and settled along the northern reaches of the Yadkin basin.

The Quiet People of the River

The first Indians who lived in what is now Forsyth County were a peaceful, simple people who may have been different from other Indians in the Southeast. They tended to be conservative and old-fashioned, and they avoided the main currents of their culture, preferring to live in the isolated side streams.

There are no written accounts about the first people who lived in Forsyth County, since they were gone by the time the first white explorers and settlers arrived in the 18th century. But we can deduce some things from research done by scientists at Wake Forest University.

They have focused on a 20-mile section of the Yadkin River near Donnaha in northwestern Forsyth County. At the Great Bend, where the Yadkin turns south, they dug through the loamy soil and found the remains of more than 100 Indian sites. From graves and trash pits came bones, pottery shards, and other remnants of an ancient society dating back almost 10,000 years.

About the time of Jesus' birth, Indians began building scattered seasonal shelters near the Great Bend. More permanent villages evolved during the next 500 years, and by 1200, a thriving society existed along that section of the river.

The 13th century was a time of great advancements for the Indians of the North Carolina Piedmont. It came at the end of a 1,700-year span that scientists call the Woodland Period. During that time, the Piedmont Indians shed their nomadic past and began making pottery, growing crops, and settling in permanent villages.

The Indians of Donnaha did all those things, just not as quickly or completely as other Piedmont tribes. For instance, they probably didn't start growing corn until around 800, centuries after other Southeastern Indians took up the tiller. Later, they discovered other types of

The Indians of the Yadkin River coiled rolls of clay into large bowls used for cooking. They smoothed the clay with paddles to remove air bubbles and to thin the walls and made impressions with fabric or corncobs. The pot was either dried in the sun or placed near a fire.

Archaeology Labs, Wake Forest University

seeds: beans, squash, gourds, sumpweed, and Jerusalem artichokes. Like other Indians, they found that farming allowed them to settle down. They lived along the Yadkin flood plain, where the soil was fertile and the periodic floods made the ground easier to work.

Other Indian tribes in the Southeast turned completely to agriculture by the end of the Woodland Period. But old ways apparently died hard at the Great Bend. Because of the abundance offered by the river and the surrounding woods, the Donnaha Indians never became full-time farmers. They continued to hunt extensively and to collect nuts and other wild foods, as their forefathers had done for centuries.

Judging from bone fragments found in the Donnaha trash pits, white-tailed deer was the favorite meal. The Indians started large, circular forest fires and drove the deer to the middle of the circle, where the hunters waited. Wild turkey, raccoon, beaver, squirrel, turtle, and fox also were important foods.

Mussel shells and fish bones fill the trash pits, attesting to the Indians' prowess as fishermen. They were especially adept at building rock fish traps in the river. Not far from Donnaha, the remains of one of these V-shaped weirs can still been seen at low water. The fishermen beat the water above the weir, driving shad, herring, alewife, and sturgeon into a woven basket that they placed at the opening between the trap's two arms.

Just as they couldn't completely stop hunting, neither could the Donnaha Indians shake the old urge to move on. Some scientists think that they probably lived in the river villages from spring to fall to plant and harvest their crops and to fish. The harvest was never enough to sustain them, so most scattered to seasonal camps in the fall to hunt and gather wild foods, leaving a few people behind in the villages.

The Indians of the Great Bend never built the large towns that some other Piedmont Indians did. Their villages ranged in size from one or two houses with 12 people to a dozen houses with no more than 100 inhabitants. All the villages at the bend probably never contained more than 1,000 inhabitants.

The houses were like their occupants: simple. They were round, with roofs of bear grass and woven mats for floors and walls. When the fleas got too bad, the Indians burned the house and made another. There were no large ceremonial halls, as there were in other Indian villages in the Piedmont, and there were no earthworks or palisades to protect the villages from enemies.

Fighting doesn't seem to have been a trait of the Donnaha Indians, unlike the Catawbas to the south, the Tuscaroras to the east, and the Cherokees to the west. Bones found in graves at Donnaha show few signs of war wounds, such as traumatic breaks. Many bones, in fact, belong to sedentary people who lived into their 40s, then considered an advanced age.

Other traits distinguish the Donnaha people from other Southeastern tribes. They didn't have elaborate ceremonies or customs, and their jewelry and pottery retained the markings of an earlier period. Neither did they believe in elaborate burials, which suggests that they didn't have a strict tribal hierarchy, with chiefs, shamans, and the like. In fact, they may have been more family than tribe.

The Indians of the Great Bend were sophisticated enough to become shrewd traders. Facing a continual shortage of the rocks needed to make tools and weapons, the Indians traded long distances for suitable material. Their trading network apparently extended to the coast, where they got marine shells for their jewelry.

Implements made of animal bones. Notice the needles on the far right.

Archaeology Labs, Wake Forest University

A "Robust" People

Life changed again for the Indians in 1540, when Hernando De Soto, the Spanish explorer, visited the Saura Indians near Asheville. The Indians of the state's interior were suddenly thrust from the obscurity of prehistory into a new age. Most didn't survive long.

After the collapse of the Spanish outposts in the country's interior in the 1570s, the Piedmont Indians had little contact with Europeans, though they traded with them through Indian middlemen. Direct contact with the English started after the colony of Charles Town was established in South Carolina in 1670. Hundreds of trappers, traders, and explorers ventured into the wilds of the Carolina interior during the next century.

John Lawson may have been the most gifted man to make the journey. A trained scientist, Lawson trekked through the Carolina Piedmont, bringing with him an immense curiosity and a keen eye for social customs, wildlife, and the colors of the land. He recorded what he saw in a remarkable journal that is still the best account of Piedmont Indian life.

In 1663, King Charles II of England gave all the land south of Virginia and westward to the "South Seas" to eight prominent Englishmen who had helped restore him to power three years earlier. These Lords Proprietors wanted to make money by encouraging the settlement of the land's vast interior, and they appointed Lawson to survey the region. Accompanied by his spaniel and an Indian guide, Lawson led a small party out of Charles Town on December 28, 1700. They embarked on a 1,000-mile, horseshoe-shaped journey that took them from the South Carolina coast through the Piedmont and eastward to the North Carolina coast.

Though he never made it as far north as the Great Bend of the Yadkin, Lawson did stop downstream at Trading Ford, where he met Saponi and Tutelo Indians. Lawson was taken with the Indians and their peaceful villages along the river, and he offered this description of the Yadkin as it flowed past the Saponi village at Trading Ford: "This pleasant river may sometimes be larger than the Thames at Kingston, [and] keeps a continual pleasant noise, with it reverberating on the bright marble rocks. It is beautiful with numerous trains of swans and other sorts of waterfowl, not common though extraordinarily pleasing to the eye.... One side of the river is hemmed in with mountainy ground, the other side proving as rich a soil to the eye of a knowing person with us as any this western world can afford."

The historic Trading Ford and all traces of the Saponi village are gone now, erased by High Rock Lake, but some of the beauty Lawson described still exists. Though the swans have disappeared, the mountains are still there, casting deep shadows on the lake's southern shores.

While Lawson was with the Saponi, Tutelo from the "westward mountains" visited the village. They were "tall likely men, having great quantities of buffaloes, elks and bears with other sort of deer amongst them, which strong food makes large, robust bodies," Lawson wrote.

The Indians, Lawson noted, were well-shaped and muscular. The men weren't much taller than the women, both being about five-foot-seven. They had black eyes and hair and tawny skin made darker by the practice of dabbing it with bear oil, which was thought to fill the skin pores, making the Indians less susceptible to the cold. Lawson was amazed at their keen eyesight, and a Tutelo showed him some "bezoar stones," a concretion found in deer stomachs. Powder from the stones blown into the eyes strengthened sight, the Indian explained.

There were other customs that Lawson found strange. He noted that the Indians of the Yadkin basin burned the bones of their prey, "as being of opinion that if they omitted that custom, the game would leave their country and they would not be able to maintain themselves by hunting." The charred remains of animal bones found in fire pits along many streams of the Piedmont are evidence of the belief.

Other Indian customs no doubt had a familiar ring. William Byrd, who surveyed the North Carolina–Virginia boundary in 1728, hired Ned Bearskin, a Saponi, to hunt for the surveying party. Bearskin told Byrd that the Saponi believed in a Supreme God, who had several lesser gods under him. The Supreme God made the earth and stars, and the others took care of their day-to-day workings.

God was just, Bearskin said, and made good people very rich and kept them healthy and protected them from enemies. Those who lied and cheated were punished with sickness, poverty, and hunger. They also were likely to be "knockt on the head and scalpt by those that fight against them."

Rewards or punishments awaited Indians after death. Good people, Bearskin said, went to a "charming, warm country, where spring is everlasting and every month is May." The woman there were "bright as stars and never scold." Game was plentiful, and the fields produced bountiful harvests. An old man sat at the entrance of this "blessed land" and examined those who tried to enter. The worthy were led through a gate to "the Land of Delights."

No such luck for the wicked, Bearskin said. They went to a "barren country, where there is always winter." Snow covered the ground throughout the year, "and nothing is to be seen upon the trees but icicles." The people there ate a bitter potato that gave them the "dry-gripes and fill[ed] their whole body with loath-some ulcers that stink and are uncomfortably painful." A woman on a monstrous toadstool passed judgment on each person entering and decided how long they should stay based on their transgressions. Huge turkey buzzards then escorted them to the "barren land," where they served their terms before being sent back to earth to try again.

John Lawson's sketch of the eastern buffalo

North Carolina Collection, UNC Library at Chapel Hill

Creatures Strange and Numerous

Lawson, Byrd, and other early explorers of the Piedmont and the Yadkin basin were amazed at the region's abundant and sometimes odd-looking wildlife. No animal was stranger to these Europeans than the buffalo, a shaggy, slow-moving creature that probably was smaller than those on the Western plains. Lawson was so sure no one would believe such an animal existed that he made detailed sketches to offer as proof. Byrd gave this unflattering description of the "American Behemoth": "His body is vastly deep from the shoulders to the brisket, sometimes six feet in those that are full grown. The portly figure of this animal is disgraced by a shabby little tail, not above 12 inches long. This he cocks up on end whenever he's in passion, and instead of lowing or bellowing, grunts with no better grace than a hog."

Buffalo migrated through the Yadkin basin for thousands of years, and the Indians depended on them for food and clothing. The

John Lawson's animal sketches

North Carolina Collection, UNC Library at Chapel Hill

vast herds were hunted to extinction by white settlers.

The passenger pigeon was another animal that disappeared soon after white settlement of the Yadkin. Great flocks of the birds descended on the river each winter. The weight of roosting pigeons sometimes toppled tree limbs. The birds were important to the Saponi, who invited Lawson to go pigeon hunting with them. "You may find several Indian towns of not above 17 houses that have more than 100 gallons of pigeon oil or fat, they using it with pulse or bread as we do butter," Lawson reported. "The Indians take a light and go among them in the night, and bringing away with them some thousands, killing them with long poles as they roost in the trees. At this time of year, the flocks as they pass by obstruct the light of the day."

Many animals Lawson saw on his journey through the Piedmont are still with us. He described opossums as "the wonder of all land animals" and wrote of owls "as big as a middling goose," whose "fearful" nighttime screechings "often make strangers lose their way in the woods."

"They Are Gone Forever"

The Saponi and Tutelo weren't as fortunate as possums and owls. Neither tribe was ever very large. Combined, they probably numbered no more than 2,700 people in 1600. By the time of Lawson's visit, white men's diseases—particularly smallpox, measles, and tuberculosis—and the ravages of rum had killed all but about 750. What the periodic epidemics didn't kill, marauding Iroquois did.

In an effort to find peace, the Indians took to the road again early in the 18th century. Some Saponi and Tutelo likely joined the Catawbas to the south, but most headed east, first to Bertie County and then to Fort Christana in Virginia, where many were gradually killed off by disease and liquor.

The survivors journeyed north beginning in 1748 to join their former enemies, the Iroquois, on reservations in New York and Canada. The last full-blooded Tutelo died in 1871.

Did he go to the Land of Delights or the Barren Land?

A schoolboy in Salem included the following in a passage he wrote about the Indians in 1825: "Their voices are no longer heard among these hills. They are beyond the penetrating power of the sun that once emitted its rays to them in these lonely groves. . . . They are gone forever."

Dates to Remember

8000 B.C. Early nomadic Indians begin to stop in Forsyth County as they follow animal herds.

500 B.C. The climate warms, and Indians start camping at seasonal sites and making pottery.

c. 1 The Indians begin settling in seasonal camps along the Great Bend region of the Yadkin River.

c. 800 Indians of the upper Yadkin begin to experiment with farming. They plant corn along the river bottoms.

c. 1000 A shift in the climate to cooler, wetter summers anchors the Indians more closely to the bottoms and makes them less mobile.

1701 John Lawson visits the Indians of the North Carolina Piedmont. His accounts of Indian life remain the best among the early explorers, and his excellent pen drawings are the only depictions available.

c. 1710 The last Indians of the Yadkin begin a 50-year exodus that eventually ends in Canada.

Names to Know

Donnaha
Bettie Pledge, a resident of northwestern Forsyth County in the 18th century, named a village in the area after her father, Donnahoo, a Cherokee chief.

Yadkin River
The river was called the Sapona in the early 18th century for the Saponi Indians, who lived in the region. The origin of Yadkin is uncertain. The best guess is that it came from an Indian word for "where the many cottonwoods grow." Numerous spellings appear in 18th-century documents, including Yatkin, Atkin, and Reatkin.

Emigrants on the Great Wagon Road stop for a noonday rest.

North Carolina Collection, UNC Library at Chapel Hill

Opening the Back Country

Most of North Carolina was still an uncharted frontier when the 18th century dawned. Beyond the few towns and villages in the coastal plain lay a largely unbroken wilderness of pine and hardwood forests that stretched to the "Blue Mountains" in the west. It was a land known only to Indians and a handful of white trappers and explorers.

The first daring settlers trickled into the interior in the 1740s, building their log huts along the Hyco, Haw, and Eno rivers. Within 10 years, the trickle became a flood, as the first great wave of American migration spilled into the back country of the Carolinas.

Many immigrants were Germans and Scots-Irish who had left their homelands in search of freedom and a better life. They arrived in Philadelphia by the boatload, soon filling all the good land nearby. They headed south through Pennsylvania and the Shenandoah Valley on a road that they widened from ancient buffalo and Indian paths.

The road eventually extended all to way to Georgia, opening up America's first western frontier as it went. It became the interstate highway of its day and was given a name to match its eminence: the Great Wagon Road. For 20 years, it carried the cargo and dreams of untold thousands of people.

Morgan Bryan, William Linville, and Edward Hughes came down the road in the late 1740s. They were among the first whites to permanently settle along the eastern bank of the Yadkin River in what is now Forsyth County. The land they chose lay strategically astride a shallow spot that became a vital link in the Great Wagon Road and the gateway to the Southeast. It eventually put Winston-Salem on the map.

Two Intrepid Explorers

As we hacked through the thick tangle of vines and spiderwebs along the riverbank on a sticky summer Saturday, a good idea was beginning to lose its luster. Ed Hill and I were searching for the Shallow Ford, the gravel roadway under the Yadkin River that played such an important role in the history of Winston-Salem. Anyone writing a book about the city, I reasoned, should first understand the importance of this historic river crossing. And what better way to know the Shallow Ford than to actually walk across it as thousands of settlers did two centuries ago?

Ed was game. He's a neurologist who lives in a 19th-century house in Old Salem and collects arrowheads, muskets, and powder horns. History excites Ed, who dressed for the occasion in a three-cornered hat and a deerskin vest and strapped a musket across his shoulder. The gun was gaining weight the farther we hiked along the river.

We had scouted the territory from an airplane a couple of weeks earlier. The ford had been clearly visible about 600 yards downstream from the bridge that takes Shallowford Road across the Yadkin. Driftwood and other debris deposited by the river had marked the ford's diagonal path between Forsyth and Yadkin counties. It was as if someone had built a fence of flotsam along the ford's edges. Our route had looked simple: a dirt path led from Williams Road to the river, and then an easy walk led upstream to the Forsyth County end of the ford.

Or so it had seemed from 1,000 feet in the air. That easy walk was turning into an arduous hike through soybean fields, up steep, sandy banks, and around tangles of saplings and briers. After an hour of searching, we still had not found the eastern end.

An island we had seen from the airplane covered that end of the ford. It wasn't there during colonial times or in the 1950s, when local historians made an expedition to the Shallow Ford. The island apparently formed after the completion of W. Kerr Scott Dam in 1962. Built upstream in Wilkes County, the dam has eliminated the disastrous floods that once raged along the river. Without the scouring of periodic floods, though, the Yadkin has gradually deposited its sediment on the Shallow Ford to form the island.

To us, that meant that there was no way to reach the ford. We could see it a tantalizing 30 yards offshore, after it emerged from the end of the island, but a gulf of swirling, muddy river water separated us from our goal.

It was time to regroup. Ed, not yet willing to admit defeat, continued the search. He left me sitting on the trunk of a fallen pine tree, staring at the island and silently cursing the Army Corps of Engineers. The mocking cries of crows perched in the trees above me filled the woods. Too bad Ed took his musket with him.

Fording a stream

North Carolina Collection, UNC Library at Chapel Hill

The Gateway to the Frontier

Travelers 200 years ago had an easier time finding the Shallow Ford. They simply rode to it. They came down the Great Wagon Road, which cut across the western end of the county, and descended toward the river on what is now Williams Road, south of Lewisville. If the Yadkin was flowing normally, they drove their wagons across a natural rock ledge 18 inches below the surface. If the river was high, they waited at campgrounds or taverns at either end of the ford until it was safe to cross.

Thousands of settlers—their lives packed in wagons or loaded on the backs of mules—made the crossing during the 15 or 20 years preceding the American Revolution, when the Great Wagon Road was the most heavily traveled road in the country. It was the only place on the river for 30 miles shallow enough for heavy wagons, and it thus became one of the road's vital links and the gateway to the Southern frontier. From the Shallow Ford, settlers could continue to Salisbury or Charlotte, through Catawba Indian country into South Carolina, or all the way to the fortified trading outpost of Augusta, Georgia.

Where the settlers went, villages, towns, and cities followed. Many cities from Pennsylvania to Georgia owe their existence to the Great Wagon Road: Lancaster and York in Pennsylvania, Winchester and Lexington in Virginia, Salisbury and Winston-Salem in North Carolina. In Winston-Salem's case, it was a quirk in geology—the Shallow Ford—that brought the Great Wagon Road here in the first place. If the ford had formed 10 miles downstream, Winston-Salem would be in Davidson County.

The road evolved slowly from dirt paths that the Indians had cut through the forest centuries earlier. Starting in Philadelphia, it gradually moved southward through Pennsylvania and the Shenandoah Valley with the tide of pioneers. The tide reached Big Lick—now Roanoke, Virginia—in the early 1740s and rolled through Rocky Mount and Martinsville.

By the end of the decade, the first wave of the great migration was about to crash into North Carolina through the back door. It came from Virginia, around the mountain that the Indians called Jameokee—"The Pilot"—and to the shallow ford on the Yadkin.

The Migration Begins

The Lords Proprietors, who never set foot in America, had a hard time selling the North Carolina interior to settlers. Their land agents were inept, and taxes were high. Weak and corrupt colonial governors couldn't protect settlers from Indian attacks, pirates, and brigands of one stripe or another.

Settlement was understandably slow under such circumstances. In 1707, even after a century of English rule, North Carolina was still very much an unknown frontier. The original Anglican, Puritan, and Quaker settlers clung to Edenton, Bath, and the other villages along the coastal plain.

The pace of growth was too slow for King George II, who forced all but one of the eight proprietors to relinquish their ownership of North Carolina. The king allowed John Carteret, the earl of Granville, to retain some of his land, but the earl had to give up all voice in governing the colony. The Granville District, as it became known, was a 60-mile-wide strip from Cape Hatteras to the Blue Ridge Mountains. It contained two-thirds of the colony's people and a great share of its wealth. It also included the land that later became Forsyth County.

Royal rule, started in 1729, brought stability, which spurred growth. An almost constant flow of immigrants into the back country during the next 30 years took the frontier to the edge of the Blue Ridge. Vast tracts were cleared in the Piedmont. Mills were built, roads laid out, towns incorporated, and trade expanded. The numbers speak for themselves. The population of North Carolina in 1730 did not exceed 30,000 whites and 6,000 blacks. By the beginning of the Revolution, North Carolina ranked fourth among the colonies, with 265,000 people.

Down the Great Wagon Road they came. Many settlers left the Northern colonies in search of cheap land. Others arrived from the crowded cities of England and Northern Ireland, from the highlands of Scotland, and from the valleys of the Rhine and the Danube in central Europe. These foreigners were fleeing religious and political persecution, drought, and failing crops. Missionary zeal and an adventurous spirit moved many others.

Germans and Scots-Irish made up the bulk of the foreigners who settled the Carolina frontier.

The first German settlers came from the Rhine River area, where the Thirty Years' War—a religious struggle between Protestants and Catholics lasting from 1618 to 1648—had been devastating. The ensuing peace wasn't much better. Thieves roamed the countryside, cities were burned, and small political wars flared up periodically. Thousands of Germans left for America.

It was success that drove the Scots-Irish from their homes. The name is something of a misnomer, since these people had little, if any, Irish blood. They were the descendants of Lowland

Scots whom England had recruited in the 17th century to farm its estate lands in Northern Ireland. The crown had another motive: it wanted the Protestant Scots to act as buffers in predominantly Catholic Ireland.

The hardworking Scots transformed Ulster. They built sizable herds of cattle and sheep and created a flourishing wool and linen industry. They were so good at what they did that Britain, to protect its own textile industry, restricted the importation of Irish wool and linen.

Added to the economic injury was the insult of the Test Act of 1703, which barred Scottish Presbyterians from teaching, becoming lawyers, and holding civil and military posts. Their churches were closed and many Presbyterians fined or imprisoned.

When the English lords raised the rent on their estates, and when famines gripped the land in the 1720s, the Scots fled to America in droves, leaving whole villages empty in Ulster.

Like the Germans, they descended on William Penn's Pennsylvania, which was known for its liberal religious laws. Estimates are that 60,000 German and Scots-Irish families—at least 300,000 people—entered the colony between 1727 and 1776. Pennsylvania simply couldn't hold all the new arrivals. Many settled there, but many more moved south to Maryland and Virginia on old paths and buffalo tracks that soon became the Great Wagon Road. Frequently, they moved several times. Then their children and grandchildren set out in search of new land.

Traveling on North Carolina's colonial roads was often hazardous.

North Carolina Collection, UNC Library at Chapel Hill

Life on the Road

A journey down the Great Wagon Road was never easy. The Indian trails were so narrow that only single packhorses could pass. The horses traveled in trains of up to 12 tied in procession. There were few inns and no ferries at the beginning, and Indian attacks were common, especially in Virginia.

The road was widened and improved as settlements sprang up, and wagons soon replaced the horse trains. Later, Conestoga wagons rumbled down the road. Made in the Pennsylvania county of the same name, the huge wagons were the U-Hauls of the migration, capable of carrying 10 tons of furnishings, food, and people.

Wagon groups typically started the journey to North Carolina in late spring or early summer. They made about five miles a day, which meant the 460-mile trip from Philadelphia to the Shallow Ford took about three months.

That's if the wagons held up and the weather was kind.

Most of the Scots-Irish and Germans lacked the skills needed to survive in the wilderness. They must have been terrified as they sat around their campfires listening to tales of Indian attacks while wolves howled in the darkness. No doubt, more than a few got lost.

Those with money and faint hearts could seek refuge in the many rustic inns that were later built along the road, but the accommodations were meager and the food deplorable. Alexander Wilson, an ornithologist, visited North Carolina in the winter of 1809, years after the settlers made the journey. If his descriptions of the inns he stopped at are accurate, one can only imagine how bad they were 50 years earlier.

The taverns, Wilson wrote, were "the most desolate and beggarly imaginable," with "bare, bleak and dirty walls; one or two old broken chairs and a bench the only furniture." Just looking at the food was "sufficient to deaden the most eager appetite." If a diner could manage to eat such swill, he had to listen to the hogs under his table: "The house itself is raised upon props, four or five feet, and the space below is left open for the hogs, with whose charming vocal performance the wearied traveler is serenaded the whole night long."

A typical log cabin in the North Carolina woods

North Carolina Collection, UNC Library at Chapel Hill

The Bryan Settlement

By the late 1740s, the Great Wagon Road reached Town Fork Creek in what is now Stokes County. A handful of settlers continued to the Yadkin River, where they built their cabins on both sides of the Shallow Ford.

Edward Hughes may have been the first. Born in Pennsylvania, Hughes, like many settlers of the Yadkin basin, moved first to the Shenandoah Valley before buying more than 600 acres on both sides of the Shallow Ford in 1747. It's not clear when he actually moved to the Yadkin, but the land was surveyed the following year, and the land titles from Lord Granville were issued in 1752. Hughes probably lived on the land before he received the titles, a not uncommon practice.

He became an important man, operating a ferry at the Shallow Ford sometime after 1753

Retracing History's Path

Someone, it seems, took a wrong turn in the search for the Great Wagon Road through Forsyth County.

The sign in front of the Rural Hall branch of the Forsyth County Public Library insists that the 18th-century highway that opened up the back country passed right through town. Another sign, this one in Bethania, notes that the road passed within hailing distance of that community.

Over the years, there has been much confusion surrounding the road, according to Rod Meyer, one of four Forsyth County men who have spent years retracing the road's earliest route through the county. The woods are full of remnants of 18th- and 19th-century roads, and Grandpa may have had the wrong one in mind when he told all those stories about the great road that ran in front of the house.

Meyer and the other researchers think they have found the route that thousands of immigrants used in the 18th century to settle the western part of the state. It didn't go through Rural Hall, and it passed miles from Bethania.

Together with Kyle Stimson, Michael O. "Mo" Hartley, and Richard Ziglar, Meyer pored over old records and maps, studied aerial photographs, and spent countless weekends walking through woods and cornfields. The men determined that the first Moravian settlers cleared the road to the Shallow Ford on the Yadkin River in 1754, a year after they arrived in North Carolina. Until then, what became known as the Great Wagon Road started in Pennsylvania and stopped near Town Fork Creek at the northern border of what is now Forsyth County. The road eventually was extended from the Yadkin to Georgia.

The route cuts through the northwestern corner of the county, and much of it is covered by portions of modern roads: Stanleyville Road, Shattalon Drive, Shallowford Road. Society has obliterated other portions. Old Town Shopping Center, for instance, lies atop the old road. So do industrial plants on Hanes Mill Road. The section through the county landfill has been unearthed and covered many times.

"Twentieth-century urban places have not been gentle to colonial roads," Hartley said.

But here and there, remnants exist. Walk into the woods off U.S. 52 near the University Parkway exit and you will see it. It's just a trench, really, a deep rut that runs a few hundred feet through the hilly land before being consumed by the asphalt of the highway. Stand quietly where the quarrelsome robins duel with the rumbling 18-wheelers nearby, and if you listen very carefully . . .

"How many wheels came down this road, how many footprints?" Hartley wondered. "It boggles the mind."

and serving as sheriff and justice of the peace. Judging from the records left by his later Moravian neighbors, Hughes enjoyed tormenting them. He often visited nearby Bethabara and created a ruckus. He once ordered the arrest of two men whom the Moravians later had to release when they were found innocent. Hughes demanded that the Moravian Church post banns for the children of two of his friends whom the church elders considered inappropriate for marriage.

Hughes apparently used creative accounting in keeping the county's books. An audit of his tax collections as sheriff showed a deficit of 475 pounds. He was ordered to pay the debt, but it's not clear if he did.

To the pleasure of the Moravians, Hughes apparently moved near Salisbury just before or during the Revolutionary War after selling or losing all his land at the Shallow Ford.

James Carter was one of Hughes's earliest neighbors. A native of Bucks County, Pennsylvania, Carter moved to the Maryland border around 1736. Eight years later, he moved to the Shenandoah Valley, where he built a mill and prospered. He headed south in 1747, stopping at the forks of Panther Creek, a few miles from the Shallow Ford. Wanderlust struck again, and Carter bought 350 acres on the future site of Salisbury in 1753.

Other settlers, such as Samuel Davis and George Forbush, built homes near the Shallow Ford before 1750. Historians later named this collection of cabins the Bryan Settlement, after Morgan Bryan, probably the most prominent of the early settlers of Forsyth County. A Quaker from Chester County, Pennsylvania, Bryan first moved to Virginia, then to North Carolina in 1748, settling on the east bank of the Yadkin River about three miles downstream of the Shallow Ford. His son-in-law, William Linville, probably came with him.

Cabins were spartan but cozy.

North Carolina Collection, UNC Library at Chapel Hill

Linville built his home a few miles away on a creek that bears his name.

A virtual wilderness surrounded Bryan and his neighbors. The closest communities of settlers were a day's ride east at Alamance and Stinking Quarters creeks, or two days south at the headwaters of Second Creek. In all, about 75 families lived scattered about the Granville tract between the Yadkin and Catawba rivers by 1751, according to colonial records. Officials certainly missed many more families, but there's little doubt that panthers and bears outnumbered people.

Settlers lived in one-room cabins made from the trees felled to clear the land. They had to make their own clothing and grow or catch all their food. Corn was the most common crop because it was easy to grow and could be put to a variety of uses. By the late 17th century, it became an important export to England. The settlers also grew indigo, wheat, rye, and barley and raised cattle.

Many early writers rhapsodized about the God-fearing qualities of the early settlers. No doubt, many fit the description, but there also were quite a few who did not. The Moravians later became distressed by their neighbors' generally low moral standards, particularly their fondness for alcohol. Francis Joseph Kron of Salem reported that drunkenness, gambling, fighting, and disregard for the Sabbath were common among the people of the Yadkin River valley. "Within a circle of 18 miles where perhaps 13 families dwell I could count as many as 20 illegitimate children, some the offspring of widows, others of single, never married women, and others, too, intruders in lawful wedlock," Kron wrote.

The growing number of orphans and illegitimate children may have been the most serious social problem confronting the frontier community. Accounts of provisions made for them fill court records of the time. Usually, the court placed an orphan in the custody of a

North Carolina pioneers performing daily chores

prominent citizen until he or she turned 21. During that time, the orphan was pretty much an indentured servant.

Eureka!

Ed's persistence paid off. He found a place along the river that seemed shallow enough to wade. We ventured in, cautiously walking through the waist-deep water. The water level gradually dropped until we were standing ankle-deep on a level bed of moss-covered rocks. The Shallow Ford.

"This is exciting," Ed said as we took pictures of each other. "We're standing on history."

We began to cross to the Yadkin County side, but the water deepened and the current began to pull at our legs the farther we walked. The crossing could be dangerous, as Moravian records attest. Wagons often overturned, with their occupants swept downstream.

I was reminded of Jesse Lee, a Methodist circuit rider who crossed the Shallow Ford in

1874. The river was up and the current strong, and Lee wandered off the ford into some rocks. "For one moment he was swimming, then plunging over the points of rugged rocks," wrote Milton Thrift in his *Memories of Jesse Lee*. "While Mr. Lee was encumbered with a great-coat, with his saddlebags on his arm, and being but an indifferent swimmer, he had but little expectation of being delivered from the danger that then threatened him; but through the good Providence of God he was brought through unhurt, and his life preserved for further usefulness."

Not possessing the good reverend's unflinch-ing faith, we abandoned the effort and headed home.

The Shallow Ford continued to be used well into the 20th century. For 150 years, it served as a highway across the Yadkin, linking boom-ing Winston-Salem with the northwestern counties that provided the city with so many of its residents and customers. Many farmers drove their loaded wagons across the ford to sell their tobacco, produce, and other wares in the city.

A bridge built to the north replaced the Shal-low Ford in 1920, and the old crossing was forgotten and left to the whims of the river.

Robert Martin, left, and Gwyn Jennings stand astride the Shallow Ford on an expedition in 1953.

Courtesy of G. Galloway Reynolds

Dates to Remember

1740s   The first white settlers arrive in the Yadkin River valley from Northern colonies and western Virginia.

1747–48   Edward Hughes, Morgan Bryan, and William Linville settle near the Shallow Ford, creating the first permanent white settlement in what is to become Forsyth County.

Names to Know

Morgan Bryan
A Quaker from Pennsylvania, Bryan was the most prominent settler in northwestern North Carolina before 1752. He arrived in the colony in 1748, settling about three miles downstream of the Shallow Ford. The settlement that grew up around the ford become known as the Bryan Settlement.

Edward Hughes
A crotchety man, Hughes may have been the first permanent white settler in Forsyth County. He was born in Philadelphia County, Pennsylvania, but moved to the Shenandoah Valley in 1746. He moved to the east side of the Shallow Ford on the Yadkin River as early as 1747. Hughes operated a ferry at the crossing and was a continual thorn in the side of his Moravian neighbors.

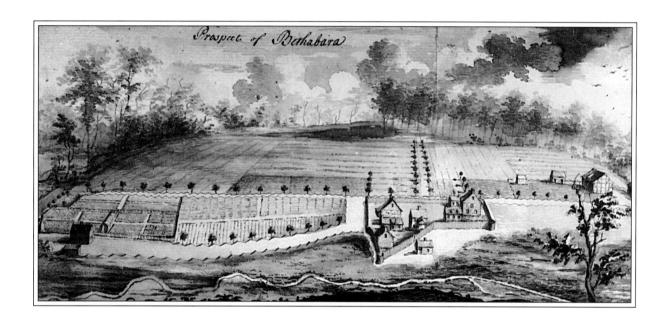

One of only two known paintings of eighteenth century Bethabara,
this watercolor, done about 1758, shows the fort surrounding the settlement.

The Moravian Archives, Herrnhut

"Reserved by the Lord for the Brethren"

Settlers didn't conquer the North Carolina frontier; they came to terms with it. Those with the courage to face the rawness of the wilderness learned to live with the isolation and loneliness. Most were content to eke out a meager existence from the unforgiving land.

Not the Moravians. They came to what is now Forsyth County in 1753 not as settlers, but as colonists. These unique people with their age-old customs came to transform the wilderness, not to be changed by it. Clearing a few acres to wrestle a little food from the ground wasn't enough. They wanted to build a community where they could protect their simple way of life, practice their religion with little interference, and live in godly, brotherly industry.

The picture of those Moravian pioneers that emerges after 200 years may seem strange to us: they were diligent, meticulous, theocratic, single-minded, and hardworking, possessing a piety that was unusual then and almost impossible to fathom now. All of those things made them seem strange to their contemporaries as well. Such traits were essential, however, if the Moravian experiment in the North Carolina woods was to succeed.

For that is what the first Moravian colonists embarked upon when they arrived at Muddy Creek. Their mission was to start a religious commune, a church-run village where everyone contributed according to his abilities and took according to his needs. They called it Bethabara, or "House of Passage," and it quickly became a success.

The small cluster of buildings and well-manicured fields withstood epidemics and an Indian war to become a haven in the wilderness. Within three years of its founding, Bethabara was the main trading center of the northwestern Piedmont. Its gristmill, pottery shed, and community store attracted nearby settlers and those passing through on the Great Wagon Road.

Church officials in Europe never intended Bethabara to be anything more than a farm. The first of the "little villages of the Lord," they decided, should be Bethania, which was founded in 1759.

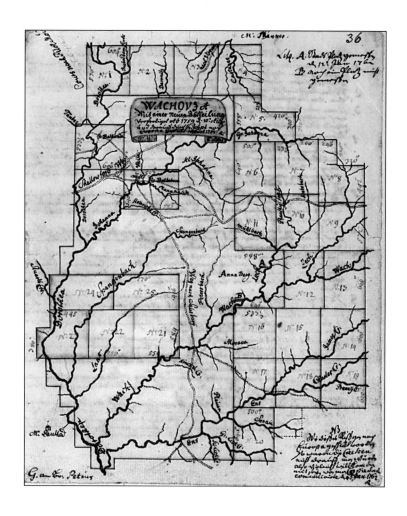

Christian Gottlieb Reuter drew this map of the
Wachovia tract in 1761.

The Moravian Archives, Herrnhut

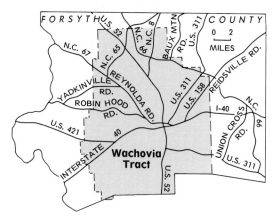

A more modern map shows the tract's location in
present-day Forsyth County.

The Winston-Salem Journal

"A Little Pilgrim Band"

Fifteen weary men stopped to rest on the summit of a small hill in southwestern Virginia on November 7, 1753. They had been on the road one day shy of a month, but it must have seemed like an eternity. They had endured atrocious weather, swollen streams, and a pitiful excuse for a road. They had to push their little wagon up steep hills and then hold onto it so it wouldn't roll too fast and crash going down. Trees had to be cleared from the path, and, at times, a new road had to be cut around ravines and deep holes.

So it was with some delight that one of the men spotted the bald knob of Pilot Mountain in the distance. As the Reverend Bernhard Adam Grube, one of the leaders of the band, noted in his journal, the men rejoiced "to think that we would soon see the boundary of Carolina and set foot in our own dear land."

Heartened by the sight, the band of Moravians pushed on. Their destination was the 100,000-acre tract of desolate wilderness in North Carolina that the Moravian Church had bought from John Carteret, the earl of Granville. It lay just on the other side of the mountain, along the banks of the Yadkin River.

The men who trudged down that lonely road were the first colonists sent to this distant land from the Moravian town of Bethlehem in Pennsylvania. It was a rather remarkable group, considering the time and place. All the men were literate and trained in a craft or profession. Among them were a doctor, a minister, carpenters, farmers, tailors, shoemakers, and millers. They possessed all the skills needed to carve a town from the wilderness.

Crossing into North Carolina on November 13, the colonists were delayed at the Dan River, which was swollen by recent heavy rains. Two men went ahead, crossing the river in a canoe, with their horses swimming alongside. Their job was to scout the Moravians' land for a place where the colonists could stay until the settlement was begun.

The remainder of the group crossed the Dan three days later and stopped at a settler's house near Town Fork Creek in what is now

Stokes County. There, they were met by the scouts, who informed them of an abandoned shack six miles inside the Moravians' land.

Rising early the next day, November 17, the Moravians hacked their way through a narrow path in the woods, cutting down trees to make a road as they went. They arrived that evening at the small, one-room log cabin built by pioneer Hans Wagner. The men "rejoiced heartily with one another," Grube reported.

Remnants of the road they took that day still wind through the woods along Bethania Station Road. Rod Meyer, the director of Historic Bethabara Park, spent months looking for the route the original settlers took to the deserted cabin that became Bethabara.

"We are on the road they would have taken on November 17, 1753," Meyer said, standing in a deep rut that runs through the woods behind the park's visitor center. "It's clearly visible here, and parts of it can still be seen north of here."

The colonists spent their first chilly night in the ramshackle cabin, as the wind whistled through the cracks in the logs and the wolves howled outside. After a meal of stewed pumpkin and cornmeal mash, most of the men prepared a lovefeast, a time-honored Moravian ceremony in which the participants share bread or cake and coffee, wine, or tea. As they worked, Gottlob Koenigsderfer scribbled hastily by the firelight, writing a hymn that certainly was the first ever composed in that part of North Carolina. He sang a verse as the lovefeast began:

> We hold arrival Lovefeast here
>   In Carolina land,
> A company of Brethren true,
>   A little Pilgrim Band,
> Called by the Lord to be of those
>   Who through the whole world go,
> To bear Him witness everywhere,
>   And naught by Jesus know.

The rhymes cheered the little band. "While we held our lovefeast, the wolves howled loudly," Grube wrote, "but all was well with us, and our hearts were full of thanksgiving to the Savior Who had so graciously guided us and led us."

The Unitas Fratrum

A long, tortuous path had led the Moravians to the woods of North Carolina. It began in the 15th century at a castle in Bohemia, where followers of John Hus met to start a religious society. Hus, a Bohemian, was branded a heretic by the Catholic Church and burned at the stake in 1415. His disciples gathered in the castle 41 years later and called themselves the Brethren of the Law of Christ. In time, they became known as the United Brethren (*Unitas Fratrum*), the Bohemian Brethren, or simply the Brethren.

They were a gentle people who believed in a religion that expressed itself by doing rather than by dogma. They patterned their lives on the simple ways of the Apostles and sought to live like primitive Christians within the framework of the Catholic Church.

That was impossible, given the church's complex hierarchy and rules. Within 10 years of forming, the Brethren ordained their own bishops, making them the first Protestant sect. The Catholic Church reacted as it would years later when Martin Luther nailed his theses on the church door. It came down hard on the tiny society, beginning a 40-year period of persecution.

The Protestant Reformation in 1517 brought peace, and the Brethren grew. By the mid-1500s, some 200 tightly organized societies practiced in Bohemia, Moravia in Czechoslovakia, and Poland. The Brethren pioneered public education. They also established their own printing press and were the first Protestant church to translate a Bible from Latin and publish it in the native tongue of their people.

Peace ended with the beginning of the Thirty Years' War in 1618. Catholic kings in Bohemia smashed Protestant homes and churches, confiscated land, and executed leaders. The Brethren scattered, fleeing Bohemia for Moravia, Silesia, and Poland. By 1627, all that remained of the church was what one of its bishops called "the hidden seed."

That seed sprouted in 1722, when Count Nicolaus Ludwig von Zinzendorf allowed refugees to settle on his estate in Saxony. The first tree was felled June 17 at a place the refugees called Herrnhut—"Under the Care of the Lord." Within five years, about 300 Brethren lived in Herrnhut. Since most came from Moravia, their neighbors described them simply as "the Moravians."

Zinzendorf lived among the refugees and became a convert. On May 12, 1727, the count offered them laws and a constitution that reflected his dictum: "I have but one passion and this is Christ." Christianity, Zinzendorf said, wasn't something to be practiced only on Sunday. It required daily good works. His doctrine described a simple life that stressed day-to-day Christian living. The renewed church began on August 13 with Zinzendorf as its leader and spiritual guide.

The Moravians professed a personal relationship with Jesus. They called each other "brother" and "sister," terms harking back to the New Testament, and their services were simple, with frequent songs and music. The lovefeast became an established part of the social fabric at Herrnhut, and the Easter Sunrise Service was first held at the village in 1732.

The communal life that was to be exported to the New World evolved at Herrnhut. The church played a central role, watching over

Count Nicolaus Ludwig von Zinzendorf, a pious nobleman, allowed Moravian refugees to live on his estate in Austria. He reorganized the church and became its spiritual leader.

Courtesy of Evangelische Verlagsanstalt

every phase of life. Everyone contributed to the common good in a communistic society modeled after those of primitive Christians. Villagers were divided into groups, or choirs, according to age, sex, and marital status. There were choirs for married couples, for single men and single women, for young boys and young girls, for widows and widowers.

Such a system was perfectly suited for missionary work. A married Moravian could travel around the world and take comfort in knowing that his family was well cared for. In the 1730s, Moravian societies sprang up in Holland, England, and Denmark. Missionaries worked among the slaves of the West Indies, the Eskimos in Greenland, and the natives of Surinam. The Moravians were the first Protestant missionaries, but unlike those who followed, they didn't try to convert whole populations, concentrating instead on individuals. They avoided theological debates and were content with just spreading the Gospels.

In the mid-1730s, the Moravians decided that it was time to take the message to America.

The History-Loving Moravians

To say that the history-loving Moravians wrote everything down would miss the point. They never threw anything away.

The result is the Moravian Archives in Old Salem, a million-page treasure trove of information that may be the best and least-known collection of early colonial records in the South.

Browsing through the archives, a researcher will find church records and maps dating from the earliest days of the Moravian settlements in North Carolina, letters from George Washington, a *New York Herald* from 1865 announcing the death of Abraham Lincoln, and travel brochures describing Winston-Salem in the 1920s.

It all stems from a simple directive in 1549, when the church ordered its pastors worldwide to "carefully collect and preserve" all official letters and historical documents. Ministers kept daily diaries and sent them, along with biographies of church members, to Moravian headquarters in Germany. There, they were reviewed and often copied and sent to other churches, so everyone would know what everyone else was doing.

The pastor of each of the Moravian congregations in Forsyth County kept his congregation's records and passed them to his successor. Many were stored in the church basement or the pastor's attic.

Such a system lasted for more than 150 years, until 1911, when the local church realized that its records were becoming too voluminous. It appointed Adelaide Fries its first archivist and designated a warehouse as the first archives building.

Adelaide Fries, a Salem native, came from a long line of Moravians. She had grown up listening to her father, John W. Fries, tell stories of the olden days. She went about her new job with relish, tackling the task with the thoroughness of, well, a Moravian.

It took a year to collect the diaries, letters, and other records from their scattered nooks and crannies. When she was done, Fries had assembled an almost unbroken record of the county's history from 1753. There were a few gaps. For instance, some pages in the Friedland church diary were missing. Tradition has it that a careless pastor used the pages to light his pipe.

There was a larger problem, though. Most of the records were written in German, the official language of the local churches until 1856. They were handwritten in a script that was hard to decipher and contained idioms unfamiliar to modern readers. If she could mine the lode, Fries knew that she could lay bare valuable historical gems.

So she embarked upon what became her life's work: painstakingly translating the most important and most interesting records into English. The result is *Records of the Moravians of North Carolina*, an 11-volume work that is among the best primary sources on any group settling in America. Fries published the first volume in 1922 and completed six more before she died in 1949. Succeeding archivists have continued the work, publishing the latest volume in 1969.

Fries, a trained historian, had a nose for news. She left out the prayers and sermons and included items that were historically significant or shed light on lifestyles and personalities. Tidbits about weather, crops, Indians, weddings, and births are scattered throughout the *Records*. They breathe life into the times and the people.

Here, for example, is an item from the Salem Board Minutes in 1787 that tells something about Traugott Bagge, a storekeeper who was one of Salem's leaders during the Revolutionary War: "Br. Bagge will at once place a lightning rod on the store, if he can persuade his wife, who is doubtful about it."

What isn't in doubt is the archives' value. Documents keep coming in. They are stored in a building on Bank Street built in 1797 and remodeled and fireproofed for the archives in 1942.

Genealogists drop by to find out about their ancestors. Officials at Old Salem, Inc., search the records to learn about the furnishings of a building they have restored.

And in a corner, a translator, magnifying glass in hand, studies an old letter written in inscrutable German script and continues the work that Adelaide Fries started years ago.

In Search of a Haven

Their first stop was Georgia, where they started a settlement near Savannah in 1735. The missionaries repaid their debts for the land and the ocean voyage by 1740, when war erupted between England and Spain. Georgia, caught between Spanish Florida and the English Carolinas, became a battleground. Rather than abandon their objection to bearing arms, the Moravians abandoned Georgia instead.

They traveled north to Pennsylvania, where the church had bought two tracts of land. The colony, with its liberal religious laws, presented the Moravians with a great opportunity. Protestant sects were disorganized. The Moravians, with their experience as missionaries and their tightly knit ministries, could have become one of the great religious forces in America if they had set out to organize congregations. Instead, they chose to keep to themselves and follow the model established at Herrnhut. They built two self-isolated towns—Nazareth, near the forks of the Delaware River, and Bethlehem, 10 miles away on the Lehigh River—where they could protect their way of life.

The towns prospered, so why did the Moravians leave comfortable Pennsylvania for the wilds of North Carolina? They wanted to spread the Gospels in an area they knew had no churches and few preachers. They also wanted to convert Indians.

"If that were the reason, then why did they choose this place in North Carolina?" wondered Rod Meyer of Historic Bethabara Park. "There were no Indians here. They were long gone by the time the Moravians got here."

Though Indians would frequently pass through the Moravian settlement in North Carolina, the Indians who lived in the Yadkin River valley had moved east at least a genera-tion before the Moravians' arrival. The Moravians did establish missionaries among the Cherokees and the Creeks in the 19th century.

The Brethren also wanted to be free to practice their religion in peace. By the 1740s, many Europeans were uneasy about the Moravian Church's missionary effort. The zeal of its missionaries was getting Zinzendorf in trouble. He was banished from his native Saxony for allegedly luring a neighbor's tenants to Herrnhut. Hundreds of Moravians were evicted from two flourishing settlements. The Moravians were attacked in print by such articles as "On How to Keep From Being Infected by the Herrnhutian Epidemic."

Across the Atlantic, Pennsylvanians were alarmed by the huge number of Germans arriving in the colony daily. The usually tolerant Ben Franklin wrote in 1751, "Why should [German] boors be suffered to swarm into our settlement and by herding together establish their language and manners to the exclusion of others? Why should Pennsylvania, founded by the English, become a colony of aliens?"

Against this background, Zinzendorf began looking for a huge tract in the New World. August Gottlieb Spangenberg, the Moravian bishop in America, explained that the church wanted a place where the Moravians could "live together as Brethren, without interfering with others and without being disturbed by them," and where they could "keep children from being hurt by wicked examples, and young people from following the foolish and sinful ways of the world."

The English Parliament eased the search in 1749 when it gave the Moravians full standing in the colonies, recognizing them as an ancient Protestant Episcopal church having "sober, quiet, industrious people." Such an endorsement made the Moravians much sought-after as colonists. Offers of land came from Labrador and the Caribbean. Zinzendorf turned them down because, he said, those places were "well suited for colonies but not for trade."

The earl of Granville was the most persistent suitor. He owned much of North Carolina and was having a hard time attracting settlers. Zinzendorf dispatched Spangenberg to the colony in 1752 to search for suitable land.

After a harrowing journey across the state, Spangenberg found 98,985 acres along Muddy Creek in what is now Forsyth County. "The land on which we are now encamped seems to me to have reserved by the Lord for the Brethren," Spangenberg wrote in his travel journal. He named it *Der Wachau*, after an estate in Austria that had been in Zinzendorf's family. The Latin form, Wachovia, was later adopted.

The earl of Granville conveyed the Wachovia tract to the church on August 7, 1753, in 19 separate deeds. The terms were 500 pounds sterling down and 150 pounds in annual rent. The church was in financial trouble at the time, and Zinzendorf started a land company to finance the move to North Carolina. He sold shares that entitled the holder to 2,000 acres in Wachovia. About half the shares were sold before the Brethren began work on Bethabara.

A Settlement in the Wilderness

And work they did. With their usual diligence, the Moravian colonists cleared three acres within 10 days of their arrival and began working the land with a plow made by one of the brothers. By spring, the 11 colonists who remained in Bethabara had planted wheat, corn, millet, oats, cotton, flax, tobacco, barley, rye, turnips, and pumpkins.

Word spread that these Germans had a doctor, a tailor, and other craftsmen. Visitors came to gawk or have a tooth pulled or a pair of britches made. "For 1° years starting in 1753, this was the busiest place in the back country," Rod Meyer said of the Wagner cabin. The original was torn down by the Moravians in 1768, but a replica can be seen at Bethabara today.

Visitors were something of a nuisance because they had to be fed and housed overnight. The gracious Moravians usually gave up their sleeping quarters in the crowded cabin for a tent outside.

New colonists—all single men—came from Pennsylvania in the spring of 1754, and the first married couples arrived the following year. By then, Bethabara was well established. The list of structures in the town is impressive, considering trees were the only thing there three years earlier: the Meeting House, the Single Brothers House, a mill, a smithy, a cooperage, two bridges, a toolhouse, a brick kiln, a pottery, a tannery, a wash house, a tailor's shop, and six homes. By the end of 1756, the small band of adventurous pioneers and their isolated cabin had grown to 65 people living in a thriving village near the major road from Virginia.

Settlers poured down the Great Wagon Road into the Piedmont. To accommodate growing settlements, old counties frequently divided. From 1752 to 1789, the Moravians lived in a dizzying succession of counties: they bought their land in Anson County, started their settlement in Rowan County, survived the Revolution in Surry County, and welcomed the new century in Stokes County.

The constant flow of people also meant steady customers for Bethabara's mill and craft shops. Farmers came from 50 miles away to the gristmill to grind flour or meal. Gottfried Aust's pottery shed often was inundated with customers. Settlers eagerly bought Aust's dishes, cups, jugs, toys, and elaborate tobacco pipes. His entire stock often sold out in hours. Demand for all of Bethabara's crafts was so great that the village opened a store where

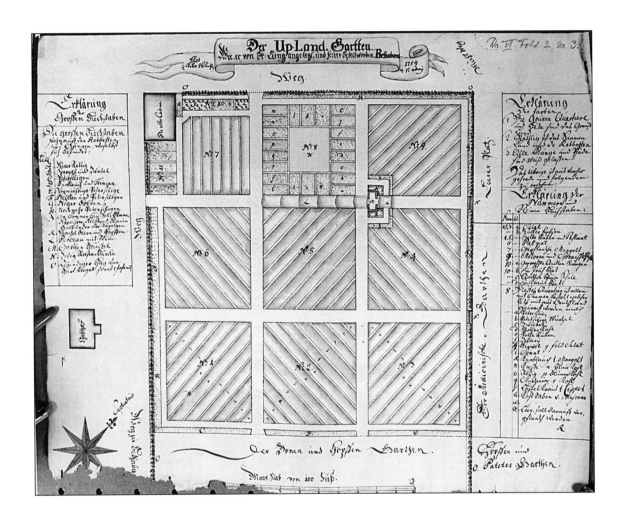

Plans for the Upland Garden were drawn by Christian Gottlieb Reuter in 1759.
The Bethabara community garden is believed to be the best documented in colonial America.

The Moravian Archives of the Northern Province, Bethlehem

The mill in Bethabara, which began operating in 1755, straddled Johanna Creek (Mill Creek).
It was a grist mill for grain, a saw mill, and an oil mill to make linseed oil from flax seed.

The Moravian Archives, Herrnhut

outsiders could do all their shopping. "It was the Wal-Mart of its day," Rod Meyer said.

Trade became regional in 1761, when a wagonload of deerskins that the Brethren had bought from local trappers left for Charles Town. The wagon returned bearing salt, lime, and other items the Brethren couldn't make or find locally. Goods were later sent to Cross Creek—now Fayetteville—and then down the Cape Fear River to the port in Wilmington.

Life in Bethabara

Amid the hustle and bustle, the Moravians managed to live the simple, pious life that Zinzendorf had prescribed. Church councils controlled all spiritual and temporal affairs in the community. Only Moravians could live in the village, and they had to be approved by the church. No one could get married, start a craft, or build a house without the church's consent. Important matters were decided by lot beginning in 1757. When a situation arose and no conclusion could be reached, the councils turned to the Lord "in childlike faith" and drew slips of paper that held an affirmative or negative response or were blank.

The Moravians needed assurances that no one would interfere with their theocratic system. The Anglican Church was, after all, the official church in the English colonies. Each county of North Carolina was established as an Anglican parish, with a vestry in charge of its spiritual affairs. The Moravians asked the royal governor, Arthur Dobbs, that Wachovia be in a separate parish. Dobbs agreed, and the General Assembly created Dobbs Parish in 1755.

Central to Bethabara's government and economy was the *Oeconomie,* the practice of common housekeeping. Everything—property, tools, livestock—was owned by the church,

which also kept all profits from craft sales. In return, the church made sure everyone was cared for. The system, meant to be temporary, later triggered resentment, but it was necessary to the founding of a large colony because it allowed villagers to work on community projects that otherwise would have gone undone. A brother could help build a road or bridge, for instance, without worrying about neglecting his corn crop. His family would still be fed. Unlike their neighbors, the Moravians were freed from the limiting prospects of subsistence farming.

From all this, it might be assumed that the Moravians were a dour bunch who led an unexciting life of drudgery under the eyes of stern church leaders. Far from it. They often sang while clearing ground, plowing fields, or building cabins. Music, in fact, was an important part of the Moravians' daily life. They sang and played instruments at church services, and a horn was used to blow signals. A brother whittled a piece of hollow tree into a trumpet in 1754 and proudly declared that "no trumpet in Bethlehem has a better tone." Later arrivals brought other instruments—trumpets, violins, even an organ—that were used to welcome new colonists to Bethabara.

Much of life centered on the church. Moravians attended church frequently, with services held in English once a month for the benefit of visitors. The pastor delivered personal sermons during the morning service on Sundays, and the sermons of Zinzendorf and other church leaders were read at other services. The last service of each day, usually held at nine o'clock in the evening, was the informal *Singstunde,* in which members sang familiar hymns.

Continuing a practice started in Herrnhut, a "scriptural watchword" from the Old Testament and a text from the New Testament were read each day, accompanied by an appropriate stanza of a well-known hymn. During times of trouble, selected brothers and sisters prayed throughout the day.

Lovefeasts were held often—when new settlers arrived, and at weddings, baptisms, and church memorials. On these happy occasions, bread or cake was passed around, followed by tea, wine, or coffee. Cornbread was even used a few times out of necessity.

Moravians were often reminded of God's wonder by simply walking through the woods that surrounded Bethabara. The famous botanist John Bartram from Philadelphia described the hillside west of the village as a "treasure-house for the botanist." Hickory, the most common tree, provided firewood and nuts that made strong yellow dye. Poplar and oak were used for lumber, and chestnut was prized for its weather-resistant wood, used in fences and roofs. Ash made strong wagons. The Moravians tapped maples for sap, which was boiled into sugar. They also stripped the bark from sumacs for dye.

Unlike many backwoods settlers, the Moravians saw the forest as a friend, not as an enemy to be pushed back. They appointed one brother as a forester to control the cutting of trees.

The woods were full of wild fruits: persimmons, cherries, plums, and crab apples. Black bears were numerous, as were wolves and turkeys, and panthers were not uncommon.

The "Dutchi Fort" and the "Time of Sorrow"

Leisurely walks in the woods came to a temporary end in 1759, the beginning of the most trying time in Bethabara's history. Murdering Indians lurked behind the trees, and a killing fever struck almost every home.

The French and Indian War (1754–63) was the last in a series of conflicts between France and England and their Indian allies for control of North America. It was fought mainly in the upper Ohio River Valley, but it exploded on the Southern frontier in 1754, when Indians killed 16 settlers along the Broad River.

A disquieting rumor reached Bethabara the following year. The Cherokees to the west, it was said, had taken up with the French. The rumor was confirmed a few weeks later when a Dunkard family from the New River arrived in Bethabara with the alarming news that 28 people along the river had been killed or captured by the Cherokees.

Settlers kept passing through Bethabara with tales of Indian massacres. Bands of Indians were said to be wandering along the Yadkin River or near what is now Walnut Cove. The Moravians decided in July 1756 to build a stockade around their village. The triangular fort was completed in 10 days, but the stockade kept falling down and had to be rebuilt twice. The palisade that now surrounds the restored village is a replica of the last fort. Smaller forts were built around the mill and the cemetery.

The Moravians tried to remain on good terms with the Indians. They had more than 500 Indian visitors in 1758 without trouble, though one party showed up with 10 scalps. Among the Indians, Bethabara was known as the "Dutch fort where there are good people and much bread."

France sent Creeks to join the Cherokees, whose hearts weren't really in the war, and the attacks got worse in 1759. Fifteen settlers were killed along the upper Catawba and Yadkin rivers, and Creeks killed more settlers along the Virginia border.

The fighting inched closer to Wachovia the following year, when a settler and his son were killed along the lower Yadkin. A company of militia sent the next day to bury the bodies was forced to turn back when it found Indians out in force. The militia spread the alarm, and refugees fled to the safety of Bethabara. "One of the refugees narrowly escaped death on the path between Bethabara and Bethania," the Bethabara church diary reports. "Two others going out against the advice of Br. Anspach, who was in command at the mill, were attacked and one of them was killed. . . . Another of the party was missing; the third escaped."

The Indians never attacked Bethabara or killed any Moravians. An interpreter who talked to the Cherokees later told the Moravians that the Indians said they had been "to a great town where there was a great many people, where a great bell rang often and during the night time after time a horn was blown so they feared to attack and had taken no prisoners."

Another traveler said he was told that "the Indians called this neighborhood Dutchi and that they said the Dutchi were a dreadful people, very large and very smart."

The stories of the bell and the horn—used by the night watchman on his hourly rounds—and the terrible "Dutchi" have become part of local folklore. They also have a ring of truth to them. "As a communal society, the Moravians in Bethabara used the bell to call people together," Rod Meyer said. "The bell was constantly ringing—to call them to a meeting, to church, to eat. From the Indians' point of view, these terrible Dutchmen didn't sleep."

Though the Indians spared the village, the "bloody flux" did not. More than 100 refugees arrived at Bethabara in 1759 alone. They camped along the stockade walls or were taken in by Moravians. The severe overcrowding triggered an outbreak of typhoid fever that summer. "Everybody was laid up, which caused great discouragement," Frederic William Marshall reported.

Eight people died, including the pastor and his wife and the village doctor. Fourteen others came close to death. Only 19 people escaped unscathed. An early historian of Wachovia called that summer the "time of sorrow."

There was little joy the following Easter when the Brethren gathered in the cemetery for the Sunrise Service amid the still-fresh graves of the fever's victims. They stood with bare heads bowed as Bishop Spangenberg looked to the sky and said, "Keep us in everlasting fellowship with those of our brethren and sisters who since last Easter day have entered into the joy of their Lord."

The Founding of Bethania

Spangenberg, who was visiting Bethabara for the first time since exploring Wachovia, came with orders to start a new settlement in a small valley, called Black Walnut Bottom, three miles to the west. Church officials in Europe had decided that Bethabara was to remain a "Unity farm." The new settlement, called Bethania, was to be the first of Wachovia's villages.

Twenty-four town lots, two tracts of meadows, and several acres for gardens and orchards—2,000 acres in all—were laid out June 30, 1759. Two weeks later, Gottfried Grabs, his wife, and their young son, William, moved into the first cabin in Bethania. Refugees in Bethabara who had expressed a desire to live with Moravians were allowed to move there.

Within three years, Bethania claimed 72 residents, three fewer than Bethabara, By 1766, some 166 people lived in the two communities. With the Indian war over and the two settlements well established, it was time to build what would become Wachovia's main town.

The Long Road of Brother Joseph

The portrait that has come down to us after 200 years shows a roly-poly man who seems more suited for the pulpit than the saddle. Brother Joseph doesn't look like a pioneer.

His fellow Moravians of the 18th century knew him better. He was just the man, they knew, to lead explorers through the wilderness of North Carolina.

Bishop August Gottlieb Spangenberg, the head of the Moravian Church in young America, could give a mighty sermon, but he was equally adept at felling a tree or fording a swollen stream. His credentials as a trailblazer were impressive. Brother Joseph, as the Moravians affectionately called him, led a party of explorers to the Moravians' new land in Georgia in 1734 and was dispatched to Pennsylvania two years later to start a settlement there.

So the 48-year-old Spangenberg was the logical choice in 1752 when the Moravians needed someone to search for suitable land in the rough-and-tumble colony of North Carolina. He picked five good men and set out from Bethlehem, a Moravian town in Pennsylvania, on August 25. They embarked on a six-month journey they would never forget, and from which some of them would never recover.

Traveling first to Philadelphia, the party then headed south—down the Eastern Shore of Maryland and through the swamps of Virginia to Norfolk. It crossed into North Carolina on September 9 and arrived in Edenton, the colony's most important town, the next day.

"On the entire journey from Bethlehem, the Lord has kept us in good health and has guided us with His eye," Spangenberg recorded in his diary.

But trouble lay ahead. Brother Joseph probably got his first inkling when he asked around town about the colony's rivers. The Moravians had agreed to buy 100,000 acres of fertile land on a navigable river from the earl of Granville. The colonists laughed at

Moravian Bishop
August Gottlieb Spangenberg

Collection of Old Salem

Spangenberg's questions. Beyond the vast labyrinth of sounds on the colony's coast, the rivers were much too shallow for anything but skiffs, he was told, and all the good eastern land was already claimed.

Undeterred, Spangenberg asked Francis Corbin, Granville's agent, for a map of the earl's vast holdings in North Carolina. The answer must have come as a shock: there was no map.

The colony was in turmoil, with the older northern counties feuding with the newer ones in the south about representation in the colonial assembly. Law and order had broken down, and crime was rampant. "There are many cases of murder, theft, and the like, but no one is punished," Spangenberg wrote.

Land titles weren't recorded. Settlers merely threw up shacks and called the land their own. Under such circumstances, surveyors found it impossible to draw a map showing what land remained unclaimed.

Such disarray must have offended Spangenberg. He was a well-educated, cultured German who had been a Lutheran minister before shunning that faith's doctrine in 1733 to join the Moravians. Like all the Brethren, Spangenberg found comfort in orderliness.

"Land matters in North Carolina are in unbelievable confusion," he recorded. "This much is sure—my lord's [Granville's] agent cannot now give a patent [land title] without fearing that when the land is settled another man will come and say, 'This is my land.'"

Francis Corbin, though, assured Spangenberg that much good land remained "in the back of the colony."

Brother Joseph bought supplies and learned what he could about the colony's largely unexplored interior. On September 18, he again put his trust in the Lord's guiding eye and led his party out of Edenton and toward the "Blue Mountains."

The summer had been hot and dry, but while Spangenberg was in Edenton, torrential rains had raised rivers out of their banks and flooded farms and forests with moving water. Dirt roads had turned into quagmires, and scum-rimmed pools had bred hordes of murderous mosquitoes.

Fever struck all but one in the party within a week. Spangenberg was so ill that he "burned like a heated stove."

Joseph Muller, the only explorer who wasn't sick, thought the bishop would die. "I went into the woods and talked it over with the Savior and begged Him, if it was His will, to give Brother Joseph back to us in time," Muller wrote.

The party huddled in a forest cabin in Granville County for two weeks fighting the fever. Spangenberg and the others were well enough to continue by October 14. They set out for the crossroads village that is now Hillsborough, where Granville's surveyor waited. The party stopped frequently for rest, and Spangenberg had to be lifted to his saddle and once even held in his seat. A member of the party became ill again and was left at a settler's home under Muller's care.

The surveyor joined the explorers, who then struck out to the southwest along the colony's main east-west road—nothing more than a path, really. They reached the Catawba River

on October 27, and Spangenberg made plans to turn off the path and venture into the forest, which he wrote was "as trackless as the ocean."

After buying more provisions and hiring two local hunters as guides, the party followed the Catawba to Quaker Meadows, near present-day Morganton. They then turned north along the Johns River and Big Wilson Creek into what are now Burke and Caldwell counties. Eighty miles from the nearest settlement, they were "in a region that has been seldom visited since the creation of the world."

What a paradise it was! The keenly observant Spangenberg described huge meadows and vast tracts of giant hardwood trees. The rich soil would grow crops abundantly, he noted, and the woods were full of buffalo, panthers, deer, wolves, and bear.

But after a month of exploring this verdant wilderness, Spangenberg was no closer to selecting 100,000 acres than he had been in

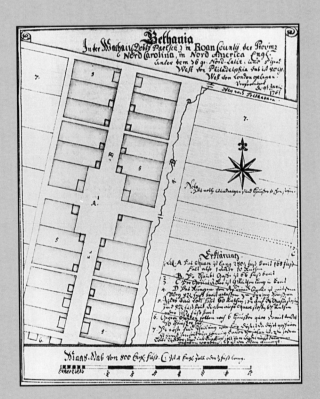

The map shows the lots in Bethania as they appeared in 1761, two years after the village's founding. The square in the middle was eliminated in 1768.

The Moravian Archives, Herrnhut

Edenton. One of the guides said he knew a path to a large river, the "Atkin," which flowed to the east. The guide missed the path and led the explorers farther up the Johns River to its mouth, near present-day Blowing Rock. There was no way out except over the mountains.

"Part of the way we climbed on hands and knees, dragging after us the loads we had taken from the backs of the horses," Spangenberg wrote. "Part of the way we led the horses, who were trembling like a leaf. When we reached the top we saw mountains to the right and to the left, before us and behind us, many hundreds of mountains, rising like great waves in a storm."

They hacked their way through laurel bushes and beaver dams. Finally, in early December, they reached a small meadow near what is now Boone. No sooner had the weary men pitched their tents than a fierce wind howled out of the mountains.

"I think I have never felt a winter wind so strong and so cold," Spangenberg recorded. "The ground was covered in snow; water froze by the fire. Then our men lost heart. What should we do? Our horses should die and we with them."

The next day dawned clear, and the warming sun burned away the men's fears. They followed a creek to a large river—the Yadkin, they thought. There was something strange about this river, however. It flowed north and then south, east and then west, and following it only led deeper into the mountainous wilderness. After several days, the guides concluded that they had found the New River, not the Yadkin.

Spangenberg realized that they were lost again. He turned the party east and south and came out of the Blue Ridge, following tiny runs that grew into creeks and then joined larger streams that flowed into the Yadkin. On December 20, they reached the river not far above Mulberry Fields, the site of the present-day Wilkesboros.

The first white people they had seen in weeks told them of large tracts to the east on the three forks of Muddy Creek. Traveling along snow-quiet trails, they found the creek on January 8, 1753. It was reasonably fertile, and there was enough of it—just under 100,000 acres. The surveyor completed his work January 13, and Spangenberg and the Moravians headed back to Pennsylvania, reaching Bethlehem in about a month.

Of the six men who made the trip, only Hermann Loesch returned to live in the new settlement. Henry Antes, on the other hand, never fully recovered from the hardships of the journey. His health gradually failed, and he died in Pennsylvania in 1755.

As for Brother Joseph, he came back in 1759 and helped select the site for Bethania. He later returned to Germany to lead the Moravian Church and write important books. He died in 1792 at the age of 88, universally respected, trusted, and beloved.

And he's all but forgotten in the city he helped found. While other important Moravians and leaders have had city streets and parks named after them, Spangenberg has been ignored. A creek flowing through the western part of the city was named in his honor, but residents found that the name didn't roll easily off the tongue, and by 1808, it had been corrupted to Spanking Back Creek. The name was tinkered with further, and 25 years later, Silas Creek first appeared on local maps in its place.

Dates to Remember

1752 Bishop August Gottlieb Spangenberg leads an expedition across North Carolina in search of possible sites for a settlement. The Moravians buy about 100,000 acres in the foothills of the Blue Ridge Mountains.

1753 The first 15 colonists leave Bethlehem, Pennsylvania, on October 8 on the Great Wagon Road and arrive in Wachovia November 17.

1755 The colonial assembly grants the Moravians' request and creates a separate parish for Wachovia: Dobbs Parish. The move gives the Moravians full control of the development of the settlement. A gristmill is completed, making Bethabara the hub of activity in the area.

1756 Palisades are built around the town to ward off Indian attack. Anna Johanna Krause is the first child born in Bethabara.

1758 The first Easter Sunrise Service is held in Bethabara.

1759 Bethania is founded.

1761 The first school for children is started in Bethania. Moravians begin exporting when they send a wagonload of deerskins to Charles Town.

1764 Frederic William Marshall arrives in Wachovia, and the search begins for a suitable site for the settlement's main town.

Names to Know

Bethabara
Founded in 1753, this was the first Moravian village in Forsyth County. The name means "House of Passage."

Bethania
The name of the second Moravian village, founded in 1759, is derived from Bethany, a village near Jerusalem at the foot of the Mount of Olives.

August Gottlieb Spangenberg
The Moravian bishop in America, Spangenberg explored North Carolina in 1752–53, looking for suitable land for a settlement. He found it in the northwestern Piedmont section of the colony. He also selected the site for Bethania.

Wachovia
Spangenberg named the land he selected *Der Wachau*, after an estate that had been in the family of Count Nicolaus Ludwig von Zinzendorf, the man who reorganized the Moravian Church. The Latin form, Wachovia, was later adopted.

Count Nicolaus Ludwig von Zinzendorf
This pious nobleman allowed Moravian refugees to live on his estate in Saxony. He drafted new laws and a constitution for the disorganized church and became its spiritual leader.

Ludwig Gottfried von Redeken, Salem's first known painter, arrived in the village in
1787 from Bethlehem, Pennsylvania, where he taught school.
He was sickly and introverted, but he had a keen eye for detail.
He painted this view of Salem from the northwest of town. He died in 1797, never
fulfilling his dream of going to Philadelphia to become a professional painter.

———

Moravian Archives, Herrnhut

Salem: Fulfilling the Dream

With the end of the Indian war, the Moravians in Wachovia turned to the unfinished business of building their main town. As its name implies, Bethabara—"House of Passage"—was merely a start. The Moravians had something more ambitious in mind. After a careful search, they chose a spot in the middle of Wachovia and called it Salem, after the Hebrew word for peace, *shalom*.

Within five years, the little town replaced Bethabara as the Moravians' religious center and the commercial hub of the northwestern frontier. It was there that the seeds planted in the wilderness 13 years earlier bore fruit.

The Moravians saw their religious convictions and peaceful temperament severely tested during Salem's founding years, first by rebellious backwoodsmen and later by the Revolutionary War. They stuck to their principles and remained neutral, and their neighbors became suspicious. Their allegiance to the new country was questioned and their pacifism scorned. Midnight riders stormed into homes and terrorized families at gunpoint, and Revolutionary leaders threatened to take their land.

Guided by prayer and aided by some swift talking, the Moravians made it through those troubling times with their town and their tenets intact. The war changed them, nonetheless. It began to transform these Germans into Americans.

The Congregation House, or Gemein Haus, was
the most important building in early Salem.

———

The Winston-Salem Journal

Moving Day

The day was pleasant and warm, more like spring than winter. The good Lord, Traugott Bagge may have thought as he loaded his family's possessions into the wagons, was smiling down on him. If the weather were a sign, then the future did indeed look bright.

Bagge and his family were leaving Bethabara on this February 14, 1772. Like many other Brethren, they were heading for a new life in Salem, the Moravians' new town six miles away. Since its *Gemein Haus*, or Congregation House, had opened the previous year, Salem had become the center of activity in Wachovia. The Salem congregation had officially formed, and the church had moved its headquarters there. Most of Bethabara's craftsmen had left to open shops in Salem. Bagge, who ran Bethabara's community store, would operate the Salem store.

A larger role awaited Traugott Bagge. This unassuming merchant would be looked upon to lead Salem through some of its most trying times. Bagge would respond with patience and perseverance, diplomacy and diligence. He would never flinch from his duty, even when a gun was pointed at his chest.

Nothing in Bagge's background could have prepared him for the job that awaited him. He had been a shopkeeper all his life, like his father and grandfather before him back in Göteborg, Sweden. In the memoir, or memorial, that Moravians keep, Bagge remembered how his father took him to the store when he was 11 "to learn the business of a merchant."

Bagge was a bright boy who was reading by age five. He mastered Latin and Greek, and even knew some Hebrew and Syriac. He quickly mastered his trade. He began reading Moravian writings at age 17 and a few years later had something of a conversion on the deck of a ship. He was returning from London to Hamburg, where he worked in his brother's store. "I surrendered myself entirely to His will," Bagge wrote of the incident, "finding very significant His words that men should give up father and mother, brother and sister for His sake, and seeing clearly that my future should be in the Unity of the Brethren."

He joined a Moravian mission in the Netherlands and was among the original shareholders in the land company that financed the North Carolina settlement. He was the only shareholder to actually move to Wachovia, arriving with his wife, Rachel, in 1768 to run the Bethabara store and keep the congregation's books.

Bagge may have recalled those years fondly as he slowly led four loaded wagons through Bethabara's streets. His first child, Anna Elisabeth, had been born in the little community, and he had earned a reputation as a skillful shopkeeper and a caring brother. Little did he know that his best years were just ahead, in the town taking shape at the other end of the narrow road.

"My Name Shall Be There"

Peace returned to the frontier after the French and English signed a treaty in 1763 that ended years of fighting in North America. With the Indian troubles over, the Moravians in Bethabara could safely take to the woods to search for a site for their major town. The church's governing body in Europe had already decided that Bethabara was to be a farming community. The Lord, the church noted, had bigger plans for the new town, which Zinzendorf named Salem.

"The Savior wills that Salem shall be the town in Wachovia for trade and the professions, and they shall be moved thither from Bethabara," the church elders said.

To run Wachovia and see to Salem's founding, the church sent Frederic William Marshall to North Carolina. The son of a German army officer, Marshall was destined for a military career until he joined the Moravians when he was 18. The product of a strict, formal educa-

tion, Marshall knew something about architecture, planning, and economics, making him the perfect choice to start a town. He arrived in Bethabara in 1764 with the title of *Oeconomus*, or financial director and business administrator, and was the most influential man in Wachovia until his death in 1802.

Marshall immediately went to work. He sent Bethabara's gifted surveyor, Christian Gottlieb Reuter, to search Wachovia's 100,000 acres for a suitable site. Several locations were rejected by the lot before Reuter came upon a site in the middle of the tract, about six miles from Bethabara. It was halfway up a hill from *der Wach,* or Salem Creek, and was shielded from the north wind. The site was high enough on the ridge for protection from floods, yet several good springs on higher ground could supply water to the town.

The site was put to the lot on February 14, 1765. Leaving such an important decision to

Frederic William Marshall

The Moravian Archives of
the Southern Province, Winston-Salem

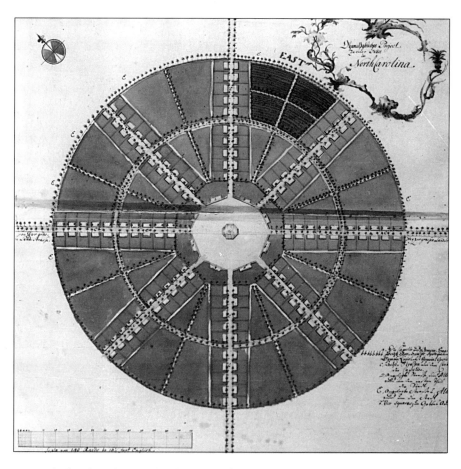

Count Zinzendorf endorsed a circular design for Salem that encouraged the isolation that Zinzendorf desired. Eight roads led to the center, where an eight-sided Gemein Haus would dominate the town.

the luck of the draw is difficult to understand today. To the Moravians, there was no luck involved. They didn't use the lot as a fortune teller uses cards or as boys draw straws. They approached it with reverence and truly believed that the result was God's wish. Therefore, they were compelled to follow its outcome. This time, the choice was approved, and the result was announced to the Bethabara congregation at the evening service. The text for the day seemed appropriate: "Let thine eyes be open toward this house night and day, even toward the place of which thou hast said my name shall be there."

Had Count Zinzendorf lived long enough, Salem may have been radically different from the town that eventually was built. Zinzendorf wanted a place where the Moravians could practice their religion in peace and quiet. His plan for the main settlement in Wachovia called for a huge, circular town nearly a mile across, encompassing 380 acres. Eight roads, like the spokes of a wheel, would lead to the center, where an eight-sided *Gemein Haus* would dominate the town. In this town, which Zinzendorf called Unitas, all buildings were to face the center in a design that encouraged the isolation the count desired. Symbolically, then, Unitas would turn its back on the outside world.

Zinzendorf died in 1760, and with him went Unitas. Spangenberg, who didn't like Unitas, took control of the church, and a more traditional European design was adopted.

The first trees were felled on January 6, 1766, and eight single brothers moved into temporary shelter 13 days later. Reuter laid out Salem's principal streets and the square in February, and workmen began building the first permanent house on Main Street in April. Working with their customary zeal, the Moravians had the town essentially built in five years.

For many years, the *Gemein Haus* was the largest building in Salem. Built of uncut stone and timber, the three-story structure stood where Main Hall of Salem College is now. The meeting hall where worship services were held was on the second floor. The building also contained apartments for the ministers, guest rooms, and the living rooms and workrooms of the single sisters.

It was the most important building in town. Its consecration in November 1771 marked the start of the Salem congregation and the end of Bethabara as the Moravians' commercial and religious center. The church shifted its recordkeeping and other functions to Salem, and the Brethren followed.

About 130 people lived in Bethabara in 1766, when the building crew was clearing the woods in Salem. Six years later, Bethabara's population had shrunk to 54 residents, while Salem's had ballooned to 120. That's certainly not very large by today's standards, or even by the standards of those times. But it is impressive considering how young Salem was, and considering that there were no real towns in the back country.

"The present building of Salem is an extraordinary affair, which I would not have undertaken had not the Savior Himself ordered it," Marshall said in 1771. "I verily believe that the rich city of London could not do that what we must accomplish—move the entire town and its businesses to another place."

Most of the craftsmen moved from Bethabara by 1772. Bagge arrived to run the store, Matthew Miksch rented a house and began making snuff and smoking tobacco, and Jacob Meyer and his wife took charge of the tavern.

Visitors kept them and other merchants busy. Actually, commerce had begun in earnest when the blacksmith and the potter opened for business in 1767. Good clay for kitchen wares and smoking pipes was found in a small meadow where the athletic fields of Salem College are

Gottfried Aust, Wachovia's first potter, was a fine craftsmen as this decorated plate, made in 1773, shows.

The Winston-Salem Journal

now. As in Bethabara, the potter's shed was one of the busiest places in Salem. On April 11, 1777, the church diary noted, "Men were in the potter's shop like a swarm of bees, coming, buying and leaving. Many could get nothing, as the first to come bought it all."

Business was booming all along the frontier. Trade in the 18th and early 19th centuries moved south through the Yadkin and Catawba river valleys to Charles Town, north through the Shenandoah Valley to Philadelphia, and east to Fayetteville and then down the Cape Fear River to Wilmington. Centrally located on the major trading routes, Salem rapidly became the largest town and the commercial center of the northwestern Piedmont.

Farmers and hunters arrived at the Salem store to sell or trade animal skins. For years, skins were the most important items exported from Salem. In 1771, Salem added tobacco to its shipment of deerskins to Charles Town and Fayetteville—then called Cross Creek. They were bartered for windowpanes, sugar, coffee, tea, lime, and other items that Bagge sold in the Salem store.

A visitor to Salem on the eve of the Revolution would have been impressed with the Old World feel of this new town on the edge of the wilderness. The solidly built houses of timber and brick were clustered around a common square, more like middle Europe than back-country North Carolina.

The visitor would have found a bustling place where the sounds of hammers and saws filled the air. The square was planted in shade trees. Sixty-foot-wide Main Street was filled with wagons and lined with shops where the visitor could have a pair of shoes made or buy britches. If he was thinking of buying land or building a house, he could hire a surveyor or order a load of bricks. He could shoe his horse at the smithy or buy it a saddle at the tannery, have a tooth pulled, get a haircut, or rest and eat at the tavern.

One such visitor was impressed with the scenery and the inhabitants. "The first view of the town is romantic, just as it breaks upon you through the woods," he wrote. "It is pleasantly seated on rising ground and is surrounded by beautiful meadows, well-cultivated fields, and shady woods. . . . Everyone was hard at work; such a scene of industry, perhaps, exists nowhere in so small a place."

The first house built in Salem,
from a photograph taken in the early twentieth century

North Carolina Division of Archives and History

Washington Slept Here . . . or There

The rider jolted to a halt in front of the tavern. He jumped down from his horse and raced inside. The president, he said breathlessly, had left Salisbury earlier that morning and was heading toward Salem. Word spread quickly through the town and into the countryside: Washington was coming.

Salem residents had known for some months that George Washington would stop in their town while on his tour of the Southern states. They had been busily preparing for the visit—fixing streets and bridges and even ordering music with English words from Pennsylvania. But until the messenger rode into town that Tuesday, May 31, 1791, the Moravians didn't know when Washington would arrive.

Frederic William Marshall, the town's chief executive, led a party of three brothers to the bridge across Salem Creek to await the president. At three in the afternoon, Washington's white "charriot," pulled by four horses, came into view on the old post road, now N.C. 150. After some brief greetings, the brothers escorted the carriage up the hill into Salem.

The town had been filling with people all day. Parents loaded their children into wagons for the ride to Salem. Former soldiers, some dressed in their old uniforms, lined Main Street. They all wanted to see the great man one last time.

As the hero of the Revolution and the leader of the young republic, Washington was already a national icon. Thousands of people had turned out to see the president during his 1,900-mile journey through the South. Bonfires, balls, and fireworks had transformed the tour into a tribute to the old soldier, who had just turned 59.

His reception in Salem may have been more subdued, but it was no less enthusiastic. As the procession approached, the crowd cheered and the band on the tavern porch came to life. One selection must have been the song that had arrived from Pennsylvania: "God Save Great Washington," played to the tune of the German hymn that was later used for "My Country 'tis of Thee."

Washington wasn't one for off-the-cuff speeches. "He greeted those who stood around in a friendly manner, showing his good will especially to the children who were there," according to the church records. He was then led to his room in the tavern.

The Daughters of the American Revolution came by 117 years later. They chose the large room on the tavern's second floor and put a plaque on the door. Washington slept here, it says.

Ken Zogry doubts it. The Daughters had no real evidence, according to Zogry, a former assistant curator at Old Salem, Inc., who has done extensive research on the tavern. It seems that the room's only qualifications were that it was the largest on the second floor and had a fireplace and windows that offered an excellent view of the town.

More logical choices, Zogry said, are the room on the tavern's first floor that church records say was reserved for "traveling families and strangers of a better class" and the small suite of rooms across from the "Washington Room." "We know he slept in the tavern, but we really don't know where," Zogry concluded.

Built in 1784, the tavern is one of two places still standing in North Carolina where Washington is known to have spent a night. The other is the Stanly House in New Bern. Compared to the usual accommodations of its day, the tavern was the Backwoods Hilton. Washington was on the road a great deal during his life as a surveyor, revolutionary, and politician. The beds in the wilderness taverns he frequented were full of fleas, and a straw mattress he was sleeping on caught fire once. In Salem, he had music with his meals and his bed didn't burn. A four-star rating, at least.

Washington had planned to spend one night, but he decided to extend his visit an extra day after learning that his friend Alexander Martin, the governor of North Carolina, was traveling to Salem to meet him. The Moravians gave Washington a tour of the town on June 1, visiting the choir houses, some shops, and the

This music was ordered from Pennsylvania to welcome President Washington.

———

The Moravian Archives
of the Southern Province, Winston-Salem

Boys School. Washington apparently had a good time. He wrote admiringly in his diary of the Moravians' industriousness and their waterworks.

Marshall and the other Moravian leaders officially welcomed Washington with a public address. They thanked "the great author of our being" for his constancy and devotion to duty and wished him continued health and success. Washington's reply, which can be found in the Moravian Archives, was short—only 14 handwritten lines. "From a society, whose governing principles are industry and love of order," he told the Moravians, "much may be expected towards the improvement and prosperity in the country in which their settlements are formed—and experience authorizes the belief that much will be obtained."

Martin arrived later that afternoon and accompanied Washington to a concert that evening.

Dorethea Elizabeth Meyer, the 13-year-old daughter of tavern keeper Jacob Meyer, was pressed into service playing the piano for Washington. According to a story about the tavern published in 1941, the president thanked the nervous girl and told her how to remove the warts he had seen on her hand. Poor Dorethea "fled in humiliation." Visitors to Old Salem can see the piano in the Vierling House today.

Or can they? According to Zogry, Dorethea probably did play the piano for the president, but not the one in the Vierling House. Evidence now shows that the piano was bought five years after Washington's visit. And Zogry doubts that Washington had the bad manners to call attention to the girl's warts.

There's another legend Zogry questions. A rare giant glass mug called the "Amelung pokal" is on display at the Museum of Early Southern Decorative Arts in Old Salem. A caption under a photograph of the pokal published in 1955 noted that Washington drank from the commemorative mug, which was presented to Marshall between 1785 and 1793.

"It's a big thing. It would require two hands to lift it. People just didn't drink from it," Zogry said. "It would be kind of like drinking from a bowling trophy."

A two-handled mug, though, may have been just the thing for a ceremonial quaff. Communion chalices used in Salem at the time were large, to prevent spills, and had two handles, which made them easier to pass to the next communicant.

Accompanied by Governor Martin, Washington departed Salem early June 2. He had breakfast at Dobson's Crossroads, now Kernersville, and spent the night in Guilford, where he toured the battlefield around the courthouse. He crossed into Virginia June 4 and headed for Mount Vernon.

In his wake, the thousands of people who saw him were left with memories that became more cherished and more embellished with each passing year. From those seeds grew the many colorful legends that bloomed like periwinkles along Washington's trail.

The Order of Things

If a visitor liked Salem enough to want to settle there, he had to be a Moravian in good standing. Like Bethabara, Salem was a theocracy, with the church overseeing every aspect of life. Three church councils regulated the town's social, economic, and religious affairs. They decided almost everything, from who could live in town to who could open a shop. They made sure that no one profited at the expense of others and that everyone enjoyed the necessities of life.

The system of common housekeeping that had irritated some residents of Bethabara was relaxed in Salem. Craftsmen worked for themselves, and families could build their own houses and set up their own households, but everyone still had to adhere to some strict rules.

Residents, for instance, couldn't own land. Within the village, lots were leased by the church. A resident could own a house, but the church owned the land. Tenants paid yearly rent equal to six percent of the value of the buildings on the land, seven percent if they didn't maintain the property.

The money went to the Salem *Diaconie*, a sort of collection agency that received rents and contributions from church members. That money, controlled by a supervisory board, was used to pay community expenses, such as repairs to the *Gemein Haus* and other buildings and the annual rent for Wachovia.

Businesses, though freer than in Bethabara, also operated under tough rules. The general store, tavern, tannery, and pottery were owned by the church. People in other trades worked for themselves, but only members of the church could open shops. The church also decided how many people could operate in a particular trade in Salem, thus ensuring a mo-

nopoly. The church set pay scales and the price that craftsmen could charge for their wares. Price controls prevented one tradesman from undercutting another and assured that items were available at reasonable cost.

Shop employees also were monitored by the church. The rules prevented craftsmen from hiring outside workers if the sons of church members were available. Usually, young men became apprentices for seven years. The apprenticeship system was vital to the well-being of the community because youngsters learned a trade and, more important, how to become responsible citizens. The apprentice was expected to work hard and be attentive to his craft. The master was expected to educate his apprentice and provide for him as he would his own child.

In a typical apprentice bond, John Henry Stultz was bound to blacksmith L. F. Eberhart. Eberhart agreed to "teach and instruct, or cause [Stultz] to be taught and instructed . . . to read, write and to cipher . . . and [to] give him a Bible and 40 dollars . . . and [to] give him two suits of freedom clothes homespun. And that he will constantly find and provide for said apprentice . . . sufficient diet, washing, lodging and apparel, fitting for an apprentice."

Such rules made for a leisurely pace. Work was done by hand, and time was measured by how long it took to complete a task. With no worry about competition, tradesmen often mixed work and pleasure. They would work in the morning with their apprentices and take the afternoon off to fish, hunt, walk in the woods, or ice skate. They met in the tavern or at Winkler's bakery to discuss the important topics of the day while enjoying a beer or brandy.

The cistern at Salem Square

The First Water System

Central water systems were relatively unheard of in 18th-century America, where most people depended on wells, fountains, and cisterns or drew their water from springs and rivers.

The Moravians were familiar with the central water systems in Germany and had built one in Bethlehem. Such a system, they knew, could supply Salem's needs more efficiently and reliably than individual wells.

Construction began in 1778 under the supervision of Christian Triebel, a carpenter, and Johannes Krause, a joiner. Pipes were made of white oak. Mains were 10 to 12 feet long, with bores of half an inch to four inches. Secondary pipes were shorter, with smaller bores.

A three-foot-deep ditch was dug from two springs northwest of town, near what is now Poplar Street. The pipes were laid in the ditch and joined with iron rings. The route followed Poplar Street to Brookstown Avenue, headed along Brookstown to Cherry Street, and continued southeast to the corner of Main and Bank streets. Outlets were placed on Main Street, and the kitchens in the Single Brothers House, the tavern, and the *Gemein Haus* were equipped with spigots.

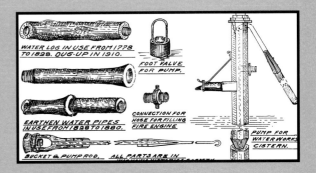

Logs were used for pipes.

The waterwheel of the second system

Drawings courtesy of The Moravian Archives of the Southern Province, Winston-Salem

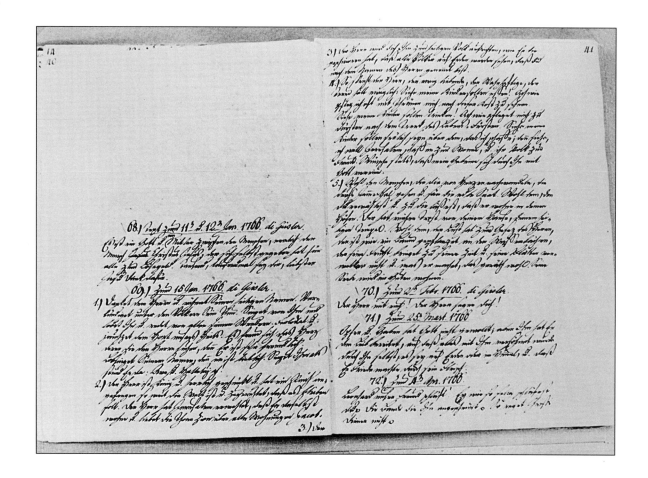

A page from the Salem church diary in 1766

The Moravian Archives of the Southern Province, Winston-Salem

The Regulator War

The talk at Winkler's during the late 1760s centered on the bands of querulous strangers who began to appear frequently in the Moravian towns. They called themselves Regulators, and they were intent on bringing down the royal government. They made the Moravians uneasy.

Trouble had been brewing on the frontier for some time. The people who settled the backwoods complained of corrupt sheriffs and justices of the peace, excessive taxes and fees, and despotic judges. These cash-poor farmers were required to pay their rent in currency rather than in farm products, and they had to travel long distances, often on poor roads, to pay taxes and file deeds at county courts.

Most irksome, though, was the General Assembly. Though most of the growth in the colony during the mid-18th century had been in the Piedmont, the legislature was still dominated by eastern merchants and plantation owners, who appointed other easterners to government positions. To backwoods farmers, the odds seemed stacked against them.

Their resentment bubbled over into riots in 1768, and the militia had to be called out in numerous counties. The peaceful Moravians deplored these "disturbances caused by a mob," as the church records reported.

The Brethren, as could be expected, tried to steer clear of the quickening current of rebellion. They paid their rent without complaint and remained on good terms with the royal government. The Regulators were suspicious. Scots-Irish settlers made up the bulk of the movement, and they seemed to take a dislike to the Moravians. Maybe it was religious differences, or contrasting nationalities and temperaments. It could have been that the farmers, who lived a hardscrabble existence, simply were envious of the disciplined Moravians and their comfortable towns.

Whatever the reason, Regulators badgered and terrorized the Brethren. Fresh off their sacking of the Orange County Courthouse in 1770, Regulators threatened Traugott Bagge with a whipping for supplying bread to government troops. A group of Regulators complained the following year that the original Moravians settlers had claimed land that belonged to them. One even contended that he owned all of Bethabara and demanded 30 pounds sterling for the title.

Moravian leaders treated the complaints with more respect than they deserved, suggesting that the Regulators take their case to court. They never did, of course. "Groundless babbling," is how the Bethabara church diarist summed up the affair. He added, "They may have wanted to try whether the terrifying name of Regulator would not frighten us into giving them what they wanted."

Inflamed by the poetry of Rednap Howell and the essays of Hermon Husbands, the Regulators took on the government. They gathered on the western bank of Alamance Creek on May 16, 1771, and were promptly crushed by eastern militia under Governor William Tryon.

The movement ended, and the name Regulator would frighten no one anymore. But the uprising was the first squall of an ominous storm that was gathering on the horizon.

Salem Academy:
"Sober Duties, Solid Realities"

A good education, the Moravians knew, was the key to a good life. In that respect, they differed little from many Christian churches that sponsored schools throughout the colonies in the 18th century. Unlike the other denominations, though, the Moravians believed boys and girls should have the same educational opportunities.

Women in colonial America cooked and cleaned and sewed. Maybe they got enough schooling to learn to read and write, but it was rare for a woman to advance beyond rudimentary skills.

The Moravians saw things differently. They had a long tradition of educating females. John Amos Comenius, a 17th-century theologian and the father of modern education, was a Moravian who believed that women had just as much intellect as men and were just as capable of learning. Because of his influence, the Moravians started girls' schools at many of their missions and opened a boarding school for girls in Bethlehem, the Moravian town in Pennsylvania.

They brought their ideas about education to North Carolina. The Moravians started the first school for children in Bethania in 1761 and opened three schools in Bethabara within the next five years—one for young boys, another for young girls, and an evening school for older boys.

There were few children in Salem during its early years. Many of the residents were single, and the married couples coming to Wachovia had left their children in Moravian schools in Pennsylvania. But plans were made to educate the children as soon as there were enough.

Christian Triebel, Salem's master carpenter, began teaching boys in his home in 1772, and Elisabeth Oesterlein taught girls in the *Gemein Haus*. The Boys School continued until the late 19th century, when it was replaced by public schools. The school for girls matured into Salem Academy and College. Salem College is the oldest educational institution in North Carolina, and the adjacent Salem Academy is the oldest school for girls in continuous operation in its original location in the United States.

Sister Oesterlein's first students were ages 2°, four, and eight. She taught them to read, write, knit, and weave, and they read the Bible and sang hymns. The school grew, and by 1788, the first Moravian girls from outside Salem were admitted. The church warned their parents that the girls must be on their best behavior and be "clean, free of itch or lice, etc." Twelve girls attended that year and were taught arithmetic, geography, music, and biblical history.

In response to numerous requests for admission from non-Moravians, church elders formally established the "Boarding School for Female Education" on October 31, 1802, and made plans for a building to accommodate 60 students. The school's goal, they said, was "to fit the scholar, by the best training, for the sober duties and the solid realities of life."

Samuel Kramsch

Wachovia
Historical Society

The first non-Moravian boarders arrived in May 1804—four girls from Hillsborough, two from Halifax County, one from Fayetteville, and one from Caswell County. Students, called "scholars," paid $160 to $180 a year for the normal courses: grammar and syntax, history, geography, English, reading, writing, arithmetic, and plain needlework. For an additional fee, they could take drawing, music, and fancy needlework.

Classes continued in the *Gemein Haus* until July 1805, when the new building—now South Hall—was completed at a cost of about $6,000. Thirty students were enrolled when the building opened. By November, more than 55 students filled it almost to capacity.

Samuel Gottlieb Kramsch, the school's first inspector, or principal, lived in the hall with his family and apparently got into some trouble. The church boards held emergency meetings in 1805 to discuss Kramsch, who had behaved "in a most improper and objectionable manner." No details were recorded, and previous histories of Winston-Salem have made no mention of the incident. It's easy to jump to conclusions, given the realities of contemporary life. But before judging Brother Kramsch too harshly, it should be remembered that what 18th-century Moravians considered "improper and objectionable" would hardly raise an eyebrow today.

Whatever Kramsch's offense, it was enough to

Main Hall of Salem Female Academy in 1873

The Photograph Collection, Winston-Salem/Forsyth County Public Library

offend the sensibilities of the church elders, who fired him and recommended that he be sent to Bethlehem. It's not clear whether Kramsch ever left Salem. It is known that he finished his days as pastor of the Hope congregation in Wachovia.

Abraham Gottlieb Steiner was hired as the new inspector and given a residence outside the school. "We shall never again let an inspector live in the school house," a bishop in Salem wrote a bishop in Pennsylvania.

The incident was kept quiet and didn't harm the school's growing academic reputation. Enrollment reached 90 in 1813, and students had to be housed in homes in Salem. There were so many requests for admission the following year that girls had to be turned away. In response to the demand, an addition to South Hall was built in 1824.

The school became the choice of many parents in the South. Sarah Childress was one of the many daughters of the South's finest families who attended the school during the 19th century. She entered the academy in 1817 and began courting James K. Polk, then a student at the University of North Carolina. Miss Childress left Salem in 1818 and married the future president. Other famous alumnae from the period included Mary Anna Morrison Jackson, the wife of Thomas "Stonewall" Jackson; Mary Denny Martin Douglas, the wife of Senator Stephen A. Douglas; and Mary Pinkney Hardy, called "Pinky," the mother of General Douglas MacArthur.

Enrollment continued to grow—to 137 by the mid-1830s and 329 in 1853. More room was needed, so the *Gemein Haus* was torn down in 1854 and Main Hall built in its place. Completed in two years,

the new building contained all the classrooms and dormitory rooms, the infirmary, and storage rooms.

Soon, even that building was overflowing. So many parents sent their daughters to Salem during the Civil War that school administrators told the families of prospective students, "We have no more beds, but if you will furnish beds we will try to take care of your daughters."

Feeding the students became a serious problem during the war. Governor Zebulon Vance sent the school sugar from captured supplies. In their old age, students would recall with amusement how their principal rode a horse at the head of a herd of pigs destined for the school's table.

The school, then called the Female Academy, was chartered for college work in 1866, and the first degrees were offered in 1890. By 1907, the school had a new name: Salem Academy and College. The academy was physically separated from the college in 1931, when new buildings for the academy were completed; it offers college preparatory courses for girls grades nine through 12.

Declining enrollment beginning in the 1970s presented the college and the academy with one of their severest tests. Only 66 college freshmen enrolled in 1990. Morale was low and faculty turnover high. Julianne Still Thrift, the first female president of Salem Academy and College, was hired the following year and began to aggressively promote the school's history and academic reputation. In 1993, the academy had almost full enrollment for the first time in years, and the college's student body rose to 850, including more than 130 freshmen.

Salem and adjacent territory on the eve of the American Revolution

---

The Moravian Archives of the Southern Province, Winston-Salem

"Permit Us to Remain in Peace"

"Our sky has remained clear in spite of the unrest in the land," Bishop John Michael Graff, Salem's minister, wrote in the church diary in May 1775. It wouldn't for long. It was the spring of Lexington, Concord, and Bunker Hill, and the storm of revolution would soon break.

In the back country, away from the battlefields and marching armies, the American Revolution was really a civil war, pitting colonists loyal to the English crown—Tories—against those who favored independence. The Moravians were spared the violence of war but endured the suspicion and partisan hatred peculiar to all civil wars.

News of Lexington reached Salem by rumor on May 8, then by newspaper accounts nine days later. The Moravians had mixed feelings about the war. They had no quarrel with England. In fact, they had friends there and were grateful for the many favors that the king and Parliament had granted them. But they also felt a loyalty to their adopted country.

Their religious scruples put them in an impossible situation. They were forbidden to take the oath of allegiance to the king, and also to bear arms against him. The Moravians weren't the fervent pacifists that the Quakers in nearby New Market were. Many brothers had, in fact, defended themselves against the Indians, and the church records make numerous references to the stockpiling of gunpowder for defensive purposes. It seems that the Brethren were pragmatic. They lived on the frontier, after all, and thieves, Indians, and marauding bears sometimes had to be shot. Their pacifism wasn't based so much on the Sixth Commandment as it was on their respect for authority. The Moravians just couldn't bring themselves to rebel against the lawful government. Bishop Graff, however, allowed each brother to follow his conscience on the matter.

The war also presented the Moravians with more worldly considerations. The church in North Carolina didn't actually own Wachovia. A church officer in London held title to the land in trust for the Moravians, who continued to pay rent on it. It was a technicality, for sure, but one that must have made the leaders in Salem uneasy. What if they backed the rebels, who then lost the war? Would the victorious English retaliate by seizing their land?

So the Moravians tried to remain neutral. Throughout the summer and fall, Tories and rebels rode into Salem asking the Moravians the same question: Are you for or against us? The Moravians assured both sides that they would remain loyal to the king and would do "all in our power to preserve freedom, so long as we are not asked to do aught against our conscience, that under no circumstances will we bear arms or personally take part in military service."

It was up to Bagge to explain to puzzled listeners how the Moravians could support King George and "preserve freedom" at the same time. Marshall was in Germany for a church synod and wouldn't return until 1780. Bagge, who headed the church council that oversaw material affairs in Salem, became the spokesman.

Those years, Bagge remembered in his memoir, were "a trying time." Tories and rebels were suspicious of the Moravians' motives, with each side accusing the Brethren of helping the other.

In one of many such instances, rebel militia rode into Salem in the spring of 1776 and charged the Moravians with supplying wagons to the royal governor. "All heads of families had to appear before the officers," Bagge wrote, "and their men, with loaded guns, stood before the doors, apparently waiting impatiently for the order to plunder." Bagge's reasoned argument and calm demeanor defused what could have been a dangerous situation.

Neither did the Moravians win many friends with their reluctance to accept the paper money issued by the revolutionary state government. That money depreciated rapidly, throwing a heavy burden on shopkeepers, many of whom suffered financially during the war. The patriots interpreted the Moravians' attitude as unpatriotic.

Bagge again: "The Brethren, especially in Salem and Bethabara, took no part in what was going on, and as our commerce continued while around us, it had greatly lessened . . . jealousy of us constantly increased."

The animosities that had first surfaced during the Regulator War were apparent at the colonial assembly in Hillsborough. Bagge and Jacob Blum went there in 1778 to plead for the Moravians' land. The assembly had passed the Confiscation Act the previous year. It allowed the revolutionary government to seize land held by foreigners, and Wachovia was technically owned by a brother in London. Bagge found "more enemies than friends" in Hillsborough.

"The unsettled people of the land had long been wanting a revolution to free them of all taxes and take possession of property of more wealthy people," the perceptive Bagge later wrote. "Many of this type became civil and military officers, others aspired to become such, and these were the men who gave the Brethren the most trouble and were the most dangerous, causing them much harm and much sorrow of heart."

He presented the assembly with a petition from the Brethren. It spoke from the heart, and its sincerity won the Moravians friends. "We have no implements of war. We do not wish to use violence against this or any power, as has been falsely charged against us," it read. "We do not covet positions of honor nor lucrative offices. . . . Permit us to remain in peace and quiet in the homes in which Providence has placed us."

The land matter wasn't settled until the Moravians transferred title of Wachovia to Marshall, a naturalized citizen of Pennsylvania. Finally, in 1782, the assembly accepted Marshall's standing as the proprietor of Wachovia.

If the Moravians' land wasn't being threatened, their convictions were. In April 1777, the colonial assembly required all men ages 16 to 60 to serve in the militia. No exemptions were made for those who objected on moral or religious grounds. The uneasy Moravians held steadfastly to their convictions until the assembly relented in 1779 and drew up an "affirmation"—not an oath—of allegiance that they could accept. The men of Salem promised to be "peaceable subjects of the independent state of North Carolina" and agreed not to aid or join the king's forces. They were exempted from military duty, though at the price of a triple tax.

For Salem, 1781 was the most eventful year of the war. Nathanael Greene's patriot army came through town on the way to fight Lord Charles Cornwallis at Guilford Courthouse. Ammunition wagons stopped to load shells, and Greene left behind his most severely wounded men to be cared for by Salem's doctor. Lawless militia and "the Wilkes men" descended on the town and "seemed to delight in excesses of every kind, including personal attacks," the church diary reports.

Cornwallis and his English army of 5,000 soldiers and an equal number of followers camped in Bethania February 9. The village, known for its rebel sympathies, was treated harshly by the British. Soldiers threatened and beat residents and took 60 cattle and untold numbers of ducks, chickens, and hogs for food.

The British left Salem unscathed when they went through the next day. In fact, Cornwallis and his officers spent a pleasant afternoon visiting Bagge and Marshall, who had returned from Europe.

Following Cornwallis's departure, "days of darkness and terror" descended on Wachovia, the Salem diary notes. Rebel troops from Mecklenburg County came to town first, followed by several wandering groups.

"When two parties of the Wilkes militia arrived there was no escape," Bagge wrote. The Wilkes men accused the Moravians of being traitors and carrying on "clandestine intercourse" with the British. Some of the sisters, Bagge reported, feared for their lives when "loaded guns were held at their breasts." Once again, Bagge talked his way out of trouble.

Five hundred rebel cavalry then stormed into town. Their leader banged on Bagge's door and threatened to wreck his house for allowing Cornwallis in.

"One evening 20 armed men came into my living room, probably with that intention, but my little children began to play with them, and they forgot their design," Bagge wrote. "Another scamp twice placed a loaded pistol against my breast; and some time before another threatened me for an hour with a bare saber, declaring he was going to cut me to pieces. The Savior, however, rescued me."

Salem Tavern, where the Declaration of Independence was posted

Survival and Change

Bagge and the Moravians survived the war but were changed by it. Though they tried to straddle the fence, there are subtle hints that their hearts were with the rebels. The Declaration of Independence was posted at the Salem tavern in 1776, the year that petitions for the king were dropped from the church litany and prayers for the American government substituted. Before 1778, the Moravians wrote of the "Continental Army" and "George Washington's Army," but "our army" soon began appearing in their writings. The war probably hastened the Moravians' entry into American culture.

As for Brother Bagge, he was elected to the state assembly as a representative from Surry County, which was created in 1773 and included Wachovia. He retired from politics after two years and settled into the life of a respected town elder.

His friend Alexander Martin, a former governor, paid him a visit on March 27, 1800, and the two old men were seen walking through town, talking quietly. That afternoon, Bagge "was taken with a fever in the chest," his memoir notes. At two o'clock in the morning on April 1, the 71-year-old Bagge died "so quietly that those who watched him did not know."

*The people of Salem file past the
Single Brothers House in what may be the first
Fourth of July parade in North Carolina.*

———

The Winston-Salem Journal

"Peace Is with Us"

The country's first Fourth of July was a quiet one. No flashy fireworks. No boisterous backyard barbecues. All the congregations of Wachovia marked the occasion with music and prayers, giving the day a solemn dignity missing from today's extravaganzas.

The Treaty of Paris, which officially ended the Revolutionary War, was signed January 20, 1783. In response, the North Carolina legislature made July 4 a day of thanksgiving. North Carolina was the only state to proclaim the day a holiday the first year after the war, and the Moravian villages in Wachovia were the only settlements in the state known to have held observances.

In Bethania, the band ushered in the first Fourth with an early-morning recital. A prayer service at 10 o'clock featured the 46th Psalm: "He has stopped wars to the end of the earth: the bow he breaks; he splinters the spears; he burns the shields with fire." A lovefeast that afternoon attracted many of Bethania's neighbors, and everyone marched through the village that evening in a candlelight procession.

Trombonists awakened Salem's towns-people, who filled the *Gemein Haus* for a prayer service. A lovefeast in the afternoon was followed by a procession through the streets that evening.

"Hearts were filled with the peace of God evident during the entire day and especially during the procession, and all around there was silence, even the wind being still," Salem's church diarist wrote.

As night fell, the people of Salem gathered in a circle, the flickering light from their candles dancing on their faces. They sang a song used in their services:

> Peace is with us! Peace is with us,
> People of the Lord!
> Peace is with us! Peace is with us,
> Hear the joyful word!
> Let it sound from shore to shore!
> Let it echo evermore!
> Peace is with us! Peace is with us,
> Peace, the gift of God.

Dates to Remember

1766 Trees are felled for Salem, the main town of the three Moravian settlements in North Carolina.

1770 The first women arrive in Salem. The first baby is born, and the sites for the tavern and graveyard are staked.

1771 The Congregation House, or *Gemein Haus*, is finished; it stood where Main Hall of Salem College is now. The Salem congregation is formally organized, with the Reverend Paul Tiersch as its first pastor. John Birkhead, the first brother buried in the Salem graveyard, is laid to rest on June 7.

1772 A school for girls, the forerunner of Salem Academy and College, opens in the *Gemein Haus*.

1773 Wachovia is placed in newly formed Surry County. The first Easter Sunrise Service is held at the Salem graveyard. It begins to attract large crowds from all over the state in the 1920s and is broadcast locally over the radio beginning in 1930. It is sent by shortwave to soldiers overseas during World War II.

1778 The first of four central water systems serving Salem is completed. Wooden pipes carry water two miles into the village.

1781 British troops under Lord Cornwallis camp in and around Bethania on their way to Guilford Courthouse.

1784 The tavern burns down in January and is rebuilt by the end of the year.

1785 The first fire engines in Salem are purchased from Germany.

1788 The Moravian Church bans slaves from living in Salem.

1789 The Moravians' first segregation policy goes into effect on Easter Sunday, when slaves are forced to sit in the back of the church. Wachovia is included in newly formed Stokes County.

1790 The Salem paper mill, thought to be the second in the state, opens on Peters Creek on the corner of what are now Peters Creek Parkway and Academy Street.

1791 President Washington visits Salem on his tour of the Southern states, spending two nights in the tavern.

1792 The first post office opens in Salem. Mail is delivered from Halifax every 14 days.

1800 Home Moravian Church is completed.

Names to Know

Traugott Bagge
The only shareholder in the land company that financed the settling of Wachovia who actually came to North Carolina, Bagge moved from Bethabara to Salem in 1772 to run the community store. He was the town's leading merchant and a guiding influence during the Revolutionary War, when he acted almost as a purchasing agent for the Continental Army. He represented Surry County in the state assembly for two years and was appointed county auditor for his services during the war. So many people attended his funeral in 1800 that the meeting hall couldn't contain the crowd.

Christian Gottlieb Reuter
Wachovia's widely talented surveyor, Reuter helped choose the sites for Bethania and Salem and drew beautifully detailed maps. He laid out Salem's streets and helped plan its water system. He also wrote the earliest account of Wachovia's flowers, animals, and geography. He died in 1777.

Frederic William Marshall
The most important man in Salem for its first 35 years, Marshall was the son of an officer in the German army and was destined by his father to enter the service. Educated at the University of Leipzig, Marshall met some Moravians when he was 18 and, with his father's consent, joined the church. He visited Wachovia when the site for Salem was chosen and returned to make it his home for the rest of his life. He held various church offices, and his knowledge of architecture was the controlling factor in the design of Salem. He died February 11, 1802. Marshall Street is named for him.

Salem
Settled in 1766, this was the principal town in Wachovia. Its name comes from the Hebrew word for peace, *shalom*.

Henry Jacob van Vleck probably painted this watercolor of Salem Square in the late 1840s.
The Gemein Haus, center, sits where Main Hall of Salem College is now.
The Boys School is on the left.

Courtesy of George Waynick

"There Is Little Love Among Us"

The communal society that the Moravians fashioned in the wilderness withstood droughts and diseases, Indian uprisings and civil rebellions. In the end, it couldn't survive in the marketplace.

Great economic changes began to shake young America in the 1830s. The Age of Industry was dawning. Northern factories churned out products that railroads carried to distant markets. Salem's craftsmen, still making shoes and britches one pair at a time, found themselves fighting a flood of cheap imports.

Salem answered with factories of its own. To bolster the town's ailing economy, the Moravian Church allowed textile mills to open on Salem's outskirts. The mills thrust the town into the vanguard of the Industrial Revolution in the South. But as in any revolution, there were casualties.

The church's carefully constructed set of rules and regulations could not survive long in the fast-paced world of steam engines and locomotives. Times were changing, and a new breed of town leader saw the theocratic system as too rigid and too old-fashioned to meet the new economic realities. These leaders questioned the church's authority to limit slavery, set prices, and lease land. The church's temporal control gradually slipped as more and more Moravians did what had once been unthinkable—they simply ignored the rules.

Thus, Salem began its transformation from a quiet congregational town on the frontier into the boisterous manufacturing giant that would emerge from the battle smoke of the Civil War.

Francis L. Fries, Salem's first industrialist, paused long enough from his hectic activities to allow Grunesweld Gustavus to paint this portrait of the young Fries and his wife, Lisetta. The painting was done in 1839, the year before Fries opened his woolen mill.

Collection of Old Salem

The First Industrialist

It's probably safe to say that Winston-Salem would not be what it is today without Francis L. Fries. In a town noted for its industrialists, he was the first. The textile mill that he built in 1840 survived well into the 20th century and was the forerunner of the factories that made the city a manufacturing giant. Fries's descendants went on to found banks and build power plants, start railroads and champion public schools.

But try to find a picture of him among the old-timey posters that hang from the walls in the restaurant that now occupies part of his mill. The other part is an elegant bed-and-breakfast where a night's lodging costs more than what the mill workers made in a year.

In fact, there are few reminders in what is now known as Brookstown Mill of the history that happened in Winston-Salem's most important industrial landmark. Some unidentified black-and-white photographs on a far wall of the restaurant show horses pulling up to the mill, and a large boiler dominates one of the dining rooms.

Fries didn't set out to make history when he opened the mill; he was more concerned with making money. Neither did he set out to change Salem. When he was born in 1812, Salem was still a church-controlled town where craftsmen worked in small shops turning out their wares by hand. When Fries died 51 years later, the old theocracy was gone, replaced by a new order dominated by steam-powered factories that would soon employ thousands of people. If such things need a father, Francis Fries, more than anyone, qualifies.

John Christian Wilhelm and Johanna Elizabeth Fries expected their eldest child to become a Moravian minister. They sent him to the Boys School in Salem and then to another good Moravian school, Nazareth Hall in Pennsylvania. It was customary for young men on such a path to stop for a while and teach. Fries did so in Salem before resigning to study law.

His career took another turn in 1836 when, at age 24, he was hired as an agent for a cotton factory that Moravian investors were opening in Salem. Knowing nothing about textiles and factories, Fries went to New England, where textile mills were well established, to study the machinery and the methods. He would continue the practice even after he became an expert in such matters, traveling north periodically to keep abreast of trends and technology.

Fries bought what was needed during that first trip and shipped it to Salem. He returned to run the cotton mill for four years. Mills and machinery were new in Salem, and Fries learned about them on the job.

He mastered the trade well enough to want to try his hand at it. He quit the cotton mill and bought a lot on Salem's outskirts. There, he built his woolen mill—literally. The remnants of a dog-eared diary from 1840–42 show that, with the help of his brother, Henry, Fries built the small, brick factory with his own hands. After it opened, he worked the machines alongside his slaves. They often worked through the night to fill customers' orders.

And thus he prospered. When Henry became a partner in 1846, F & H Fries Company was born. The mill was enlarged and cotton milling added. The company made Confederate uniforms during the Civil War and survived Reconstruction. The family business lasted into the next century, building new mills along the way.

The success of the Fries mill signaled the end of the old ways in Salem. Craftsmanship was no longer enough. Surviving in the Age of Industry required flexibility, machinery, and capital.

The Boom and the Breakdown

The years following the Revolution were good ones in Salem and the surrounding countryside. Everywhere in town, it seemed, a building was going up: a new tavern to replace one destroyed by fire, the Single Sisters House, the Boys School, an expansion of the Single Brothers House.

In 1800, workers finally finished the church. They had been at it for two years, laying more than 144,000 bricks. The Salem church, which would later be known as Home Moravian, was consecrated on November 9. Measuring 92 feet by 46 feet, and with lower walls three feet thick, the building was the grandest in the back country and a fitting symbol of the church's prominence and prosperity.

And authority. The church was the town, and the town was the church. Running things was the *Aufseher Collegium*, a church council that was the equivalent of a board of aldermen. It administered most of Salem's temporal affairs.

Need a musical instrument? The council first had to approve. "Several of the musical Brethren of the Collegium ask whether it would be permissible to buy a large drum to be used with the wind instruments," the council's records for April 15, 1812, show. "Collegium cannot consent, believing that it would give offense."

As could newspapers. The council readily approved the print shop requested by John Christian Blum in 1827 but had reservations about his proposed newspaper, "which [has] various unpleasant results for local individuals, for the congregation town, and for the Unity itself, in which this would be a new thing."

The council finally agreed, and Blum's *Weekly Gleaner* began publication. The council's fears were groundless, as it turned out. In a town of less than 500 people who all attended the same church, everyone knew everything "newsworthy" about everyone else. Blum's paper lasted less than a year because there was little in it that anyone would buy to read.

To the members of the *Collegium* and the other church councils, Salem was more than just a town. It was, they truly believed,

Francis Fries's woolen mill in 1864

North Carolina Division of Archives and History

ordained by the Lord, and the people who lived there weren't merely residents, but brothers and sisters.

This made decisions difficult sometimes, as when people complained in 1838 about service at the tavern. "We discussed the situation and realized that in spite of all his good qualities, Br. Sensemann seems to lack a certain something which makes the stay for travelers in our tavern more comfortable and pleasant," the *Collegium* reported. "We shall have to appoint another tavern keeper in the course of time, so much is certain. However, before this step is taken, we are going to try to make up for Br. Sensemann's missing tavern keeper's qualities by appointing a skillful barkeeper. If this fails, it will be time to find another tavern keeper."

The council did so, reluctantly, a year later.

The church's authority was widespread and complete, and no one questioned it. Why should they? Things were going well. The population was slowly increasing—to 477 in 1824—and new shops were opening all the time. Dozens of trades were represented in the town's 30-odd shops.

But an ill wind began to blow in the late 1820s. It would gather strength and finally sweep away the congregational town. Cyclical economic depressions, droughts, and failing wheat harvests became the norm during the next 20 years. The pastor of the Salem congregation wrote in the church's annual record that 1827 was a difficult year for Moravians, as "hard times" had depressed trade and the craftsmen hadn't prospered. The

The slaughterhouse run by the Single Brothers

The Photograph Collection, Winston-Salem/Forsyth County Public Library

Weekly Gleaner reported in November 1828 that the state's "local currency is deranged and money scarce."

Added to the shortages and depressions were new threats brought to town on the country's roads, canals, and railroads. Improved transportation began connecting the country to the town and the town to the city. Local markets became regional ones by the 1830s, and regional markets went national.

It meant that the products rolling out of the burgeoning factories in the Northeast could be sold in Salem stores. It was a boon to consumers, who enjoyed more variety and lower prices. But to the craftsmen of Salem, who operated small shops and made their products by hand, the competition meant economic ruin. A church committee reported in 1849 that the factories supplied a "considerable number of items" more cheaply than the Salem craftsmen could make them.

The shopkeepers began to view the church's strict rules as obstacles that prevented them from competing. They couldn't cut prices, join in partnerships, or take other steps to meet the threat without the church's approval. Many began to seriously question the church's authority, and young men started to show a preference for leaving town rather than working as apprentices.

The theocratic system had always had its critics. Even during the postwar boom, there were some in Salem who wondered what had been gained by the war with Britain.

"For some time various persons have begun to oppose man-made rules, calling for American Freedom," the church's Congregation Council reported in 1785. "Such remarks show a great lack of understanding, for in the so-called free lands as well as in others there must be proper submission to authority, without which no human society can endure. For example, a journeyman must act in all things according to the instructions of the master workman in the shop. If anyone claims the above mentioned freedom against the rules of the town, he hereby proves that it would be better for him to live elsewhere."

That's exactly what Joshua Reuz did. Tradition has it that he became so upset with Salem's strict rules that he moved two miles north to a spot he called Liberty. The road from there to Salem eventually became known as Liberty Street.

But in the 1830s, the complaints weren't limited to a few eccentrics and malcontents. Almost everyone, it seemed, thought the traditional ideas that had nurtured Salem were out of step with existing conditions. And for the first time, people openly violated the church's rules. Craftsmen, for instance, cut costs and lowered prices to stay in business. Some broke the rules by entering into partnerships, which allowed them to make more goods at a cheaper price. A shoemaker, for instance, became partners with a shoemaker outside Salem—strictly against the rules.

Other tradesmen started selling items not reserved for them by the church. A coppersmith, for instance, sold iron and tin goods not made in Salem. The tinsmith in town complained, and the coppersmith relented only after being threatened with expulsion from Salem.

The records of the church councils at the time are full of such incidents. The church occasionally took action, but usually it didn't.

The bickering and flaunting of regulations prompted Henry Leinbach to observe in 1834, "Rough times, these. It appears that there is little love among us anymore. Indeed, I strongly suspect that as a communion we will not hold together anymore. Times are hard, and many people do not do as they wish others to do unto them."

Life in Salem's First Textile Mill

The bell at Salem Manufacturing Company sounded at dawn, and all along Factory Hill, candles flickered on in the windows of the company-owned apartments and houses. People hurriedly dressed and made breakfast in the 30 minutes they had before starting another day in one of the state's first textile mills.

They worked until sunset on most days, with just a short break for lunch. Their jobs were tedious, repetitious, and sometimes dangerous, and their pay often didn't cover the rent and their bills in the company store. Their behavior outside the mill was closely watched by their Moravian bosses, who viewed them suspiciously and treated them like second-class citizens.

Welcome to the beginning of the Industrial Revolution in Salem. Much has been made of the village's manufacturing tradition, of Salem's important place in the South's industrial heritage. But for the people who created that tradition, who were stationed on the front lines of that revolution, there was nothing grand about it.

Most came from Stokes, Davie, Guilford, and Davidson counties, where droughts, depressions, and failing crops devastated small farmers during the 1830s. People were attracted by the mill's offer of steady pay and a house for any family that provided three or four workers.

Young women left the farm to earn money to send home. Some, like Elizabeth Loggins, who arrived in 1838, were widows, or had been abandoned. They came with their children and lived in company boardinghouses. Loggins ran her boardinghouse while her two teenage daughters worked as spinners in the mill. Company rules required her to take in as many boarders as the mill decided and to feed them "plain, wholesome and cleanly food."

Families living in company houses usually sent their children to work in the mill. Mothers stayed home to care for their families, while fathers sought employment outside the mill.

The workweek was long and tiring—80 hours in the summer and 70 in the winter. The mill operated six days a week, closing at four on Saturdays. The grueling schedule was toughest on the children, some of whom were as young as 10. Swollen ankles from constant standing were a common ailment. Many of the children were so tired that their supervisors had to beat them to keep them awake.

Woman and older girls made up the majority of mill employees. They worked as spinners and weavers, earning anywhere from $.75 to $1.75 a week in 1841. That was about the average salary paid by other mills in the state. It was more than women could make as domestics in Salem, but about a third less than what common laborers earned in the state's copper and gold mines, and almost three times less then what textile workers in New England made.

Men were supervisors, machinists, and firemen for boilers. Skilled men, such as mechanics, could earn as much as $4 a week. Supervisors received $10 a week, or about what craftsmen in Salem made. Children swept floors and worked as doffers for about $.75 a week.

These wages, pitiful as they seem, allowed some families to buy small farms and acquire some independence from the mill. Most remained close to the mill, however, using the wages earned there to supplement their farm income.

Often, though, mill wages weren't enough to pay a family's expenses. The Nathaniel Casey family was typical. Casey and his wife, Mary, both 55, lived in a mill house on Factory Hill in 1845. Casey and his four children worked in the mill and brought home $262.37 that year. Workers like the Caseys depended on the company for all their necessities. The rent on their mill house and their bills in the company store totaled $427.77, leaving the Caseys indebted to the company. This system, which would be seen throughout the South after the Civil War, created a debtor class over which the mill exercised complete control.

Workers had to be back in their apartments or homes by dark and had to get the mill's permission to travel any distance. If a worker quit her job, she had to leave the boardinghouse. That effectively tied her to the mill. Workers, especially those belonging to families, were required to give a month's notice before quitting, but the mill could fire them on a week's notice.

From the Moravians' point of view, such rules were necessary to protect their way of life. They thought many of their neighbors were immoral, and they feared the mill workers' bad habits would corrupt the community. So the Moravians ostracized them by putting them in houses outside the village and by trying to control their movements.

The workers, of course, resented such treatment. They didn't leave any written records, but their actions speak for how they must have felt.

They snubbed the Moravians' religion, for instance. The church sincerely tried to lead the mill hands in the right direction by opening a Sunday

Employees of Salem Manufacturing Company lived in mill houses like these, which were east of the factory.

Collection of Old Salem

school for them and by closing the mill every other Tuesday night to allow them to attend services. When the mill opened in 1837, the Salem pastor wrote in the church diary that he hoped the church could "succeed also in caring for the spiritual needs of the numerous strangers who come as workers in the factory."

While they enjoyed the lovefeasts on Christmas and New Year's and appreciated the Sunday school for its educational benefits, the workers had little to do with the church. Most didn't understand the German sermons and hymns, and they found Moravian services formal and boring compared to Baptist and Methodist services.

The workers may have been sending a message to the mill bosses: You may control our lives inside the mill and in the company houses, but you won't control our religious lives as well. After two months, the mill resumed Tuesday operation when it became apparent that the workers didn't share "that relish for our Moravian service, which was believed to exist."

Neither did they relish their treatment in the mill. The company's board of directors didn't hesitate to fire workers or slash salaries whenever cotton prices rose or yarn prices fell. It closed the factory for weeks at a time to repair or install machinery, and the workers had to struggle through those times without pay.

Considering the low wages and the layoffs and shutdowns, it is hardly surprising that the mill workers quit in droves and took off when they felt like it. They might leave for a week, suffering from the "summer complaint," or disappear for an afternoon to go fishing. They returned home to help their families with the planting and to attend Methodist camp meetings, funerals, and weddings. The Moravians thus learned one of the first lessons of the Age of Industry: unreliable jobs breed unreliable workers.

And sullen workers, who apparently weren't as respectful of their bosses as the Moravians would have liked. The bosses thought the workers drank too much in the mill houses and viewed the workers as contentious rule breakers. The board of directors declared that it would no longer stand for the "whims, caprices and insolence" of its employees. It admonished the mill hands in 1841 that it and the president of the company "should be treated by those engaged in the establishment with due respect."

Price list for Salem Manufacturing Company

The Moravian Archives of the Southern Province, Winston-Salem

The
Revolution Begins

Something needed to be done to revitalize Salem's ailing economy. The Moravians decided to follow the example of capitalists throughout the South and open a cotton mill. The price of cotton was low, and the needed machinery could be purchased in New England, the center of the country's textile industry. No doubt, the 15- to 20-percent profit that other Southern mills were enjoying attracted the Moravians.

Some residents of Salem, though, regarded the mill as a threat to the village. They feared the effects that a large number of non-Moravians working in the mill would have on the morals of the community, and they opposed creating a factory outside the church's control.

The church councils considered the matter carefully in 1836 and finally decided to sell investors 2° acres west of town. To ensure that the congregation maintained control over the mill, the church bought 100 of the original 250 shares. Twenty-nine prominent Moravians bought the balance at $200 a share.

When it opened in the fall of 1837, Salem Manufacturing Company became one of only a handful of mills operating in the state. North Carolina, which would one day become the country's leading textile state, was slow to embrace the new industry.

The first mill was started in Lincoln County in 1813, followed by small mills on the Tar River near present-day Rocky Mount and on Rock Fish Creek near Fayetteville. By the 1840s, mills were springing up in what would become the heart of the industry, along the Deep and Haw rivers. Though the steam engine had been developed for textile mills in 1793, most North Carolina mills depended on water for power. The Salem factory was one of the few mills in the state that used steam.

It opened with 40 employees, who ran 1,032 spindles and 26 looms and turned out yarn, sheeting, bed ticking, and napkins. Within a year, 105 people worked in the factory, and by the early 1840s, the mill was larger than most in the state and equal to the average mill in New England.

Business was good at first, but excessive competition and the high price of cotton in the late 1840s ate into profits. The mill closed in 1849, and Governor John Morehead bought the property at public auction a year later. He moved the machinery to a textile plant that he owned in Leaksville. The building in Salem was used as a gristmill before F & H Fries bought it. In 1880, the firm built a new factory on the site and moved its cotton manufacturing there under the name Arista Mills.

Despite its failure, Salem Manufacturing Company started Salem down the road to industrialization. It attracted a large number of outsiders, who were the first workers in Sa-

lem to produce articles on machines for a national market. It was a work force vastly different from the one in the Salem shops. The mill hands, mostly women and children, weren't Moravians. Most worked for low wages and with little hope of improving their status.

The Salem mill was important for another reason: it gave Francis Fries his start.

Fries left Salem Manufacturing Company in 1840 and asked the Moravian Church for permission to build a steam-powered woolen mill behind his father's house in the village. He planned merely to prepare wool for the spinning and weaving traditionally done by the wives and daughters of the area's farmers, or by slaves on his father's plantation outside Salem. Bowing to neighbors who were worried about smoke from the proposed mill, Fries bought lot 103—on the corner of what were then New Shallowford and Salt streets—from the church. He and his brother, Henry, got to work building the mill.

They carded their first wool on June 17 and began making yarn four months later. Fries soon added looms and dyeing equipment and by 1842 was offering an assortment of wools, yarns, and cloths of different colors and prices. A heavy jean, added the following year, became the mainstay of the line for years.

A year after it was formed, F & H Fries Company employed seven whites and 16 slaves. By 1860, it had 77 employees and slaves and produced $87,300 in woolen and cotton goods. Twenty years later, it was a modern industrial firm with a market that spanned the country.

As the numbers show, blacks made up a significant part of the work force in Fries's mill. His insistence on using blacks forced the village to come to terms, once and for all, with the thorny issue of slavery.

African-Americans in Salem

The Moravians in Salem celebrated the opening of their *Gemein Haus* in 1771 with a baptism. All baptisms were special to the Moravians, but they must have judged this one to be particularly important because they saved it for the building's dedication.

Two Brethren led the convert into the chapel. His name was Sam, and he was a black man. The church had bought him two years earlier because he had impressed Moravian leaders with his desire to find the Lord.

Sam answered the required questions that November 17 and received absolution. He was baptized and given a name more befitting his new religion: Johann Samuel. Like any other male Moravian, he would be called "brother."

The moment moved many of the 300 people who were there. "The presence of the Savior was deeply felt by the congregation, including the many friends and a few Negroes," the pastor wrote in the church diary. "Many said the impression upon them would never be forgotten."

Make no mistake, Johann Samuel was still a slave, still a piece of property to be bought and sold like the horses he tended. But if nothing else, he stepped out of the obscurity of slavery that day to become the first black in North Carolina baptized a Moravian.

The founding Moravians, judging from the records they left, weren't entirely comfortable with the institution of slavery. Most came from Europe, where human bondage was a part of the dim past, and the whole idea tended to offend their religious sense of work. They certainly couldn't ask someone else to do a job—no matter how small—that God had ordained them to perform. They also worried about the example it would set for the children.

Unlike the neighboring Quakers, though, the Moravians felt no moral need to free slaves. One brother was instructed by the church to tell his slave, who wanted to convert, that baptism wouldn't make him "a free man and equal to his master."

The Moravians apparently took a pragmatic approach to slavery. They may not have liked it, but they accepted it as the way business was done. Faced with an ever-growing village and a continual labor shortage on the frontier, the Moravians found that slaves could be used in unskilled jobs, thus freeing the Brethren for more demanding tasks. The church leased slaves and, at times, bought a few outright, but the number of African-Americans living in Bethabara and Salem before the 19th century was small.

If they weren't like the Quakers, the early Moravians were the next best thing. Though they did not treat blacks equally, they at least treated them kindly. Frederic William Marshall explained to the church governing council in Germany in 1770 that "not many brothers and sisters have the gift of handling slaves without spoiling them."

During much of the 18th century, the Moravians allowed blacks to worship with whites. They could be baptized and confirmed and could attend school with white children. Blacks also received the same medical care. That was fairly liberal treatment for its day, which made the Moravians much sought-after by blacks as owners. Slaves leased by the church sometimes begged church leaders to buy them before their leases expired. A few were bought after they expressed a desire to be baptized.

Attitudes toward blacks began to harden as the Moravians became more like their neighbors. By the 1780s, blacks weren't allowed to carry guns, and the church urged white masters to dress their slaves inexpensively. Fearing the effect slaves would have on young brothers' work habits, the *Aufseher Collegium* banned slaves from living in Salem in 1788. The church began its first segregation policy on Easter Sunday the following year, when blacks were ordered to sit in the back of the church. The Congregation Council, in reaching the decision, considered the "customary thought of the people in this country." In other words, that's what everybody else was doing. Separate religious services for blacks began in Wachovia in 1801.

This growing racism confused the Moravians, as shown by the actions of the Congregation Council. It had second thoughts about the new policies, which applied to all slaves. Black Brethren, the council thought, should not be included. "They are our brothers and sisters and different treatment of them will degrade ourselves . . . and will be a disgrace to the community," the council minutes relate.

No matter. As the town grew, and as old-timers were replaced by younger Moravians who were more accustomed to slavery, more and more townspeople asked that they be allowed to keep slaves. Some townspeople even devised schemes to get around the church ban, forcing the church boards to meet in 1814 to discuss its rules on slaves. The boards affirmed the ban on slaves in Salem, concluding that allowing them in town would make women "work-shy and ashamed of work" and increase the difficulty the church was having persuading young men to become apprentices.

People continued to defy the rules, and the Congregation Council fought back with new ones in 1820 that made owning slaves uneconomical. The council prohibited slaves from learning professions, since that would decrease "the industriousness and ingenuity of whites" and lead to "the sad custom of laziness." The council also limited each household to one domestic slave, but only after the slaveholder had applied to the church and posted a bond.

The council also reserved the right to demand that slaves be removed from town for almost any reason.

The new rules were just as controversial as the old ones. Francis Fries, his father, Wilhelm, and Christian Vogler were the main opponents. They all bought and kept slaves without getting the church's permission. Arriving in Wachovia in 1809, Wilhelm Fries bought a black woman—without asking the church—to help with the housework after he began taking in boarders from the school for girls. Vogler didn't ask the church when he leased a black smithy to teach his son the trade.

Francis Fries was in school in Pennsylvania at the time, and letters from his parents show their feelings toward the church's rules on slaves. His mother, Johanna, referred to the "silly" church board in a letter in 1828. "They are ridiculed in the village and think they are the only wise ones," she wrote to her son.

Wilhelm noted in a letter two years later that the church board had demanded he sell his slaves. "I answered that I preferred to go to the country [where he owned a plantation] rather than do that because we have to live," he wrote.

Slavery in the Mills

Francis Fries and the directors of Salem Manufacturing Company used slave labor to varying degrees. The tensions this created were central to the controversy over church regulations against slaves in Salem. The manufacturers considered slaves cheaper, more docile, and more dependable than white workers, who were insolent and forever leaving the mills to go fishing or help their families on the farm. Slaves couldn't leave and could be beaten without fear of reprisal.

A supervisor of the cotton mill suggested in 1838 that fired workers should be replaced by slaves, with whom "more punctual obedience could be enforced." The suggestion ran counter to the church's restriction on employing slaves in Salem. After much debate, the board of directors—comprised of all church leaders—decided to remain true to the church's rules, but agreed to allow the use of four slaves for menial tasks. The board preferred paid white labor when it was available.

Fries had other ideas. He thought slaves belonged in his mill and was willing to challenge the church's rules. He convinced church authorities he wasn't breaking the rule against teaching slaves a trade, since his slaves filled the role of unskilled labor. The argument was ludicrous because slaves performed the same tasks as whites—they worked as carders, spinners, carpenters, and nurses. But the church accepted it. By 1850, Fries owned 23 slaves, who made up half the work force in the mill. Ten years later, his company owned 47. Fries paid his slaves, and many opened their own businesses on the side, making chairs and brooms or buying chewing tobacco in bulk and selling it by the plug.

The church hoped that allowing Fries to use slaves would not be seen as a precedent. It was. Tradesmen complained that Fries was being allowed to defy church rules, and many bought slaves without asking permission. Finally, in 1845, the church threatened to revoke the lease of anyone violating the slave rules. It turned out to be the last effort by the traditionalists to preserve the congregational town envisioned by its founders.

The Congregation Council was more concerned with economic realities. Council members believed that the rules should be applied evenly, that all members should be treated as Fries had been. The majority of the council opposed abolishing the rules and voted instead to amend them to allow slaves in trades and to require those owning slaves to post bonds. When no one came forward with bond money, church leaders tired of the fight. The Congregation Council abandoned all the slave rules in 1847. The Moravians had become by then pretty much like their neighbors. Blacks, who once could become members of Moravian society, were nonentities.

Abolishing the slave rules was the beginning of the end of the congregational town. The other pillars of the church's theocratic system quickly crumbled. The monopoly system was abolished in 1849; tradesmen could open shops and sell what they wanted without the church's permission. The church relinquished its last vestige of temporal authority in 1856 when it repealed the lease system; anyone could live in and own land in Salem.

Thus, the church came face-to-face with the new economic order and was finally overcome.

Abraham
The Life of a Black Brother

To slaves living in Salem in the 18th century, baptism offered more immediate rewards than eternal salvation. It conferred on them a measure of dignity and respect and offered a better life. It turned Sambo, the Mandingo warrior, into Abraham, the Moravian brother.

Abraham was among a number of slaves baptized into the Moravian Church in the late 1700s. Though baptism didn't change Abraham's status as a slave, it did bring him into the close social world of the Moravians and allowed him to live and work alongside his white brothers.

Jon Sensbach, a historian at Old Salem, Inc., has spent years researching black life in early Salem. From his work, we know that Sambo was born a Mandingo about 1730 on the African Guinea coast, a region of western Africa that consists of present-day Senegal, Gambia, Guinea, and Sierra Leone. His African name is unknown, but the Moravians called him Sambo before his baptism.

The Mandingo were descended from a powerful empire whose culture had spread along the coast of western Africa. They believed in a supreme, omniscient God, and their religion was communal—a person's faith could not exist separate from the community.

By the 18th century, Mandingo rulers no longer dominated the region. They fought wars with their neighbors, selling their prisoners to white slave traders. Sambo was captured in one such war and sold to European slavers.

He was first shipped to a French colony in the West Indies to work on a sugar plantation. He was then taken to Virginia and bought by Edmund Lyne, who brought him to Bethabara in 1771.

The Moravian Church, needing slaves for its growing settlement, purchased Sambo for 64 pounds. Heinrich Herbst, the tanner, had asked for permission to buy a slave because he was having trouble finding steady help. The church rented Sambo to Herbst, who put him to work in the tannery, first in Bethabara and then in Salem.

Sambo didn't accept his new life docilely. He tried to run away in the summer of 1775, but he was captured in less than three weeks and returned to Salem. He was punished, but his defiance continued. The church elders reported in May 1776 that he went without permission to a brother's house, where he "frightened them with his impudence, for which he must be flogged."

Then Sambo had a change of heart and asked to become a member of the Moravian Church. While his precise reasons will never be known, church membership offered Sambo a chance to improve his life. He could live with his white brothers, maybe even marry and start a family. It may well be that Sambo simply wanted a chance to worship as part of a community. Many of the Moravians' communal practices may have seemed familiar to him.

State law at the time prohibited blacks from starting their own churches. Those desiring organized religion had no choice but to join white churches. Many Christian denominations drew black converts for the first time in the 1770s.

Sambo began attending congregational meetings and dropped his previous reluctance to learn German prayers and verses. The elders noted in December 1779 that "Sambo has already expressed at various times his desire for baptism. . . . We have noted meaningful signs of grace working in his heart." He was baptized a year later, at the age of 50, and given the name Abraham.

Baptism allowed Abraham to participate fully in all lovefeasts, prayer meetings, and church services. As a single man, it's likely that he slept and ate at the Single Brothers House. He also began preaching to other blacks in Wachovia.

As it did with white brothers, the church arranged Abraham's marriage. He married Sarah, a slave in Bethania who was given to Herbst so she could marry Abraham. Sarah received religious instruction but was never baptized. Abraham's memoir reveals that he was "very troubled" about her soul. They had no children.

Their daily life is open to speculation. Their clothing was plain and their home sparsely furnished. They probably spoke English, and Abraham prayed in German.

He died in 1797 and is buried in God's Acre. His simple tombstone bears a crudely carved inscription:

ABRAHAM NEGER
Guinea
d. 1797 A 67

He lies a few feet from Herbst, his master for 26 years.

Saving St. Philip's Church

Michael Jordan, an Englishman, was visiting Salem in 1774 when he passed on. Not being a member of the Moravian congregation, Jordan was buried in the small cemetery for "strangers" south of the village.

More than 200 years later, Leland Ferguson was looking for his grave. Ferguson, an archaeologist, spent a couple of summers digging in front of St. Philip's Church in Old Salem. He was trying to find the graves of about 150 people—most of them Moravian slaves—who were buried there in the late 18th and early 19th centuries. Ferguson's dig was part of a long-overdue effort to save the most important landmark of black history in the city.

"All of this is part of our effort to learn what went on here," Jon Sensbach said in front of the church as Ferguson uncovered old graves in 1991. "This area was a major complex of life for blacks in and around Salem."

Sensbach is a historian who has studied black life in early Salem. St. Philip's, he knows, was at the center of that life.

For too long, the aged building sat on South Church Street forgotten and neglected. Water from a leaky roof streaked the inside walls. The foundation settled, and vandals broke windows and plundered the interior. It didn't seem a fitting end for the worship hall of the nation's oldest black Moravian congregation and the oldest surviving African-American church in North Carolina.

The church traces its history to 1822, when women missionaries in Salem established a congregation for slaves who had been baptized into the Moravian Church. Monthly services were held at farmers' houses.

"Thirty Negroes gathered to lay up the logs for the church for Negroes," the Salem diary reported on September 27, 1823. "The Female Missionary Society has with pleasure undertaken to bear the expense. All went well."

A small log church was built beside the strangers' graveyard, where local slaves also were buried. The church became the center of black religious, social, and educational life. The white single sisters opened a Sunday school in the church in 1827. Dozens of slaves learned to read and write there until a state law four years later banned teaching those skills to slaves.

The congregation outgrew the small building, and a larger brick church was built in 1861 just to the north of the old log structure. Two classrooms and a choir loft were added in 1890. The black congregation worshiped in this church, under white ministers, for almost 100 years.

Fifty-two years after it was built, the church got a name. Before 1913, it was known as the "Negro congregation" or the Colored Salem Moravian Church. Evidence suggests that the church was named for Philip the Evangelist, an early Christian convert who baptized an Ethiopian.

The St. Philip's congregation moved to a new building in the Happy Hills community in 1950. It moved to its current location on Bon Air Avenue when U.S. 52 was built 17 years later.

The old building, which is owned by the Salem congregation, was used to store plumbing fixtures and old furniture. Periodically, someone would bemoan the deterioration of the building and announce a move to save it. Though sincere, each effort died for lack of money.

Finally, in 1989, a group with some muscle formed to rescue the old church. Its membership included representatives of Old Salem, Inc., the Moravian Church, St. Philip's Church, and the Historic Properties Commission. It received some grant money for archaeological and architectural studies, and it has compiled oral histories of current and past congregation members and teachers. Because of the group's efforts, the building was added to the National Register of Historic Places in 1991.

The goal is to restore the building as a museum and add it to the tour of Old Salem, said the Reverend Cedric S. Rodney, the pastor of St. Philip's.

"To bring it back to life—this would be something to talk about for years," he said.

The black Moravian Church that became known as St. Philip's dominated South Church Street in the 1860s.

Collection of Old Salem

Dates to Remember

1801   Separate church services for blacks begin in Wachovia.

1802   The Girls Boarding School, the forerunner of Salem Academy, formally opens.

1820   Church elders pass rules against slaves working in Salem.

1822   The single sisters start the Salem Female Mission Society to work among black slaves. The first black Moravian congregation is formed.

1823   The first African-American Moravian church is built on Church Street. The log building is replaced by a brick church in 1861. It is enlarged in 1890 and named St. Philips in 1913.

1827   A Sunday school is started in Salem to teach slaves to read and write. A state law passed four years later bans teaching literacy to slaves.

1828   John C. Blum publishes the first edition of *Blum's Almanac*. The Goslen family purchases the almanac in 1926 and continues to publish *Blum's Farmers and Planters Almanac*.

1834   John Nissen opens his wagon works in Waughtown. Over the years, the company turns out thousands of sturdy wagons that move the tobacco that fuels Winston's growth.

1837   Salem Manufacturing Company opens, marking the start of the industrialization of Salem.

1840   Francis Fries opens a woolen mill that uses slave labor, setting the stage for the abolishment of all church restrictions on slavery. Free public, or "common" schools open in the county for all white children.

1843   A volunteer fire department is organized in Salem.

1846   F & H Fries Company is formed.

1847   Church rules controlling slavery are abolished. A branch of the Bank of Cape Fear opens on Bank Street.

Names to Know

Francis L. Fries
The town's first industrialist, Fries opened a woolen mill in 1840 on the corner of Brookstown Avenue and South Liberty Street—then New Shallowford and Salt streets. He was also the chairman of the county's first board of commissioners. He died in 1863.

Henry Fries
He joined his older brother at the woolen mill, and F & H Fries Company was born. A lifelong bachelor, Henry devoted his life to the company. He ran the mill until he died in 1902.

John Philip Nissen
The grandson of Salem's pioneer wagon maker, Nissen opened a small wagon works on Waughtown Hill in 1834. Fueled by the burgeoning tobacco trade, the wagon business boomed, and by the mid-1870s, the wagon works was spread over 600 acres. His sons, Will and George, took over the business after Nissen's death in 1874. Will sold the business in 1919 and used the proceeds to build the Nissen Building—now the First Union Building. The wagon works closed in 1948.

Johann Samuel
This slave, bought by the church in Salem, was called Sam before he was baptized in 1771 and given a name more in keeping with his new faith. Johann Samuel was the first African-American baptized by the Moravians in North Carolina. He and his wife, Marie—also a baptized Moravian—were freed by the church in 1801. Samuel leased a farm from the church in Hope or Friedberg and died in 1836.

Main Street in Salem in 1866

Wachovia Historical Society

Building a Town in War's Shadow

Despite hard economic times, Stokes County continued to grow. Enough residents lived in the county by 1849 that the state legislature split it in two, creating a new county from its southern half. They called it Forsyth, and it included the Moravian towns.

A county seat and courthouse were needed. The Moravian Church agreed to sell land to Forsyth for a new town. After much debate, the church made a momentous decision and sold about 54 acres a mile north of Salem Square. The proximity of the new town to Salem linked the fortunes of the two forever.

Winston, as the new town was called, grew slowly at first. Even 10 years after its founding, there were still just a few stores and houses, a church here and there, and a modest courthouse. Residents of the more prosperous and more populous Salem had little reason to travel the mile up Main Street to Winston unless they had legal business to conduct at the courthouse.

It would take the calamity of the Civil War to open the way for the new town.

Public Meeting at Winston,

On December 29th, 1860.

A Meeting of the citizens of Forsyth County, irrespective of party, will be held at Winston, on Saturday the 29th of December, inst., at 11 o'clock, a. m., to take counsel together on the alarming condition of the country.

South Carolina has seceded from the Union. Commissioners from Alabama, and Mississippi are now at our State capital inviting North Carolina to do the same thing. A great question is now before the people,—no less than Union or Disunion.

Believing that there is safety in the voice of the people, all our fellow-citizens, without regard to party, are earnestly invited to attend.

MANY PEOPLE.

December 20th, 1860.

A placard announces a public meeting in Winston in 1860 to discuss secession.

The Moravian Archives of the Southern Province, Winston-Salem

"The Parting
of Husband and Wife"

The wagons came first—40 of them, filled with clothing, food, and other supplies. They rumbled slowly along Main Street in Salem and down the hill to the bridge across Salem Creek outside town. Next came the brass band, playing appropriate martial tunes. The men followed, marching precisely in files to a war they thought would end before they got there.

None of the men marching in those orderly rows on that beautiful late-spring Monday in 1861 knew the horrors they were about to encounter. The Civil War had just begun, and joining the Confederate army seemed the honorable thing to do. These farmers, clerks, mechanics, and carpenters were the first men in Forsyth County to join the army, and it seemed only right that the county send them off in style.

So there they stood at seven in the morning on June 17, in front of Salem Academy. The volunteers had formed into three companies and given themselves quaint names, like the Forsyth Rifles and the Forsyth Grays. It was all part of the naivety of the times,

when men were sent off to war with parades and brass bands, when the names Sharpsburg, Gettysburg, and Fredericksburg had yet to take on a gruesome aura.

Alfred H. Belo and the company he had formed—the Forsyth Rifles—had the place of honor at the front of the troops. Belo was the son of Salem's most prominent merchant, Edward Belo, whose new house on Main Street had recently been the scene of one of those touching ceremonies that marked the war's beginning. Some young ladies in Salem had made a flag for Belo's company and presented it to the men on the steps of the massive house. That flag is now on display in the Confederate Museum in Richmond.

Behind Belo that day were Rufus Wharton's Forsyth Grays, followed by Frank P. Miller's company. The crowd that gathered in Salem Square and along Main Street quieted as the Reverend George F. Bahnson stood on the academy's top step. He prayed for the men and warned them about "the temptations of a soldier's life."

"It was truly a solemn and affecting scene

to witness this religious ceremony on the departure of our brave volunteers . . . surrounded as they were by a large number of distressed and weeping family and friends," Salem's *People's Press* reported. "At the close of the ceremony, when the order of march was given, a scene presented itself which will be remembered: It was the parting of husband and wife, brothers and sisters, parents and children, perhaps forever."

The men marched toward Salem Creek to join their wagons, and a large group of relatives and friends followed.

"At the final parting, cheer upon cheer rent the air in honor of these brave men who were going forth to peril their lives in defense of Southern soil," the newspaper noted.

The men headed for Danville, Virginia, where they were mustered into the 21st North Carolina Regiment. The war, they soon learned, wasn't a place for bands and parades.

A New County and New Town

For the fourth time since surveying their land in North Carolina, the Moravians found themselves in another county. They had surveyed land in Anson County, built homes in Rowan, and prospered first in Surry and then in Stokes.

Each time, the state legislature had created a new county by dividing the older, larger one. The state did it again on January 16, 1849, when it passed a law that created a new county from the southern half of Stokes. The legislature named the county for Benjamin Forsyth, a Stokes resident who had died in the War of 1812.

The law creating the new county also named a board of county commissioners, headed by Francis L. Fries. The board was charged with finding at least 30 acres for a county seat and courthouse. Salem, with 700 people, was by far the largest town in the new county, which made it the logical choice for the courthouse. The Moravian Church rejected the idea because it objected to whipping—a common punishment handed out by the courts of the day—and didn't want whipping posts built in Salem.

Church leaders debated what land to sell the new county. Traditionalists, fearing the effects of a rowdy county seat on Salem, wanted the church to sell land two miles from Salem Square. Progressives worried that Salem would wither if it were that far from what was to become the county's commercial center.

The latter argument prevailed, and on May 12, the church sold the new county $51\frac{1}{4}$ acres a mile north on Main Street. The price was ridiculously low: $256.25, or $5 an acre.

The tract was bounded on the north by what is now Seventh Street, on the south by First Street, on the east by Church Street, and on the west by Trade Street. Thomas J. Wilson, a lawyer, owned the only house on the property, on the corner of Second and Main streets. He had bought his lot from the church in 1847 because he wanted to live in the country.

Wilson soon had neighbors. The county commissioners reserved a 200-by-198-foot parcel atop the hill on Main Street for the courthouse and divided the rest of the tract into 71 lots, which they sold at public auction. Robert Gray, a merchant from Randolph County, bought the first lot—number 41, on Main and Third streets just south of the courthouse square—for $465. There, he built his house and one of the first stores in town.

The auction raised almost $9,000, which the commissioners used to build the courthouse. The two-story brick building was fronted by four pillars, each 30 feet high. It opened December 16, 1850, and the new town was in business.

If it only had a name. The town went almost two years as "that place just north of Salem." Some thought it should be named Salem, while others argued the town needed its own identity. The court tried to settle matters by ordering a popular vote to name the town, but the order was somehow lost. Finally, the General Assembly passed a bill on January 15, 1851, that named the town after Major Joseph Winston, a Revolutionary War hero from Germanton. The town was incorporated eight years later with William Barrow as its first mayor.

The first Forsyth County Courthouse

———

The Photograph Collection, Winston-Salem/Forsyth County Public Library

Joseph Winston and Benjamin Forsyth

In one of the stranger twists of local history, the seat of the county first settled by pacifistic Moravians was named for a war hero.

Ben Dixon MacNeill pointed out the irony in a sarcastic profile of Winston-Salem that appeared in the *North American Review* in 1930. The Moravians, he noted, more or less sat out the Revolutionary War because of their religious convictions. They also wanted nothing to do with the rowdiness that usually comes with county seats. The Moravian Church, he wrote, agreed to sell land for the county's new town with the stipulation that there be no whipping post outside the courthouse.

"The commissioners were not wholly supine," he noted. "In defiance of probable ecclesiastic disapproval in the matter, were it brought to their attention, the town was named Winston, in honor of one Maj. Joseph Winston, whose patriotic blood-letting occupy some space in the earlier annals of the state."

MacNeill could have thrown in Colonel Benjamin Forsyth, a hero of a later war, had he thought about it.

The truth is, cities and counties have been named for less notable people.

Joseph Winston, in particular, came from distinguished stock. His ancestors arrived in Virginia from Yorkshire, England. Winston was born in 1746 in Louisa County, Virginia. He and his cousin Patrick Henry spent much of their boyhoods together.

The French and Indian War gave Winston his first opportunity at real fighting. The story is told that, at age 17, he was wounded in a raid on an Indian camp. Shot twice and left for dead, he was carried to a hiding place by comrades and survived for three days on nothing but berries. Winston recovered, but one of the musket balls remained in his body and pained him for the rest of his life.

He moved to Surry County, North Carolina, in 1769, settling on a fork of the Dan River, where he and his wife raised at least 12 children. Winston became a leader in his community and was elected to represent the county in the provincial congress at Hillsborough. He was made a major in the Surry militia and was sent to the Halifax Congress in 1776 to vote for independence from Britain.

When the fighting started, Winston led a group of volunteers against Tories at the Battle of Moores Creek Bridge. He fought Tories again at Kings Mountain in 1780, and his Surry men were in the front line at Guilford Courthouse the following year.

Winston was awarded a sword by the grateful General Assembly, and voters sent him five times to Raleigh as a state legislator. He also served in the state convention that ratified the Constitution.

He died April 21, 1815, and was buried at the family cemetery in Germanton. His remains were moved to Guilford Courthouse Military Park in 1908.

A comrade in the Revolution described Winston this way: "He was a man of stately form, old-school manners and of commanding presence. His home was in the lofty mountains of Stokes and Surry, whose cloud-capped summits seemed within a squirrel's jump of heaven."

Benjamin Forsyth made his home in Stokes County, moving there from Virginia in 1794. He married Bethemia Ladd three years later, and they had six children. A state legislator in 1807 and 1808, Forsyth bought and sold land vigorously and was one of the first land brokers in the county.

When the War of 1812 began, Forsyth was the captain of a rifle regiment. He was sent to the northern frontier, where he established a reputation for bravery and daring. Especially good at leading raiding parties in search of supplies and prisoners, he was present when the Americans captured Fort George in Canada in May 1813.

He was promoted to major and was commissioned a lieutenant colonel on April 15, 1814. Killed in a skirmish near Oldetown, New York, on June 23, 1814, Forsyth was buried with honors in Champlain, New York.

Winston's Early Years

Winston grew slowly, unlike Salem, which was essentially completed in five years. Except for the courthouse, there was really nothing to recommend the place. Even so, the editor of the *People's Press* was excited by what he saw in the new town. "An occasional walk to our adjoining neighbor Winston never fails to impress us with the growing importance of that place," he reported in January 1852. "New and tasty buildings have been erected in 1851 and others are in progress. The citizens of Winston mostly display that neatness in the erection of their dwellings which strikes the beholder."

The most striking was the home of Judge D. H. Starbuck, who had bought lots 50, 51, and 52 on Main and First streets during the original auction. The brick mansion that he built in 1851 amid a beautiful grove of trees was one of the first palatial homes in Winston. Starbuck lived there until his death in 1887. His son, Henry R. Starbuck, sold the property to Winston-Salem in 1920 for its new city hall.

The *People's Press* commented in its February 8, 1851, edition on a building of a different kind: "The prison house—not yet completed—is a rather gloomy looking place. May the mere sight of its grated windows prove a terror to evildoers and its cells ever remain tenantless."

If Robert Gray's memories were accurate, the prison had plenty of customers. In a speech he gave in 1876, Gray recalled early Winston as "the scene of many broils and some tragedies, all proceeding from the sale, in barrooms and groceries, of spirituous liquors—the prolific source of contentions, crime, and misery."

As a deterrent to such behavior, one of the first laws passed by the town commissioners dealt with drunks. They were to be thrown into jail until they sobered up and then tied to the whipping post outside the courthouse to receive 15 to 39 lashes.

Hezekiah Thomas, then, must have had his hands full. The town's first police officer, Thomas had to arrest drunks and protect the citizens against assorted criminals. He was also required to stop at each corner at night and sound his trumpet to let residents know that he was on the job and ready for action.

Aside from its bars, Winston lacked forms of diversion in the years before the Civil War. Men would gather around stoves in the stores that Gray, William Barrow, Harmon Miller, and Frank Gorrell had built near the courthouse by 1860. Some would find solace in Peter Wilson's hotel and "house of entertainment" at Liberty and Third streets.

Those more spiritually inclined had a number of churches to choose from. The small Methodist Protestant Church stood at Liberty and Seventh streets and the Presbyterian at the end of Third on Cherry Street. Methodist Episcopal Church, later Centenary Methodist, on Sixth and Liberty, drew the biggest crowds for hearty singing and shouting.

Nothing, though, compared with court week. People from all around gathered at the courthouse square, though few had any legal business to conduct. They came to talk politics and swap gossip and maybe a horse or two. Farm families rode into town on their locally made Nissen and Spaugh wagons, carrying dried fruit, fresh eggs, honey, and butter to sell around the square or to barter with the merchants. Some farmers camped in the vacant lot where the O'Hanlon Building now stands, laying out their multicolored quilts, their pots jingling from the backs of wagons.

A shrill blast from a tin horn in the distance meant that the stagecoach from Fayetteville was lumbering up the Western Plank Road,

Winston and Salem's major link to the rest of the world. Before the road reached them in 1852, the towns were isolated. There were no navigable rivers and few roads, and the railroad stopped in Raleigh.

The state legislature created the Fayetteville and Western Plank Road Company in 1849 and gave it $120,000 to build a wooden highway from Fayetteville to Salisbury. It was one of 84 such companies that the General Assembly authorized by 1860. Only the Fayetteville and Western road ever reached its goal.

To get on the road, communities had to buy shares in the company to help finance construction. Salisbury was lukewarm on the idea, hoping instead to lure the railroad. So the road's promoters turned to Salem, where Fries led the effort. The conservative Moravians bought $26,500 in shares. Some buyers added conditions, pledging money only if the road came near their farms or businesses.

Work on the road began in Fayetteville on October 4, 1849. The road reached Salem by way of Carthage, Asheboro, and High Point. The planks ended at the Salem town limits because the Moravians didn't want rattling boards to disturb church services. The planking started again north of Salem, and the road continued up Main Street to Winston. There, it angled west to Bethania, where it ended in 1854.

Eight feet wide and with planks three inches thick, the road cost an average of $1,500 a mile to build. The company hoped to turn a profit by charging tolls. A rider on horseback paid a penny a mile, while a wagon and four horses paid four times that amount. Tolls were collected at 11 buildings, spaced about 11 miles apart. For a wagon and two horses, a trip from Salem to Fayetteville cost $2.25 and took three days. A stagecoach could make the trip in 18 hours at a cost of $9. Parks along the way provided places to pull over and spend the night.

More than 20,000 wagons used the road in 1854, when it was called "the Appian Way of North Carolina." They hauled hay, corn and meal, beef tallow, beeswax and honey, hides, roots and herbs, dried berries, and cured meat.

The popularity of the road was short-lived, however. The railroads started reaching the counties that the road served by the mid-1850s, and the plank road couldn't compete. Neither could it withstand the heavy traffic without requiring constant repair. And because the planks weren't nailed down, the ride wasn't for the weak-hearted or those with ailing kidneys.

Mark Twain once commented after traveling down a plank road that the ride would have been nice "had not someone thrown down boards along the way."

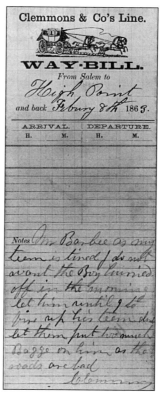

E. T. Clemmons owned the biggest stagecoach line in the area during the Civil War. His coaches and wagon carried passengers, mail, and freight to dozens of towns in North Carolina and southwestern Virginia. One-way passenger fare from Salem to High Point was $3.

North Carolina Division of Archives and History

John Philip Nissen's factory turned out wagons known for their durability.

North Carolina Division of Archives and History

Nissen Wagon Works

The Photograph Collection, Winston-Salem/Forsyth County Public Library

Spach Brothers Wagon Works

The Photograph Collection, Winston-Salem/Forsyth County Public Library

Children worked in Nissen's factory

The Photograph Collection, Winston-Salem/Forsyth County Public Library

John Philip Nissen and William E. Spach operated rival wagon works in Waughtown. Nissen's factory was larger than Spach's. He employed more people and turned out more wagons.

Nissen Wagons

The Photograph Collection, Winston-Salem/Forsyth County Public Library

And the Band Played On

The musicians settled into their metal folding chairs in Salem Square and began tuning up, their instruments competing with the cicadas that chirped noisily in the trees. It was the Fourth of July 1990, and the Salem Band was about to play a concert. No one would shoot at it this time.

Conditions weren't nearly as sedate for the original band members, whose concerts were often accompanied by cannon and musket fire. They played in the 26th North Carolina Regimental Band, the most famous of the three brass bands from Wachovia that marched off to the Civil War. The band was in Richmond in 1862 when the Union army was turned away at the gates of the Confederate capital. It witnessed the slaughter at Fredericksburg, followed Robert E. Lee into Gettysburg, and entertained the dispirited troops in the trenches of Petersburg. Captured as Lee retreated toward Appomattox, the band members spent the closing days of the war in a Federal prison.

That's not exactly what Julius Lineback had in mind when he joined the band in March 1862. Lineback listened when fellow Salem resident Sam Mickey talked to him about organizing a regimental band. Lineback wanted to do his duty, but he wasn't too keen on becoming a convenient target. "So I was open for some other engagement," he wrote in his history of the band, published in 1904. Lineback resigned his position as bookkeeper for F & H Fries Company and became one of the eight original "band boys."

They elected Mickey captain and left Salem on March 5, 1862, arriving the next day at the camp of the 26th North Carolina Regiment in the eastern part of the state. Lineback had packed his bass horn in a long black box, which prompted some of the hospital stewards to ask if he had brought his own coffin along.

The band's initial duties were rather mundane— playing at daily guard mounts and dress parades and giving short concerts each night and on Sunday mornings.

The routine was broken on March 13, when news arrived that 13,000 Yanks were coming. "We had not expected to so soon run up against the serious side of army life and heartily wished that the disturbing element had kept quiet some time longer," Lineback wrote.

The band members spent an anxious morning on a flatbed rail car awaiting a locomotive to pull them to safety, as cannonballs from enemy ships

The original members of the Twenty-Sixth North Carolina Regimental Band pose while in Salem on their first furlough in July 1862. They are, from left: Samuel T. Mickey, A. P. Gibson, J. O. Hall, W. H. Hall, A. L. Hauser, D. T. Crouse, Julius Lineback, and Joseph M. Fisher.

Wachovia Historical Society

screeched overhead. The engine finally arrived and took them to Goldsboro.

They reached Richmond on June 26. "We marched through the city trying to play several pieces and not doing ourselves much credit, as some of the boys were rather poor at memorizing music and could not play much without notes," Lineback remembered.

The band members remained at a hospital in Richmond while the regiment took part in the Seven Days Battle. They assisted the surgeons, fed the wounded, and carried wood and water. Throughout the rest of the war, the bandsmen served as stretcher bearers and hospital assistants.

But they had come to play their instruments. The men were accomplished musicians who were quite comfortable playing military marches, popular Confederate tunes, operas, waltzes, polkas, hymns, and Moravian chorales. Lee himself praised them. "He considered our band one of the best in the army and hoped that we would do all we could to cheer up the men," Lineback wrote.

The band was captured in April 1865, and its instruments were confiscated, except for Mickey's cornet. The men were sent to a prison camp at Point Lookout, Maryland, and were released one by one to return home.

Back in Salem, the band re-formed as the Salem Band, and it has been playing ever since.

The tuning was over, and the leader—one of Sam Mickey's descendants—stood and began playing the cornet that his ancestor had carried with him in that long-ago war.

The Civil War

A pall settled over Christmas 1860 as notions of brotherhood and peace were overshadowed by talk of disunity and war. It was a somber crowd that filled the courthouse December 29 in what was until then the largest meeting ever held in Forsyth County. The people came to discuss what the newspaper described as "the urgent state of affairs facing our country."

Republican Abraham Lincoln had been elected president in November, bringing to a head the festering issue of slavery. South Carolina had responded by seceding from the Union on December 20, and other Southern states had threatened to follow. The country was faced with a painful choice: war or dismemberment.

The people in the courthouse made it clear that they wanted neither. They unanimously passed a resolution that branded South Carolina "hasty and reckless" for resorting to secession, which "was no remedy for a single grievance." The Union, the crowd urged, should be preserved. It advised that North Carolina align itself with moderate states like Virginia and Tennessee if war came.

It wasn't the first time the county's 11,000 residents had made their feelings known on the subjects of slavery and secession. Forsyth, which had previously been solidly Democratic, had abandoned the party in 1860. John Bell, the presidential candidate of the Constitution Union Party, had carried the county. The secession issue in Forsyth was seen as largely a Democratic issue. Most people in the county didn't own slaves and were loyal to the Union. Moravians also felt a strong attachment to their Brethren in Pennsylvania.

County voters repeated their position in February 1861, when they overwhelmingly defeated a measure calling for a special session of the General Assembly to vote on secession. The proposal failed statewide by 651 votes.

Sentiment changed on April 15, 1861, when Lincoln called for 75,000 volunteers after the fall of Fort Sumter in Charleston. Slavery wasn't an issue now; county and state residents saw Lincoln's call to arms as a threat to their liberties. The *People's Press* noted that the residents of Forsyth County were united and "ready to oppose the aggression and defend their homes and firesides to the last."

North Carolina seceded on May 20—the last state to do so—and Salem and Winston began girding for war. The militia started enrolling all white men ages 18 to 45, and three volunteer companies formed in two months and marched off to war. Women gathered in homes to make uniforms and collect war supplies.

The enthusiasm lasted about 18 months. The army drained the county of its men, leaving women and men too young, old, or sick for fighting to tend the farms. Government policies and the decline of industrial and agricultural production triggered shortages and galloping inflation. Weariness, bitterness, and outright disloyalty followed.

By 1863, unpopular government policies, such as the draft and the suspension of the writ of habeas corpus, alarmed people and made many wonder who the real enemy was. The government's practice of taking food and horses from hard-pressed farmers was particularly loathsome.

Julia Conrad Jones, who lived in Bethania, described a train of army wagons that descended on the community, loading up with corn, wheat, bacon, and eggs. "They got three sacks of hay from us," she wrote to one of her sons serving in the army. "[They] were not satisfied with what we could spare, but came and took corn too. You know how little we can spare. I do not know where we are to get more."

The war also fueled animosity between classes. Laborers and workers were hit hardest because they couldn't afford to hire substitutes to serve in the Confederate army. They resented those who could and thought that the war was being fought to aid the rich.

Mrs. Jones, who sent two sons to war, particularly disliked the speculators, who seemed immune to the draft. "The brave and noble are gone and the ignoble are getting rich," she wrote one of her sons.

The Confederate defeats at Gettysburg and Vicksburg in 1863 added to the war-weariness. Many people, like Carolyn Fries, realized that further fighting was futile. "The tide of the war has changed," she wrote her future husband at the front. "For some time we had been successful everywhere, but we certainly cannot boast of our position at present. If 'the darkest hour is just before the dawn,' the day cannot be far distant."

A month after those defeats, more than 1,200 people jammed the grove outside the county courthouse for a peace rally and demanded an end to the war. The fighting, they said, was benefiting only "the speculator, the extortioner and high-paid officers, civil and military, who are fattening on the carnage of war and destruction of civil and religious liberty."

Loyalists held a rally of their own a month later. Twenty-five people attended.

The gubernatorial election of 1864 offered Forsyth County voters a clear choice: William W. Holden, a vigorous newspaper editor who wanted peace at any price, or the incumbent, Zebulon Vance, a veteran who ran on a platform of "fight the Yankees and fuss with the Confederacy." Holden got about 45 percent of the vote in the county. Forsyth's soldiers gave Vance the county, but the civilians at home clearly were tired of war. Statewide, Vance outpolled Holden by more than four to one to win reelection.

Life on the Home Front

Deserters roamed the woods, stealing horses and looting houses. Inflation devalued money until it was nearly worthless, but there wasn't much to buy, anyway. Crops went unplanted or withered in the field because all the able-bodied men had been drafted. Weariness weighed heavily on those who remained at home.

"I become chilly whenever I think of the blood that has already been spilled, the thousands of brave men and boys that must yet be sacrificed," Julia Conrad Jones wrote in a letter to her son Jimmy in 1864. She echoed the feelings of most people in Forsyth County during the last years of the Civil War. "I am not a Tory, but I do wish this war would stop."

Julia and her husband, Dr. Beverly Jones, lived near Bethania on the Abraham Conrad plantation, the largest in Forsyth County. Their letters and diaries tell of the hardships that most people in the county endured during the war. They describe the fear that parents felt for their children on distant battlefields and reflect the despair that settled on the people at home as the war seemed to go on forever.

It had started so brightly and with such high hopes. Like other Southerners, Forsyth County residents enthusiastically supported the war when it began in 1861. They staged parades to send off their brothers and husbands and boyfriends. They collected food and clothing, wound bandages from old sheets, and strung cloth from clotheslines to make "oilcloth" to keep the soldiers dry in the rain.

Every young man was itching to fight. Most feared the war would end before they got their chance. Virgil Wilson, Julia's nephew, wrote her from Yadkinville in 1861 to tell her that her son Abraham wanted very much to join the army: "If he were my boy, I would give him a rifle and say, 'Go and die if need be in Old Dominion.' He is plenty old enough to shoot a Yankee and protect himself."

Abraham, the eldest of the Joneses' 10 children, joined the Confederate army in September 1862 and was sent to eastern North Carolina. His family almost certainly scanned the casualty lists that ran weekly in Salem's *People's Press*: "R. E. Richardson of Walkertown, wounded slightly . . . Peter Rawls of Winston, wounded in the legs and left in the hands of the enemy . . . We regret to report that our friend W. E. Pfohl was killed. . . . "

For the Joneses, the bad news came on May 7, 1863, in a letter from an officer in Abraham's regiment. Their son, he told them, had been captured. "He was a good boy . . . ," the officer wrote. "AG has his own coat and blanket. I have got the rest of his clothes. I will take good care of them. I expect it will be some time before he is paroled."

He was released seven months later and returned home in poor health. His parents nursed him, and Abraham went back to the army and spent the remainder of the war on the battlefields of eastern Virginia. He survived.

As did his brother Jimmy, who entered the army in 1863. Alexander, another brother, wanted to join two years later but needed his parents' permission because he was only 17. Julia wouldn't hear of it. "I cannot give you up," she wrote her son, who was attending a military school in Hillsborough.

No one was safe, though. Alexander and other cadets were ordered to guard Union prisoners in the rain. He caught pneumonia and died at home in 1865.

As the war dragged on, most of the county's men between the ages of 18 and 45 were drafted. The manpower shortage forced many businesses to shorten their hours or close. The *People's Press* informed its readers in October 1864 that its last employee could not get a deferment and was about to be drafted. "Should our patrons receive no papers, they may know the reason—suspended by state authority," Levi Blum, the paper's editor, wrote. He didn't miss an edition.

Farmers weren't as lucky. Fields lay fallow, creating serious food shortages. Julia Jones's niece in Yadkin County wrote her in 1862, "I know many who have crops and no one to tend them but themselves. To leave them now would be ruinous. It seems to me that they can as well serve their country by making bread as any way." She later wrote asking her aunt for food.

Women, children, and old men were left at home to raise crops and bear rampant inflation and shortages of almost every necessity. Bacon was 20 cents a pound in 1861 and $1 a pound at the close of the war. A bushel of corn was $2 in 1862 and $25 in 1865. Corn was so scarce that Francis Fries, the owner of a textile mill in Salem, offered to trade cotton for it. The traditional Moravian lovefeast cost $125 without coffee, which was impossible to buy at any price.

The *People's Press* ran a regular column in 1863 called "Practical Hints for Hard Times," which offered readers substitutes for items that could no longer be purchased. Rabbit fur, it advised, could be used instead of wool, and feathers stuffed between two layers of cotton made a warm quilt jacket. "Confederate pins"—cactus or prickly pear thorns—could be substituted for the real thing.

Those at home had more to worry about in 1864 than the lack of wool or straight pins. Deserters from the Confederate army and draftees who refused to report—"skulkers"—hid in the woods or in abandoned farm buildings, such as those at the Flynt farm near Bethania.

"Now I am afraid we shall be overrun with deserters and skulkers," Julia wrote Jimmy in May 1864. "The few sheep and pigs we have will no doubt be slain by those at Flynt's."

The deserters became bolder and more numerous by 1865. Dr. Jones wrote to Alexander in March that a neighbor's barn had been burned by deserters. "The deserters have had things quite their own way in this county, stealing and burning," he wrote. "They go from house to house and take what they please."

Burglaries rose dramatically. Smokehouses were favorite targets because meat was scarce. Looting and fires became so common that the *People's Press* urged town officials to bolster night patrols and hire more police.

"People are much disheartened and think it would be best to give up to the Yanks now," Julia wrote Alexander in March 1865. "They have hung on to the eleventh hour. . . . I fear the day is not distant when we will be overrun if not a subjugated people."

That day did come, a month later.

"Peace has succeeded war," Blum wrote in his *People's Press*, "and the people, the great mass of people throughout the county are breathing easier."

But it would take time before life returned to normal. O. J. Lehman, a cornet player in the Confederate army, returned home to Bethania on April 19, 1865. He was shocked by what was left.

"And Oh what a change since we left our old home nearly four years ago. No one here but old men and women. The state government had been overthrown. . . . All laws were a thing of the past. . . . Banks all closed and bankrupt, no money and but a few of the necessities of life could be had," Lehman wrote almost 40 years later. "I full remember the first meal that my mother prepared for me on my arrival, which consisted of corn bread made with water, a very little salt, brown cow peas poorly seasoned (meat was very scarce), sorghum molasses and coffee which was made from parched sweet potatoes, parched rye. The meal was enjoyed and relished more than a $1 meal at the restaurant at the present time. Under these circumstances what was to be done? It was root hog or die."

SALT TICKET.

FORSYTH COUNTY NORTH CAROLINA.

	Whites.	Blacks.
Number of persons composing my family.	2	10

Weight of PORK or BEEF annually put up for family use, *1200* Pounds.

Amount of SALT on hand. ....

I hereby certify, upon honor,
to the correctness of the above.
(Signed.) .... *W. F. Randleman* ....

The above ticket has drawn ..... *½ bushel* ..... for ..... months supply.

SALEM, N. C. *Dec. 3d* 1862.

This salt ticket entitled the bearer to 1,200 pounds of salt.

The Moravian Archives of the Southern Province, Winston-Salem

The Yankees Are Coming!

"Sister and I sat reading and sewing until 1 o'clock when word reached us that the Yankees were in Yadkinville," Carolyn Fries Shaffner wrote in her diary on April 1, 1865. "We immediately commenced packing as we were certain that they would burn the factories and we feared the house would go also."

Word that Union cavalry was raiding western North Carolina sent Salem and Winston into a panic. The mayors of the two towns agreed on April 2 to formally surrender their communities in the hope of mollifying the Yankees and sparing the towns.

General George Stoneman was relatively kind to the towns he and his troopers visited. They had invaded the northwestern part of the state in late March, destroying warehouses in Boone and Wilkesboro and some cotton factories in northern Iredell County. Stoneman had issued strict orders against looting and the destruction of private property, and his men had obeyed.

They turned into southwestern Virginia and then headed for Danbury in Stokes County. They passed through Germanton on April 9, heading south.

The news stirred a commotion in Salem, remembered Edward Blum, who ran a print shop in the town and helped his brother, Levi, edit the *People's Press*. "This caused a sensation, and men and women were busy hiding silver and gold and valuable jewelry in various ways," he wrote in his reminiscence of the war's final days.

Silverware and jewelry were hidden in holes dug around Home Moravian Church, and two fine black stallions were spirited away to the basement of the Female Academy's Main Hall.

As Stoneman's men approached on Monday, April 10, John Blackburn, the clerk of court in Winston, belatedly decided to protect the court records. He stuffed the most valuable papers into sacks and scurried around town dropping them at various homes.

Blackburn then joined the delegation that rode to Salem's outskirts to await the Union troopers and surrender the town. The group included Joshua Boner, Salem's mayor, and the Reverend Robert de Schweinitz, the principal of the academy.

Stoneman's brigade, under Colonel W. J. Palmer, rode down the road about five in the afternoon. What happened next is part of local folklore.

De Schweinitz had tied a white handkerchief to his cane, but the soldiers paid him no mind. They grabbed the reins of his horse, and Colonel Palmer went for his pistol.

The principal boldly stood his ground. "I am de Schweinitz," he said.

The surprised Palmer put his pistol back in his holster. "I had a teacher of that name when I was in school in Lititz," he said, referring to a Moravian school in Pennsylvania.

Palmer, a Pennsylvanian, may have had pleasant memories of the Moravians, which may account for his troopers' kind handling of Salem.

The reception that the troopers received in Salem was another possible reason. A member of Palmer's brigade wrote later of the entrance into town, "Here we met with a most cordial reception, very different from the usual greetings we receive. The ladies cheered us and brought out bread, pies, and cakes. . . . The people showed much enthusiasm at the sight of the flag we carried, and many were the touching remarks made about it. Old men wept like children and prominent citizens took off their hats and bowed to it."

Another soldier remembered the young ladies at the academy, who unfurled a United States flag from their windows.

The single sisters reacted differently when they spotted the enemy riding down Main Street, Edward Blum remembered. "At the Sisters House, the good sisters were considerably excited . . . ," he wrote. "Some gesticulated in their excitement, showing their white handkerchiefs. A report was made to [Palmer] that the inmates of the women's lunatic asylum were out on the street and needed looking after. A general laugh followed upon the explanation and [was] readily understood as several of the staff and the general himself were acquainted with Moravians in Bethlehem."

Fears that the Yankees would lay waste to the towns were unfounded. Palmer's men behaved tolerably well for the 24 hours they were in Salem. They took food and some horses and had a good laugh when the son of C. L. Rights, the town clerk, hollered out his window, "You can't get our horses! We got them hid in the cellar!"

They didn't ransack houses or burn anything. In fact, Palmer sent men to protect Fries's textile mill, which was looted by residents. Thousands of pounds of cloth were taken, Blum said, "without leave or license and not for the use of either army but taken for the benefit of people who had not really contributed for the boys in the army. But such is the way of the world. . . . The Yanks were disgusted with the greed and stopped the work."

Henry Fries, a partner in the firm that owned the factory, placed placards around Salem a few days later addressed "to the Honest People of Forsyth." Some people had taken merchandise under the mistaken impression that Union troops were planning to burn the factory, Fries said in the placard. They had returned those articles. "I am sorry to say, however, that some persons removed articles, not for protection against destruction, but for their own use. These people are simply thieves." And familiar thieves, at that. Fries had found out that much of the property was in the hands of people he thought were "good, friendly neighbors."

After the troops departed, word reached Salem of General Robert E. Lee's surrender at Appomattox. "We can indulge in wild speculation what is in store for us," Carolyn Fries Shaffner recorded in her diary, "and the prospect for our future is anything but cheering."

For all its pain and sorrow, the Civil War marked a turning point in the history of Winston and Salem by making the industrialization of the two cities possible. Emancipation swept away forever the economy that had supported the antebellum plantations. Throughout the 1850s, the owners of those plantations had fought against better transportation routes and laws favorable to manufacturing. That fight ended with the Civil War.

Though North Carolina would remain agricultural well into the 20th century, freeing the slaves made available the one thing industrialization needed—cheap labor.

The boom was about to begin.

Forsyth's "Proudest Day"

The 1,000 people crammed into the tiny courthouse square strained to hear what 11-year-old Mary Fountain was saying. She stood on the steps of the courthouse in a white dress festooned with flowers and garlands of evergreen.

"We are here to cast a veil over the foibles of the past," she began, "and to hallow the second advent of American freedom and liberty to the sons of North Carolina."

With that, the United States flag was hoisted up the courthouse flagpole on May 20, 1865, four years to the day after the state had seceded and the flag had been removed. The Salem Brass Band played "The Star-Spangled Banner" amid a 12-round salute from a cannon.

"As the flag reached the top and spread its ample folds to the breeze a shout went up . . . ," the *People's Press* reported. "The joy was so overwhelming that many of the old and young shed tears of joy freely, as cheer after cheer went up in honor of the occasion. It was the proudest day in the history of Forsyth County."

Dates to Remember

1843   The Salem Vigilant Fire Company, the area's first organized fire department, is formed.

1849   The monopoly system is abolished in Salem. Forsyth County is created by carving off the southern end of Stokes County. The Moravian Church sells 51 acres a mile north of Salem for the new county seat.

1850   The first courthouse opens in the yet-unnamed county seat.

1851   The General Assembly names the new town in honor of Joseph Winston.

1852   The Western Plank Road reaches Salem, linking the region with the major shipping port of Wilmington. It is extended to Bethania within two years.

1855   English replaces German as the official language of the Moravian Church.

1856   The lease system is abolished in Salem. The town is incorporated with Charles Brietz as its first mayor. Francis Eugene Boner starts Winston's first newspaper, the *Western Sentinel*.

1859   Winston is incorporated, and William Barrow is elected its first mayor. Gas street lamps are installed along Main and Church streets in Salem.

1865   Union cavalrymen under Colonel W. J. Palmer camp in Forsyth County. They raise a little hell and steal some horses but don't burn anything down.

Names to Know

Edward Belo
He's best remembered for the big white house on Main Street in Old Salem that bears his name. Belo quit his job as a master cabinetmaker to open a small store in his family's home on Main and Bank streets. He replaced the house with the present one in 1860. A store, the first "department store" in Salem, occupied the first floor, and the Belo family lived on the second floor. The iron animals on the parapet were made at Belo's foundry, north of town. Belo served on Salem's first board of commissioners and was vice president of Wachovia National Bank when it formed in 1879.

Robert Gray
Born in Randolph County, where he owned a store for many years, Gray moved to Winston in 1850 and became one of its most influential early citizens. He bought the first lot in town and built one of Winston's first stores there. A member of the first board of commissioners, Gray was elected mayor in 1861. He died 20 years later and is buried in Salem Cemetery.

William E. Spach
He opened a wagon works in Waughtown in 1854 that rivaled the nearby Nissen works. The two turned out wagons that were renowned for their durability and dependability. Smaller than its rival, Spach Brothers Wagon Works employed just two people in the 1870s, but it turned out about 20 wagons a year. The wagons cost about $100, or $20 less than a comparable Nissen wagon. The company stopped making wagons in 1928 and turned to furniture.

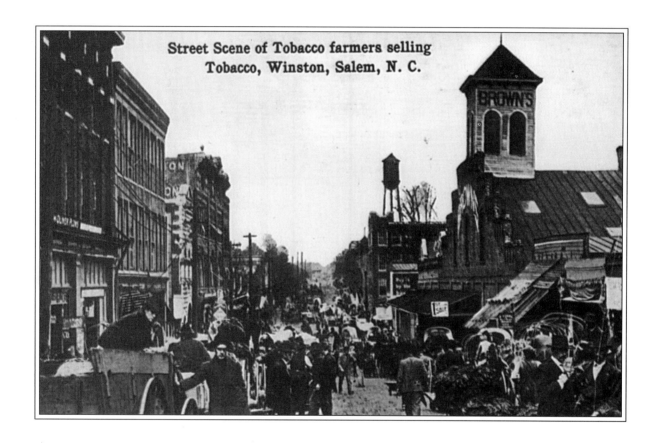

Main Street during the tobacco market, about 1890

The Photograph Collection, Winston-Salem/Forsyth County Public Library

The Crowning of King Tobacco

It is a benchmark, one of those convenient points in the history of a place that marks an unmistakable change. Gettysburg was never the same after The Battle; Johnstown was never the same after The Flood. The catalyst was not as dramatic in Winston—just a 28-mile spur railroad line to Greensboro. But the coming of the railroad in 1873 marked the start of almost 50 years of phenomenal growth that transformed sleepy Winston into a bustling, boisterous boom town.

The railroad ignited the boom, but tobacco fueled it.

Tobacco was to Winston what steel was to Pittsburgh and oil to Houston. Tobacco was king. It turned a hardscrabble town best known for its dried berries into a bustling city that was one of the manufacturing giants of the New South. It attracted restless, resourceful men such as Pleas Hanes from Davie County and Dick Reynolds from Virginia, who built factories that became businesses of international importance.

Winston's population swelled more than 1,500 percent during those 50 years, as thousands of people flooded into town to work in the tobacco factories. Many were black tenant farmers lured in on boxcars with stories of ready pay and steady work.

What was good for business apparently was good for the town. So no one complained when those who ran the factories also began running the town council and the school board. The company town was beginning to take shape.

The Biggest Blood in Winston

Richard Joshua Reynolds rode into Winston on horseback in 1874, took off his hat, and scanned the dusty little town—as the statue of him on Main Street attests. Presumably, he was looking for a place to build his tobacco factory. The company he started the following year on a lot about the size of a tennis court would one day sprawl over 100 acres of downtown and dominate Winston-Salem's psyche as well as its real estate.

Reynolds came to Winston merely to take advantage of the little town's rail connection, but his tobacco company ended up defining the city. The two grew up together, and their histories are so intertwined that it's impossible for most people to think of one without the other. People who know nothing about Winston-Salem know that it is the home of R. J. Reynolds Tobacco Company.

The company's leaders would come to dominate the city's politics and social structure. Its founder set the pattern. R. J. Reynolds was so influential that it was 41 years after his death in 1918 before company officials summoned the nerve to hang the portraits of other chief executives next to his in the boardroom. By the time he was 40 years old, Reynolds was Winston's leading citizen. He was called on to lend his support or his money to numerous projects. Reynolds helped start a savings and loan, served on the town board, championed public schools, and fought J. P. Morgan's railroad monopoly. His money helped build a school for blacks, an opera house, and a YMCA.

Josephus Daniels, the publisher of the *News & Observer* in Raleigh, described his friend this way: "He was a strange man, Dick Reynolds was, a bold, daring and audacious man with little education and little polish. . . . North Carolina has not produced another merchant of such vigor and success."

Raised on a plantation in what is now Critz in southwestern Virginia, Reynolds grew up in comfortable surroundings. His father, Hardin, had amassed a small fortune making chewing tobacco and running a store. He was one of the largest planters in Virginia when the Civil War started, and one of the few not bankrupted by the war. When he died in 1882, Hardin owned more than 8,000 acres in Virginia and 3,000 in Stokes County in North Carolina.

R. J. Reynolds had opportunities that other children of the time and place didn't. He attended a private school but didn't care much

Opposite page:
R. J. Reynolds in 1872, two years before he moved to Winston

Reynolda House Museum of American Art

for books. An eye defect that apparently prevented him from visualizing words probably had a lot to do with it. He was bright and quick-witted, though. In an often-told story from his Civil War–era boyhood, a teacher asked Reynolds what covered the mountains. "Rocks and deserters," he replied.

Emory and Henry College didn't interest Reynolds. He left after two years because he didn't do well in any subject except math. A business college in Baltimore was good for about six months.

Books may have eluded Reynolds, but he knew tobacco and people. Riding a wagon through the mountains of Virginia, Tennessee, and Kentucky, he peddled his father's chewing tobacco. He found times tough, money scarce, and the tobacco almost impossible to sell. So he traded it for anything of value—animal hides, beeswax, tallow, yarn, old furniture, jewelry. He then auctioned off the items, often selling them for more than the tobacco was worth.

Selling tobacco that way was at best uncertain and at times unprofitable. To succeed at this business, Reynolds decided, he needed access to a railroad. Since there was none in Critz, he packed up and rode the 60 miles to Winston, where the Northwest North Carolina Railroad—now Southern Railway—had completed a spur line to Greensboro in 1873. He came, Reynolds said later, "for the benefit of the railroad facilities, and on account of this town being located in the center of the belt in which the finest tobacco in the world is grown."

Reynolds was only 24 years old when he arrived. He had $7,500 to his name. He immediately bought a lot next to the railroad tracks on Depot Street—now Patterson Avenue—from the Moravian Church for $388.50. Reynolds built a two-story wooden factory—the "little red factory" of lore—for $2,400, hired 12 seasonal black workers, and was in business.

It wasn't much of a business at first. Reynolds sold about 150,000 pounds of chewing tobacco his first year—minuscule by later standards. By 1879, business was good enough that he added to the factory and bolstered the work force to 75 employees. From then on, he built additions or new factories or bought out competitors every two years. At the time of Reynolds's death, his company owned 121 buildings in Winston-Salem.

Reynolds once said that he would retire when he made $100,000. But in 1892, when his net worth more than doubled that figure, he embarked on the most aggressive part of his career. He replaced his original factory with a six-story plant that was the largest building in Winston. It had steam power, electric lights, and a smokestack that cost more than the first factory. Number 256 is the oldest Reynolds factory still standing. In August 1990, the company sold the building to Forsyth County, which had not decided what to do with it at the time of this writing.

Production quadrupled. Shortly after the turn of the century, Reynolds's company gobbled up most of the other tobacco factories in town. It was the major industry in Winston, producing 25 percent of the country's chewing tobacco. The introduction of immensely popular Prince Albert smoking tobacco in 1907 gave the company its first national product, and Reynolds billboards began appearing on Union Square in New York.

Called R.J.R. by the time he was 30, Reynolds was the most eligible bachelor in town before marrying Katharine Smith in 1905. Six-foot-two and with dark hair and eyes, he often was chosen to lead parades and emcee balls and other social events.

His brother Harbour Reynolds was impressed when he visited in 1884. "Dick is the biggest blood in Winston," he wrote their mother.

He and his company would only get bigger.

A somewhat romantic view of R. J. Reynolds's first "little red factory"

R. J. Reynolds Tobacco Company

Station at the growing city, Winston-Salem, N. C

213757

The Union Railroad Station on Chestnut Street, between Third and Fourth streets, was a busy place in 1910.

North Carolina Division of Archives and History

Railroad tracks in Winston's manufacturing district, about 1890

The Photograph Collection, Winston-Salem/Forsyth County Public Library

Reconstruction and Dried Berries

Reynolds rode into a town that was just beginning to awaken. Nothing much had happened in Winston and Salem since 1860 because of the Civil War and Reconstruction. Though almost 25 years old, Winston still had a decided frontier flavor. Its unpaved streets were dusty in the summer and bottomless quagmires in the winter, and wood-frame buildings were the dominant architectural style. Hitching posts and horse troughs lined the courthouse square, which was ringed by a dilapidated fence. Its gate always stood open, and cattle, hogs, and sheep roamed at will. Sheep made a habit of sleeping under the large portico at the south end of the building.

About 500 people lived in Winston. Throw in Salem and the population was still less than 2,000. Like Southerners everywhere, they had come through some difficult times after the war shattered the region's economy. "Stores were closed with no goods or wares, so we did without," O. J. Lehman, a resident of Bethania, remembered.

Flour, at $20 a bushel, was almost as scarce as jobs. Men willing to work hard for little pay could find work as farm hands, but even those limited opportunities disappeared in 1868, when heavy rains destroyed the cotton crop and many farmers went bankrupt.

Dried fruits and berries provided the main source of money for the villages before the late 1870s. Boxes of fruit lined Winston's streets, waiting to be shipped by wagon and later by train. Pfohl and Stockton, one of the town's leading merchants, did $50,000 worth of business a year in dried fruits. A New York newspaper reported in 1877 that Salem had shipped 3 million pounds of blueberries during the preceding three years, worth $500,000. The industry remained strong until the 1880s, when the introduction of canned and evaporated fruits killed it.

But by then, tobacco was king, and it would usher in an exciting time of unparalleled growth and prosperity.

Early Days of Tobacco

Tobacco is first mentioned in the Moravian records in 1755, when Brother Loesch bought "a couple of hundred tobacco plants" from a Mr. Banner. The importance of tobacco as a cash crop in North Carolina decreased after the Revolution. The Napoleonic Wars cut off markets in France and England, and westward expansion in the United States created new tobacco-growing states. The result: prices plummeted to an average of about four cents a pound in 1850. With the invention of the cotton gin, many North Carolina farmers gave up tobacco for cotton.

Eli and Elisha Slade changed all that when they planted their "bright-leaf" tobacco in a Caswell County field in 1852 or 1853. The new yellow-leafed tobacco was vastly superior to the kind then being grown. It transformed the state by allowing farmers to compete with the burley leaf of Kentucky. New flue-curing techniques replaced the old method of curing by open fire, and the result was a thin, milder-tasting yellow leaf.

The first large quantity of bright leaf was grown in the northern part of Forsyth County in 1858. Farmers found that the silty soil was particularly suited for the new tobacco. Forsyth farmers raised about 250,000 pounds of it in 1870. This is not particularly impressive when compared to the million-pound crops of some eastern counties, but it set the stage for a new era.

It began on February 14, 1872, when the horn sounded at Winston's first permanent tobacco warehouse. The small frame structure on the corner of Church and Third streets was Thomas J. Brown's second attempt at opening a warehouse in Winston. A native of Caswell County, Brown had moved to town in 1869 to open a tobacco warehouse in an old livery stable on Liberty Street. Though he had distributed seeds to entice local farmers to grow bright leaf, Brown had been forced to close the warehouse because not enough tobacco was grown to support an auction house. Sensing the coming of the railroad from Greensboro, he tried again.

"Any three ol' wimen 'tween the co't house and Nissen's shops kit smoke in their pipes all the 'backer as'd ever be sold in that thar house," one local wag predicted in the newspaper.

They would have had to smoke a lot of tobacco. Brown's Warehouse—whose motto was "Honest dealing, close attention and fair treatment to all"—became the most successful of the numerous tobacco auction houses that opened in Winston. It was so successful that in 1884, Brown built a new warehouse on Main Street that covered 18,000 square feet.

Depending on which version of what happened on opening day in 1872 is true, Brown either had his doubts or knew immediately that his warehouse would be a winner. In the warehouse for its opening were Brown's bookkeeper, his auctioneer, three buyers, and two black floormen, Dick and Pard Mack. By one account, farmers and their families poured into town and filled the warehouse with tobacco. In the other version, Brown was disappointed when only two farmers showed up on a raw, wet day.

Tobacco is piled high inside a Winston factory in 1901.

North Carolina Division of Archives and History

However the opening went, Brown sold about 250,000 pounds of tobacco that first season, an amount sold in a few days on today's market. Buyers from Danville and other towns in southwestern Virginia bought most of the tobacco because there were no local manufacturers.

With a railroad, a good local supply of leaf, and an auction house, Winston was ready for a tobacco factory. Hamilton Scales hauled his equipment into town on Nissen wagons in late 1872 and built a 500-square-foot factory. To ensure a supply of leaf, Scales and S. M. Hobson opened another tobacco warehouse the following year.

Thomas L. Vaughn built the second factory in 1873. He was followed later that year by Pleasant Henderson Hanes and his brother, John. They moved from Davie County, where Pleas Hanes was a tobacco salesman for a small company in Mocksville. The brothers opened P. H. Hanes & Company, which billed itself as "the largest manufacturer of plain goods in the world." With 600 employees who could handle more than 3 million pounds of tobacco, Hanes became Winston's biggest tobacco factory and largest employer before the brothers sold their business to R. J. Reynolds in 1900.

Reynolds opened the fourth factory, and dozens more followed. By 1890, some 35 factories turned out 9.6 million pounds of chewing tobacco a year. None of the factories, though, was very large. Only Hanes, Reynolds, Brown & Brothers, and Bitting & Hay were worth at least $75,000.

Winston was establishing a reputation, as John Hanes noted in 1890. "We now boast with pride of the number and magnitude of our factories, and our output of chewing tobacco is larger than any city in Virginia or North Carolina," he said. "Our manufactured tobacco is regarded by jobbers everywhere as [the] standard . . . and the name of Winston on a box of the same is a guarantee of its merit."

The growth of the town's economy attracted thousands of new residents. Most of the immigrants—black and white—were farmers fleeing bleak conditions on the farm. Winston saw its population grow a record 544 percent in the 1870s, to 2,854. Ten years later, more than 8,000 people lived in Winston and Salem. When the new century dawned, the two towns could claim almost 14,000 residents.

Lacking skills that meshed with the industrial society they were helping create, the new arrivals took jobs that required little, if any, skill. That meant long hours and low pay, with almost no chance of advancing to management. Workers were most unhappy with the long workdays, complaining in a survey by the Bureau of Labor Statistics that they had little leisure time with their families. Their condition was "growing worse all the time," they said.

One blacksmith said he had done more work in two years than his father, also a blacksmith, did in seven. At age 29, he considered himself "broke down."

The average wage of an unskilled worker in Winston was $.81 a day in the 1880s. Many of the jobs were seasonal, and bills—wood was $2.50 a cord and coal $8 to $9 a ton—were high.

Debts and misery were widespread, a printer said, in summing up the conditions of the working man. "It takes all a poor man can make to live at the wages he gets," he said, "and he generally falls in debt in the winter and has to scratch throughout the summer to pay for his winter supplies."

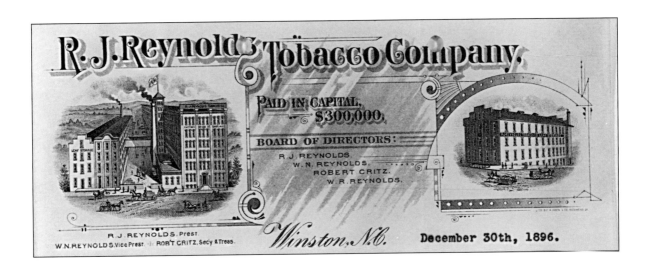

The letterheads of the two largest tobacco companies in Winston in the 1890s

North Carolina Division of Archives and History

Inside the Early Tobacco Factories

On a spring day in 1890, a couple of hundred black people lined Fifth Street. White foremen from R. J. Reynolds Tobacco Company went down the line inspecting each person, pressing forearms hardened by years of work on tenant farms. The blacks came from South Carolina. They had been loaded into boxcars and lured to Winston by Reynolds recruiters, who told them stories of ready work and steady pay.

The farmers probably weren't told how dreary the work was or how little they'd be paid, but it wouldn't have mattered to most of them. Almost anything was better than the farms, where only the work was steady.

After the inspection, the foremen assigned each person a job in one of the company's factories. The big, strong men would push hogsheads of tobacco across factory floors. "Mules," they were called. Other men would shovel coal or stir tobacco leaves in steaming kettles. Some of the women would learn to grade tobacco, and others would get the tedious job of removing the woody stem from each leaf.

Most of the people would work 10 or 11 hours a day in humid factories. They would make less than four dollars a week.

Stories were later told about the patriarchal R. J. Reynolds walking through his factories and giving his employees a raise on the spot. No doubt, wages and conditions improved in all the tobacco factories over the next 30 years. R. J. Reynolds Tobacco Company led the way with drinking-water systems, lunchrooms, day nurseries, medical departments, profit-sharing plans, and the like. The company became a model employer, offering high-paying jobs to generations of workers.

But for the thousands of blacks who poured into Winston in the 1880s and 1890s to work in the town's dozens of tobacco factories, conditions were grim. Yet still they came. They saved what little money they could and then sent home for their families.

The tobacco factories relied almost entirely on blacks. The work was done mostly by hand, and whites preferred to hire blacks for manual labor. In contrast, the textile mills of the day, which were already highly mechanized, employed only whites because blacks were considered unsuited for working with machinery.

Lacking electricity and heat, the earliest tobacco factories closed in the winter. That made for a highly transient and unreliable work force. Workers often stayed just long enough to buy a new suit of clothes before returning home. Those who remained through the season left when the factories closed and returned when they reopened in the spring. The larger factories added electricity and steam in the mid-1880s and machines to dry the tobacco a few years later and remained open year-round.

The work itself hadn't changed since antebellum days, when slaves on plantations had made most of the twist and plug chewing tobacco—the primary products of Winston's factories in the 19th century. Twists were braided ropes of tobacco, and plugs were pressed rectangular pancakes, usually flavored with honey, licorice, sugar, or brandy.

The tobacco entered the factories in wooden barrels called hogsheads. The leaves were unpacked and treated with steam to make them pliable and easier to handle. They then were sent to the untying line, a long table that usually ran the length of the room. Pickers removed trashy leaves and foreign matter and saved the better leaves, called wrappers, which were used to cover the finished plugs. The rest of the leaves—the filler—were used to make the chewing tobacco.

Classers on the untying line graded the wrappers as to color, size, and type, while gangs of stemmers—usually women and the most numerous group of workers in the factory—sang and chanted in rhythm as they removed the woody midrib of the tobacco.

Befo' I'd work fur Reynolds R. J.
I'd walk all night an' sleep all day,
Walk all night to keep from sleepin'
An' sleep all day to keep from eatin'.

The leaves were dried until completely dehydrated and then immersed in a sugar or

Workers remove the woody stems from tobacco leaves.

The tobacco is boiled in licorice and dried.

The leaves are braided into twists.

licorice solution for flavoring. In the flavoring room, black men tended large steaming kettles, constantly stirring the mixture with large wooden paddles. Still steaming, the tobacco was carried to the roof of the factory for sunning, which also made it sweeter.

After it was completely dry, the tobacco was sprinkled with various flavorings and sent to the lump room. The lumpers, usually black men, stood on one side of a tall workbench and used scales and gauges to shape rough rectangular plugs of uniform shape and weight. They then covered the plugs in the wrappers.

Shapers in the prize room put the plugs in a press that formed them into pancakes. The pancakes were oiled to prevent sticking and pressed again. Young black boys affixed tin tags to the plugs and put labels on them and tax stamps on the boxes of finished product.

The hours were long and the work dirty, uncomfortable, and sometimes dangerous. Having a hand or finger crushed in a press wasn't unusual. The workers were mostly young and single, with most under 30 years old. Children as young as 10 worked at various jobs in the factories, usually at the insistence of their parents. Foremen whipped children, but their parents rarely objected. Very small children accompanied their mothers to work, sleeping in corners or trying to help pick or stem tobacco.

A weak state law in 1903 barred children under 12 from working in the factories, but it was rarely enforced. The law met stiff opposition from the manufacturers. Bailey Brothers, one of Winston's largest tobacco companies, complained to the state labor commissioner, "Children are very serviceable in tobacco factories as stemmers, an it don't hurt them. In fact, they need employment to keep them out of mischief. . . . We are opposed to any legislation on the labor question as we think it will regulate itself."

The tobacco companies also fought federal laws banning child labor. Finally, in 1919, Congress passed a law prohibiting the hiring of children under 14 and limiting those between 14 and 16 to eight hours of work a day.

Drawings courtesy of
North Carolina Division of Archives and History

Men busy making boxes for plug tobacco

The Photograph Collection, Winston-Salem/Forsyth County Public Library

Men and boys built the boxes and barrels used to ship Winston's tobacco products.

The Photograph Collection, Winston-Salem/Forsyth County Public Library

Copyright 1916
by R. J. Reynolds
Tobacco Co.

Your money buys quality

Quality has been the only inducement ever offered to smoke Prince Albert. Coupons or premiums have never been used with it. Prince Albert can in no way be affected by national or state restrictions on the use of coupons and premiums.

Quick as you light up some Prince Albert tobacco you'll realize how much you appreciate its freedom from bite and parch which are *cut out* by the patented process by which it is made.

Prince Albert is to be had everywhere tobacco is sold in toppy red bags, 5c; tidy red tins, 10c; handsome pound and half-pound tin humidors, and, in that clever pound crystal-glass humidor with sponge-moistener top.

PRINCE ALBERT
the national joy smoke

will meet every pipe or cigarette desire you ever had. It has a fine flavor that you'll like better the more you smoke.

You certainly owe it to yourself to give this tobacco a thorough test because *then only* will you know *yourself* that Prince Albert is so good. And you will know why Prince Albert is today smoked by men all over the world—it is so cool and friendly.

R. J. REYNOLDS TOBACCO CO., Winston-Salem, N. C.

Advertisements like this made Prince Albert a national best seller.

North Carolina Division of Archives and History

The southeast corner of Third and Church streets

Collection of Old Salem

P. H. Hanes & Company on East Third and Church streets was the largest tobacco company in Winston before 1900.

North Carolina Collection, UNC Library at Chapel Hill

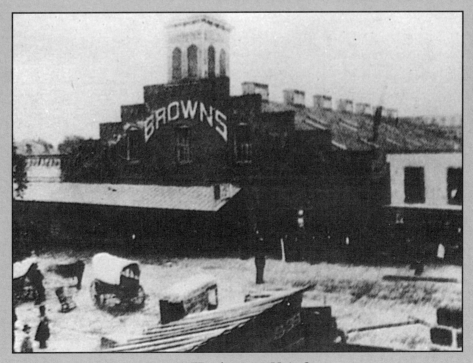

Brown's Warehouse on Main Street

The Photograph Collection, Winston-Salem/Forsyth County Public Library

Grimy faced workers take a break.

Collection of Old Salem

Workers outside the Wachovia Flour and Grist Mill

The Photograph Collection, Winston-Salem/Forsyth County Public Library

Charles and Christian Fogle started a construction company that practically built Winston.
In 1890, a typical year, the company built 45 houses, two tobacco factories,
three stores, a livery stable, a church, a county jail, and Park Hall at Salem Academy.
Above, the men paused long enough to have their picture made that year.
Christian Fogle is standing fifth from the left.

———

Collection of Old Salem

Carnival on Old Town Street

From their earliest days, Salem and then Winston were trading centers, supplying farmers for more than 50 miles. The new railroad and the busy tobacco factories and warehouses solidified Winston's place as the commercial heart of northwestern North Carolina.

During the annual tobacco market, the streets were a maddening crush of wagons, as thousands of farmers came to town to sell their tobacco. Most of the warehouses were on Old Town Street, the busiest in Winston before the turn of the century. The town commissioners, recognizing the commercial importance of the street, renamed it Trade Street.

Farmers and their families slept and ate in the warehouses or in their wagons parked outside. After selling their tobacco, many farmers had the only cash they would see all year, and they were in a buying mood. Peddlers and medicine men like Josiah Roberts worked the crowd on Old Town Street. "You should go to Winston-Salem about two weeks after the market opens. Heaven knows, if there ever was a medicine racket it's operated there," Roberts said. "You can learn more about the rackets and pitching on Trade Street in two days than you can in two months in Durham. The people have money and are in a carnival mood, buying and spending."

Peddlers sold watches, rattlesnake oil, and blood purifiers. Doc Chesire said he lived all year off what he made during the market season. "Those people in Winston will bite on anything," he remembered. "I believe they'd bite their own finger if you told them."

Tobacco money also meant shoes for the kids, a pretty dress for Mama, and maybe that new plow at Brown-Rogers & Company hardware store.

The farmers and their families didn't have to go far to find a general store. Some of the largest of the 18 stores in town were right there on Old Town Street. Vaughn and Prather, a thriving grocery store, was on the corner of Fifth. H. D. Poindexter, another store, was on the far corner, at Fourth Street. The huge Hinshaw and Medearis Building, also on Fourth, had two steam elevators and seven departments that sold everything from shoelaces to parlor furniture.

The most beautiful general store, though, was Pfohl and Stockton on Main and Third streets. Built in 1876, the three-story brick structure had an ornate Italianate facade and arched windows, a striking contrast to the drab appearance of the other stores. It also may have had the first telephone—of sorts—in Winston. Henry Foltz, an employee, remembered that two tomato cans were attached to waxed string and that one of them was stretched to J. E. Mickey's shop three blocks away. "It was actually possible to understand some words," Foltz wrote in his recollections of the period.

While the farmers browsed the hardware store or snuck off to one of the eight saloons on Third Street, their wives crowded the Temple of Fashion, the first store in Winston specializing in women's clothing. Some may have gone just to catch a glimpse of M. H. Langfeld, the store's young owner and the town's leading dandy. Langfeld, cane in hand, was a handsome figure in his high silk hat, long, black Prince Albert coat, white vest, and light-colored pants. "He was quite a ladies man but sometimes lacked discretion," Foltz remembered, "and some very amusing incidents of his experience while here are no doubt still remembered by some of our older people."

The men could head for Jacobs Clothing, considered the finest men's clothing store in northwestern North Carolina. Built by Joseph Jacobs in 1876, the store at 215–247 Main Street was known as the "Jacobs Block."

What money they didn't spend, the farmers could use to open a savings account in Wachovia National Bank, one of the two banks in town. Wachovia opened in 1879 when William Lemly carted the safe and furnishings of First National Bank of Salem up Main Street to Winston. Lemly had been the cashier of the Salem bank, which closed when its president, Israel Lash, died. The new bank started with $100,000 in capital in a building on Third Street. In 1888, it moved half a block north, to the corner of Third and Main. The seven-story brick building was Winston's first skyscraper.

The Salem Grocery Store on the corner of Main and Academy streets

The Photograph Collection, Winston-Salem/Forsyth County Public Library

W.A. Lemly, the president of Wachovia Bank in 1888, talks to customers in the left window.
James A. Gray, Sr., the head cashier, stands in the other window.

———

Wachovia Corporation

Opposite page:
George Brooks, James A. Gray, Sr., and R. J. Reynolds stand outside Wachovia National Bank in 1889.

———

Wachovia Corporation

"We'll Try Again"

Mary Wiley, center, was the daughter of Calvin Wiley, who pushed for public schools in Winston. A beloved teacher at West End Graded School, she stands with pupils outside the school.

When Calvin Wiley stepped to the front of the Methodist church on February 2, 1871, little did he know that he was about to embark on a nine-year crusade to start a public-school system in Winston.

He was a newcomer to town, having moved from Tennessee the previous year to open an office of the American Bible Society. A good salesman of the Good Book, Wiley was even better at selling public schools. He had been their foremost advocate in the North Carolina General Assembly back in the 1850s, when he represented his native Guilford County. Wiley had been such a persuasive supporter that he was chosen the state's first public-school superintendent. When the office was abolished in 1866, Wiley had moved to the mountains of Tennessee to become a Presbyterian minister and sell Bibles. Back in his home state in 1870, he returned to stumping for an old cause.

Wiley explained to the people in the church the benefits of education and why the town should provide free schooling for its children. "It is the duty of every citizen in town to aid in the work of the establishment of the schools," he said.

Children in Winston could attend private school or one of the public schools in the county. Free county schools for whites ages five to 21 had opened in 1840, when the area was still part of Stokes County. On the eve of the Civil War, about 2,500 students had attended "common" schools in Forsyth County. The few schools were overcrowded, and some parents complained about the difficulty of getting children to far-off schools over poor roads. Closed during the war, the county's public schools hadn't reopened until 1869.

The people at the church thought Winston's children would benefit by attending schools closer to home. They elected Wiley to head a committee of 20 people, which then petitioned the General Assembly to authorize a local tax for a school system. The law passed in 1879, but the tax had to be approved by town voters. Wiley and the committee campaigned hard for the tax, but voters defeated it in 1881.

Newspaperman James A. Robinson described Wiley's reaction: "We can see Dr. Wiley after each defeat of his cherished project, as he dry-smoked about an inch and a half of a small-sized cigar, as was his wont, and rolled it between his lips, with his keen black eyes flashing sparks of enthusiasm and saying [on] the day of defeat, 'We'll try again.'"

They did, in 1883, and this time the tax passed by 83 votes.

At the same election, the voters also chose Wiley to the new school board, which included William A. Whitaker, James A. Gray, Sr., James Martin, and Pleasant Hanes. Wiley, of course, became the board's chairman.

The men met at night, usually at Wiley's house, to go over the budget and building plans. They also walked the streets studying vacant lots suitable for school buildings.

They particularly liked the lot on the corner of

West Fourth and Broad streets, and it was there that they built the town's first public school, West End School. The land and building cost almost $25,000, which was more than what had been raised by taxes. A number of people had to loan the school board money to make up the deficit.

The two-story brick building opened September 9, 1884, with 275 students. Measuring 190 feet by 170 feet, the school contained nine classrooms and a library with more than $4,000 worth of books. Coursework consisted of history, music, physiology, civics, algebra, geography, arithmetic, and grammar. Calisthenics were a regular part of the day, with dumbbell drills and Indian clubs for the older boys. Students attended chapel regularly to sing hymns and recite Scripture.

Children brought their lunch in baskets and ate under the trees in front of the school. Cucumber pickles were swapped for ham biscuits, layer cakes for fried pies.

The state had declared in 1869 that "separate schools for the races are a necessity," thus easing the fears of whites, who thought carpetbaggers would force integration of the schools. The Winston school board didn't have money to build a black school, but it arranged to have black children taught in the basement of First Baptist Church. Depot Street School, on what is now Patterson Avenue and Seventh Street, was built for black children in 1887 with money from Northern philanthropists.

That was also the year Wiley went on a fateful trip to South Carolina. On his way home, his train wrecked, and he was forced to stay in a swamp until rescued. He died at home of typhoid fever.

Central Graded School on Bank and Church streets

The Photograph Collection,
Winston-Salem/Forsyth County Public Library

Wiley didn't live to see his fledgling school system reach maturity. By the time Winston and Salem consolidated in 1913, almost 7,000 students attended 12 schools. Eight years later, the same school system that had borrowed money to open its first school had a budget of more than $1 million.

The rapid growth had its drawbacks, however. A study of public schools done in 1918 by the University of North Carolina found Winston-Salem to be near the bottom of the list in attendance, expenditures, and maintenance. Its teachers were the lowest-paid in the country. A college graduate with 22 years of experience could expect to make about $562 year, while black teachers were paid no more than $446. The study recommended higher pay for teachers, changes in curriculum, and the hiring of a health officer, a business manager, and an attendance officer. The cost of implementing all the recommendations was estimated at more than $177,000.

Winston-Salem voters responded the following year by approving $800,000 in school bonds to add more schools and make the recommended improvements.

The city again came to the rescue in 1933, after the state had taken control of public schools. City schools found themselves severely strapped for money. Janitorial services were cut, and overcrowded classrooms forced many teachers to quit. Fearing that the quality of education was suffering, citizens voted to tax themselves to supplement the city's schools.

Calvin Wiley would have been proud.

*The Woodland Avenue Graded School
for blacks opened in 1910.*

The Photograph Collection,
Winston-Salem/Forsyth County Public Library

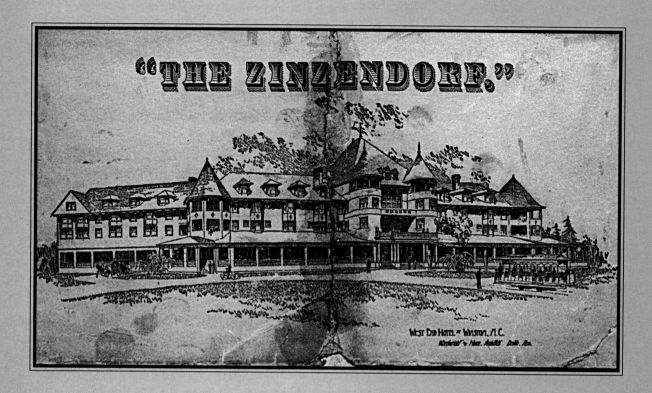

The Hotel Zinzendorf

The prominent businessmen who formed the West End Hotel and Land Company in the 1880s had dreams of turning the undeveloped West End into a tourist resort. Those dreams rested on the Hotel Zinzendorf, a rambling 300-foot-long structure that they built on the crest of a hill near the present intersection of West Fourth and Glade streets. Opened on May 18, 1891, the hotel was the grandest in North Carolina. It had 100 rooms, all heated by steam, and bathrooms on each floor. Guests could sit on the north veranda and look at Suaratown Mountain in the distance or dance in the evenings to the music of a 12-piece orchestra. The hotel was surrounded by woods that were a favorite hunting spot for Winston's prominent men. R.J. Reynolds, William A. Blair, and others bagged a few wild turkey and quail on Thanksgiving Day, November 24, 1892, and brought them to the hotel to be cooked for their dinner that day. "They got cooked all right," Blair later said, "but they were never served." A shout of "Fire!" came from the laundry room in the rear of the hotel about 11 o'clock that morning. Fire fighters from Winston and Salem rushed to the hotel, but water pressure was too low to fight the fire. Made of wood and cedar shingles, the building burned in about two hours. The heat from the fire was so intense that it cracked windows two blocks away. What posessions that could be salvaged were piled onto what is now Grace Court.

Guests and townspeople watched helplessly as the grand hotel was engulfed in flames.

The Photograph Collection, Winston-Salem/Forsyth County Public Library

The dream was reduced to chimneys and a pile of ashes.

Wachovia Historical Society

The King's Unintended Son

Blacks who expected their lives to improve immediately after the Civil War were in for a shock. Though a Freedmen's Bureau opened in Salem to help the recently freed slaves, there were too many whites like O. J. Lehman of Bethania. He probably expressed the opinion of many whites when he wrote in his recollections of the period that the newly enfranchised blacks had become "troublesome." Whites worried that their land would be divided and given to their former slaves.

"The Negroes were the masters and we whites were underdogs," Lehman wrote. "This state of affairs could not continue—the Anglo-Saxon race would not submit to it. Under the existing circumstances, an organization called the Ku Klux Klan was formed."

Made up primarily of Confederate veterans, the secret organization began in Tennessee and spread throughout the South after the war. Its mission was to terrorize blacks back into submission.

Many prominent whites in Forsyth County were arrested for being Klansmen, Lehman wrote. "They met in the dark hours of the night, clad in long flowing white robes, determined to regulate matters. They notified and threatened the Negroes who had become obnoxious also some white people who urged the Negroes on . . . ," he remembered. "Some of the ringleaders were beaten unmercifully."

The black population of Winston and Salem remained small until the opening of the tobacco factories. Blacks from farms in Virginia and the Carolinas then rushed to work in Winston. More than 5,000 blacks lived in the two towns in 1900. Within 10 years, blacks made up 40 percent of the towns' population of 22,000.

Those who came to work in the tobacco factories during the latter part of the 19th century settled around the northern and eastern parts of the city, within walking distance of the factories. Tenements ran from Sixth and Chestnut streets down to Fifth Street, and along Third, Fourth, and Fifth between Chestnut and Depot streets. Sixty-three percent of the tobacco workers lived in those two districts.

Some moved north of town to Boston Cottages, a development of rental houses for blacks along Thurmond Street. Others went out to Liberia, the earliest of Winston's outlying neighborhoods. Once part of a plantation owned by a Moravian, the land was sold to blacks starting in 1872. Many residents worked as maids, cooks, janitors, and gardeners at Salem College, which was just across Salem Creek. Others worked in the tobacco factories. Described as a "sweet" neighborhood by residents, the area first appeared as "Happy Hills" on a 1908 map.

Because of the tobacco industry's phenomenal growth, Winston became the home of a prosperous and growing black middle class. Black attorneys, doctors, druggists, ministers, barbers, insurance agents, teachers, funeral directors, woodworkers, and cafe owners bought substantial houses in Columbian Heights or along East 14th Street. Among the cities of the Southeast, Winston and Durham were known as places where blacks could prosper.

Patterson Avenue from Third Street north to Liberty and east to Main was the business and social heart of the black community in the early 20th century. In the Goler Building, at Patterson and Seventh, blacks could visit a doctor, get a haircut, and then eat lunch at a cafe on the ground floor. The Emma Building next door contained lawyers' offices and a print shop. Down the street were drugstores, two movie houses, beauty shops, and three funeral homes.

The first school for blacks was built in 1867, about where Happy Hills Park is now.

Wachovia Historical Society

The Forsyth Rifles quelled riots like the one in 1895 and fought in the Civil War and World War I.

Wachovia Historical Society

Fraternal organizations such as the Knights of Pythias and the Masons met at Pythian Hall, on Seventh and Chestnut streets. The YMCA opened in 1911 in a small rental building on Church Street.

"We had it all," said the late Joe Bradshaw, who spent a lifetime studying local black history. "It's just that white folks never knew about it."

Segregation saw to that. Thanks to federal laws enacted after the Civil War, blacks in Winston and elsewhere enjoyed a great deal of freedom through the 1890s. They voted and actively participated in the political process. In 1881, the popular Israel Clement was the first of at least eight blacks elected to the Winston Town Commissioners.

Racial harmony grew strained as blacks continued to move to Winston. A riot erupted in 1895 when police officer M. M. Vickers was shot and killed by Aaron Tuttle, a black teenager who scuffled with Vickers after refusing to leave the sidewalk to allow a white woman to pass.

While Tuttle was awaiting trial, rumors spread through the black neighborhoods that whites planned to lynch the teenager. Some 300 to 500 blacks gathered in front of town hall on Saturday night, August 11. When they refused to disperse, the sheriff called out the Forsyth Rifles, a militia unit that had served in the Civil War. The militia fired point-blank into the crowd, but there's no record of how many were killed. The fighting ended around four o'clock the next morning.

The town commissioners later that day requested that Charlotte send a Gatling gun to Winston. The gun arrived by train but was never used. It now is one of the prized exhibits at the North Carolina Museum of History in Raleigh.

Democrats won statewide elections in 1898 and restored white supremacy in North Carolina. They enacted poll taxes and voter eligibility laws that made it almost impossible for blacks to vote. Blacks were disfranchised by 1900 and gradually became second-class citizens, as the city passed laws that effectively separated the races. In 1912, Winston was among the earliest cities to follow the lead of Richmond, Virginia, in designating city blocks black or white depending on the color of the majority of residents. The law forbade anyone of the opposite race to live on the blocks.

King Tobacco's unintended son—Jim Crow—was born.

"For Service Rather Than Success"

The lonesome hillside was the place where Winston stored its gunpowder when Simon Green Atkins went there in 1892 with his family and a mission. Within a few years, he transformed the hilltop south of town into a thriving African-American community of painted houses and neat gardens. Its centerpiece was the school Atkins founded to educate the thousands of blacks who poured into town.

Winston-Salem State University, which grew from that small school, is a lasting monument to Simon Atkins's zeal for education. Columbian Heights, the middle-class black neighborhood that developed around the school, sprung from his belief that good schooling started in good homes.

Born a slave in Chatham County in 1863, the talented and ambitious Atkins was teaching at Livingstone College in Salisbury when he caught the eye of the Winston school board, which needed a principal for its black elementary school. Atkins took the job.

Arriving in Winston in 1890, he found a bustling town where blacks arrived almost daily to work in the tobacco factories. Most lived in one- or two-room shacks with no running water and few other conveniences. Atkins realized that if his students were to succeed, they needed better housing. He also knew that he couldn't do it on his own.

"Self-support, self-respect, and self-defense," Atkins often said to his students, but he knew they could do little without the support of whites. "It is impossible for the colored people of the state to be elevated except with the aid and goodwill of their white neighbors," he wrote in a letter to a friend in 1899.

One of Atkins's great gifts was his ability to gain the respect and trust of white business leaders and politicians despite the stark racial boundaries that existed in Winston at the time. He showed that in 1891 when he appeared before the Winston Board of Trade to ask for help in starting a black college. Atkins also suggested that a suburb be developed near the school for the increasing number of black professionals.

Eleven prominent white men formed the Inside Land and Improvement Company, which assembled the land that became Columbian Heights. Atkins chose the name from the Columbian Exposition of the Chicago World's Fair in 1893. The area soon became the place to live for black doctors, lawyers, professors, ministers, and skilled craftsmen. Atkins and his family may have been the first residents. Their house on Cromartie Street was later moved to its present location off Martin Luther King Jr. Drive.

Atkins's attempt to enlist help for his school was equally successful. Slater Industrial Academy, named for a white philanthropist from New York who donated money to the school, could not have opened in 1892 without the help of Henry E. Fries, William A. Blair, and other local white leaders who freely gave their time and money. Offering high-school and industrial courses, the school started in a one-room frame building with 25 students and one teacher. Its first permanent building, Lamson Hall, was built by the students in 1896.

Atkins, the principal, stated his school's mission at a Methodist ecumenical conference in 1901: "We want to educate people for service rather than success . . . and prepare them to be brothers among the people." Educators, he went on, should abandon the notion that all blacks should be trained for field work and little else. "Let him be a man, and everything else will take care of itself," Atkins said.

He worked diligently raising money and support for Slater and built a school that became the center of black learning and culture in Winston-Salem. Slater entered the state school system in 1895. Its name was changed to Slater Industrial and State Normal School two years later. It began offering teaching certificates in 1905, and the General Assembly made it a four-year college 20 years later. Winston-Salem Teachers College became Winston-Salem State College in 1961. The evolution was completed eight years later when the school became a university.

Failing health forced Atkins to retire in 1934, and he died a few weeks later, on June 28.

"His character was above reproach: honest, industrious, humble and yet aggressive and conservative," said Henry Fries, who worked with Atkins for more than 30 years. "He felt he had a mission to perform. . . . We shall never look upon his likes again."

Simon Green Atkins with students of Slater Industrial Academy

The Photograph Collection, Winston-Salem/Forsyth County Public Library

Lamson Hall, the first permanent building at Slater, was built by the students.

Joseph Bradshaw Collection

Slater students

The Photograph Collection, Winston-Salem/Forsyth County Public Library

Student carpenters and brick masons at Slater

———

Joseph Bradshaw Collection

The brickyard at Slater

———

Joseph Bradshaw Collection

*Cadets at Davis Military Academy play ball
on the school grounds.*

*Davis Military Academy moved
to Winston from Lenoir County
in 1890 when local citizens
pledged $20,000 for buildings
and donated land for a campus
on the northwest edge
of the city.
The school closed in 1909
when the Methodists of
Winston bought the buildings
and the grounds for a
children's home.*

*Parades by the cadets at
Davis Military Academy were familiar
sites in the streets of Winston.*

The disaster's aftermath drew a crowd of gawkers.

Courtesy of Frank Tursi

The brick and concrete walls crumbled under the weight of the water inside the reservoir.

The Photograph Collection, Winston-Salem/Forsyth County Public Library

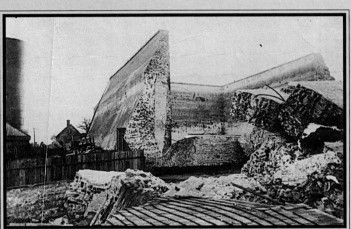

"The Saddest Chapter in Our History"

The newspaper said that it struck like a "thunderbolt." To those living near Winston's reservoir on November 2, 1904, it was more like a tidal wave.

Built in 1882 on the hill where Trade and Eighth streets intersect, the rectangular brick-and-cement reservoir supplied all the town's drinking water. People who lived near it complained about water seeping from under the walls, but the town had always considered the structure safe.

To meet the demands of the growing population, the water system was expanded in 1903. Two powerful pumps were added to bring water from a new dam on Frazier Creek to the reservoir and a new metal holding tank nearby. It was a recipe for disaster.

Unable to withstand the increased water pressure, the north wall of the reservoir collapsed at 5:20 that November morning. About a million gallons of water rushed down the hill, where black families lived in one-story rental houses. Eight of those houses were swept away and dozens were damaged. Nine people were killed, including the entire William Poe family, whose bodies were found a mile away at the foot of Trade Street. At least eight other people were seriously injured. Stories of miraculous survival abounded: a black man and his wife rode the crest of the wave on their bed and were carried unharmed to the bottom land around Peters Creek, where Northwest Boulevard now winds.

It was Winston's worst disaster—"The Saddest Chapter in Our History," the *Union Republican* reported. The flooded area around the reservoir "looked like a pond," a city official said.

The description stuck, and the black neighborhood around the old reservoir has since been known as "The Pond."

Above:

West Fourth Street, looking east from Broad Street, about 1890

Left:

Umbrellas ward off the sun's rays as people stroll along the intersection of Fourth and Main streets about 1896. The building with the tower is Brown's Warehouse on Main Street.

The Photograph Collection, Winston-Salem/Forsyth County Public Library

A large crowd gathered at the courthouse square on Tuesday, October 3, 1905, for the unveiling of the Confederate moonument.

The Moravian Archives of the Southern Province, Winston-Salem

A festive occasion draws a crowd on Main Street near the turn of the century. The picture was taken from the Wachovia National Bank Building on Third and Main. The second Forsyth County courthouse is on the left, and the Town Hall, festooned with bunting, is on Fourth and Main.

Reynolda House Museum of American Art

Winston's first town hall on Fourth and Main streets was torn down for the Reynolds Building. Its clock is now in the steeple of Calvary Moravian Church.

The Photograph Collection, Winston-Salem/Forsyth County Public Library

"Giddy Youth and Sober Old Age"

Twenty-two million Americans lived in cities and towns in 1890. Cities had come into their own, and Winston was among them.

Two railroads connected the town and its tobacco factories to outside markets by then. At the urging of R. J. Reynolds and other industrialists, Francis H. Fries, the son of Francis L. Fries, took time out from his duties in the family's textile mills in Salem to build 122 miles of track from Winston to Roanoke, Virginia. The Roanoke and Southern Railroad—now the Norfolk and Western—opened in 1889, connecting Winston with important tobacco markets in southwestern Virginia.

Winston also was beginning to look and act like a city. The first modern street paving began in 1890 with the laying of Belgian blocks along Main Street. A public sewer system to replace the private privies was completed the following year, after the city had received numerous complaints about foul odors. Mayor Albert B. Gorrell and the town board had inspected privies on the east side of town and found them in awful shape. The hollow below the Brown & Brothers factory was "in such a foul condition and so offensive that this secretary is not a scholar enough to describe it," their report had noted.

When Colonel Joseph A. Bitting connected the 15 miles of wire to the dynamo on March 25, 1887, the first flash of electric streetlights in Winston dazzled spectators. They were equally impressed a few weeks later when, during a severe thunderstorm, all 37 streetlights flashed for five minutes and then went out.

Another festive occasion was the running of the city's first electric streetcars on July 17,

Francis H. Fries

The Photograph Collection,
Winston-Salem/Forsyth County Public Library

1890. "Although the machinery was all new and the track just laid, everything worked like a charm . . . ," the local *Union Republican* reported. "For the past few nights, there has been a perfect jam of merry pleasure seekers spinning up and down the line, and the streets thronged with spectators."

By 1907, streetcar lines extended from the courthouse in all directions: north along Liberty Street to the Piedmont Fair Grounds, south down Main to Nissen Park, east along Third to City Hospital, and west down Fourth to West End. That neighborhood, located at the end of West Fourth Street, was the first of the city's western suburbs.

People lived downtown during Winston's early development to be close to work and within reach of the fire department. Cherry Street was lined with fashionable houses. West Fifth Street from Pine—now Marshall—to Broad was called "Millionaire's Row" in the 1890s because it was the home of many of the city's wealthiest residents.

Street paving, streetcars, and the appearance of Model-T Fords in 1908 triggered the first suburban exodus. People moved "out to the country," to such far-off places as Washington Park and West End, which developed around Grace Park, given to the city by tobacco manufacturer W. A. Whitaker and named for his wife.

Unlike Salem, little planning or care went into the early development of Winston. Design was left in the hands of busy capitalists leafing through building guides. Stores, homes, and gaudy factories leaped up from every corner. The result was a hodgepodge of buildings that one historian said resembled "a huge hastily built mining camp."

Beginning in the latter part of the 19th century, Winston's capitalists demanded that more care and attention be paid to the city's architecture. Public and commercial buildings began to reflect the city's growing might and confidence.

The new courthouse that opened in 1897 was the most stunning building of the period. It had become apparent by the 1880s that the original courthouse was too small to meet the needs of the growing town, and the county had hired noted architect Frank P. Milburn to design a building worthy of Winston. He came up with an ornate Romanesque structure with towers and turrets and circular staircases that many people in town thought looked like a Russian church.

Adelaide Fries, who became one of the city's

Courthouse square has undergone many changes since the first Forsyth County Courthouse was built in 1850. That courthouse was torn down in 1896 as shown above.

The Photograph Collection, Winston-Salem/Forsyth County Public Library

*A beautiful Romanesque building that better reflected the might of Winston
at the turn of the century replaced the first courthouse.*

The Photograph Collection, Winston-Salem/Forsyth County Public Library

noted historians, was only 26 when she first saw the building, but she understood what it represented. "Standing on a slight eminence in the heart of a busy little city, this handsome structure of granite, buff brick, and brownstone is a great contrast to the modest building whose place it took as is the present county seat, with its widespread suburbs," she wrote.

Winston's first city hall had none of the splash or dash of the courthouse across the street. It was "a gloomy-looking brick structure," remembered Clement Eaton, who, as the son of Winston's longtime mayor, Oscar B. Eaton, spent a lot of his boyhood in city hall. Located on the corner of Main and Fourth streets, the three-story building opened in 1893 and was at least utilitarian, containing the fire and police departments, the jail, a market, an armory, and city offices. A clock in the large tower faced in four directions.

Winston was no doubt growing, while Salem had changed little since the Civil War. With its railroad and the tobacco factories, Winston replaced its older neighbor as the center of commerce. Salem still had the Fries textile mill, which had installed electric lights in 1881 and was shipping regularly to markets all over the country. Tenements for the workers surrounded the mill, and Salem thugs sometimes threw rocks through the windows to torment the "lintheads" inside.

But by and large, the Moravian village was settling into old age. Like a parent, it continued to have a calming influence on its boisterous offspring to the north.

"Sober old age and giddy youth, quiet and bustle, the middle of the last century and the keenest development of the bustling end of this century—these are Salem and Winston . . . ," an observer wrote in 1899. "The resident of Salem takes his visitors over to Winston to see the huge tobacco factories and the fine modern buildings, but does not forget to tell him that the taxes there are considerably higher than in Salem. The resident of Winston drives his guests down the long shady trees of Salem, points out the quaint old buildings and tells their history—how Washington stopped there and Cornwallis there—but does not tell about the taxes."

Diversions in both towns were simple. Families read together in parlors, and children played the piano and other instruments for their parents. Free band concerts on the courthouse lawn always attracted a crowd, as did the mineral springs south of Salem on Marshall Street. The springs were a favorite gathering place for young people, as this item from the *Twin-City Daily Sentinel* in 1897 suggests:

> Four large wagons filled with straw and jolly people left the city last evening about seven o'clock for the springs, which place was reached by eight o'clock. The young ladies had not failed to take along that all-important part of a straw ride or picnic, the lunch basket, and on this occasion it was very full and the contents very choice. Supper was served and an hour or two pleasantly spent at the springs, after which the party journeyed homeward. Upon reaching the city the wagons were driven around the square, while sweet melodious voices awoke the neighborhood.

The coming of the circus was a grand event. The Barnum & Bailey and Ringling Brothers circuses made regular stops in Winston. "The parade through the streets, accompanied by the thrilling music of the calliope, furnished free entertainment to the poor and the rich, the Negroes and the whites," Clement Eaton recalled.

F & H Fries Company in the 1880s consisted of, from left, a gas works, a woolen mill, a cotton mill, a smoke house, and an office.

———

The Winston-Salem Journal

The hydroelectric plant that Henry W. Fries and his nephew Henry E. Fries built on the Yadkin River near Clemmons in 1898 was the first in the south to transmit electricity long distances. It was later purchased by Duke Power Company and is still in operation.

The Photograph Collection, Winston-Salem/Forsyth County Public Library

Above: Winston's first golf club poses in 1898 on a course on Liberty Street.

Courtesy of Frank Tursi

Below: Electric cars started puttering around town after the turn of the century.

Collection of Old Salem

The miniature railroad at Nissen Park in Waughtown always drew a crowd.

———

Collection of Old Salem

Salem students gather around the spring house in 1903.

The Photograph Collection, Winston-Salem/Forsyth County Public Library

Streetcars amble down Liberty Street about 1910.
The Phoenix Hotel is the large building on the left, at the corner of Liberty and Fourth streets.

The Photograph Collection, Winston-Salem/Forsyth County Public Library

Streetcar conductors on courthouse square

Collection of Old Salem

Thomas A. Edison, center, attended the opening of Winston's electric streetcar system in 1890.

———

The Photograph Collection, Winston-Salem/Forsyth County Public Library

Fourth and Liberty streets in 1909

———

The Photograph Collection, Winston-Salem/Forsyth County Public Library

The Rise of Reynolds

Winston's businessmen can be forgiven for thumping their chests and boasting of their economic prowess in 1906. The city's rise from a sleepy hamlet where goats and pigs wandered the courthouse square to an energetic city at the forefront of the state's industrialization was indeed head-spinning. The numbers tell the story. Winston's factories led the state by turning out $11.3 million in products, a 132-percent increase in just six years. The town's capitalists had more money invested in manufacturing than the next six largest industrial cities in the state combined.

"We are in a class by ourselves," the Winston Board of Trade, the forerunner of the chamber of commerce, boasted in a pamphlet.

So was R. J. Reynolds Tobacco Company. Because of the astuteness of its founder, the company entered the 20th century as the biggest business in town and one of the leading manufacturers in the South.

The number of tobacco factories in Winston topped out at 39 in 1897. Twelve remained two years later. Fierce competition in a crowded industry and the cutthroat tactics of James B. Duke's American Tobacco Company broke their backs.

Formed in 1890, American was one of the biggest monopolies in the country. It was despised by wholesalers, who were forced to do business with it; by farmers, who blamed it for low leaf prices; by warehousemen, who saw it as a threat because it was large enough to buy leaf directly from farmers; and by the public, who thought it was keeping prices high. By undercutting independents and pressuring retailers, American drove competitors to bankruptcy or forced them to sell out. With its sub-sidiary, Continental Tobacco Company, it cornered the plug tobacco market by the late 1890s.

Though he publicly railed against Duke, Reynolds willingly joined the trust in 1899. An astonished Josephus Daniels, an avowed enemy of the Duke trust, asked Reynolds why he sold to Duke. "Sometimes," Reynolds replied, "you have to join hands with a fellow to keep him from ruining you and to get the under hold yourself. . . . I don't intend to be swallowed. Buck Duke will find out he has met his equal, but I am fighting him now from the inside. . . . If you will keep your eyes open, you will find that if any swallowing is done, Dick Reynolds will do the swallowing."

Armed with capital from the sale, Reynolds bought out the other tobacco manufacturers in town. The first to go was T. L. Vaughn and Company, Winston's second-oldest tobacco company. Vaughn was so distraught over being forced to sell to Reynolds that he retired to the country, reported Nancy Stockton, his niece. "It made my uncle so mad he built a house in Buchanan, Va., on a river so he could spend the rest of his life hunting and fishing," she wrote. "Someone built a tannery upstream and poisoned the water. Poor uncle and poor fish. Sad tale."

P. H. Hanes & Company and Brown & Brothers sold out within a few days of each other in late December 1900. The Hanes brothers, who owned the largest factory in Winston, had watched fires destroy their main plant twice. Tired of battling flames and the Duke trust, they sold the business to Reynolds for about $1 million. With his share of the money, Pleasant Hanes started P. H. Hanes Knitting Company in 1901, with 50 sewing and 12 knitting machines. His brother, John, began Shamrock Mills in an old tobacco plant on Marshall and Second streets. The forerunner of Hanes Hosiery, the company began making men's and children's socks in 1900. John Hanes replaced

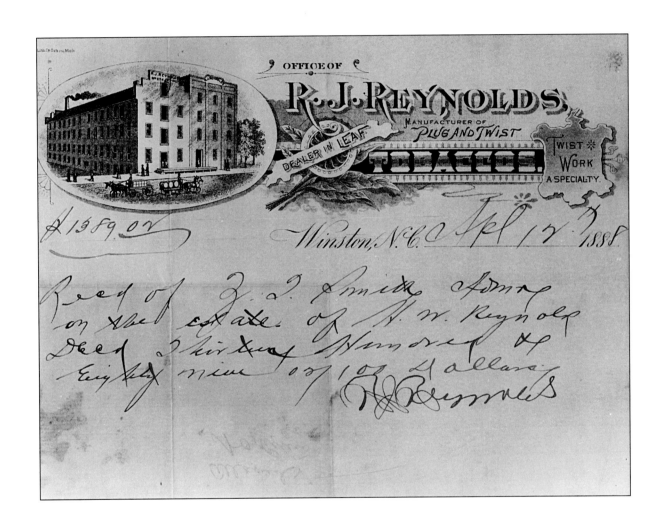

R. J. Reynolds's scrawl of a signature led many who didn't know him to think he was illiterate.

Reynolda House Museum of American Art

By 1897, when this picture was taken, R. J. Reynolds was "the biggest blood in Winston."

R. J. Reynolds Tobacco Company

the old tobacco plant with a new mill in 1911. An architectural oddity, the mill had a saw-toothed roofline, with six-foot-high windows designed to let in northern light. The building has found new life as the Sawtooth Center for Visual Design.

The bearded Bill Taylor, the founder of Taylor Brothers, resisted selling out. He is reported to have told Duke, "Go ahead and form your trust. Taylor's whistle will be blowing our hands to work long after all of you are dead and forgotten, suh."

Reynolds prospered mightily in the trust. Along with buying out other tobacco companies in Winston and Martinsville, Virginia, he built 14 major factories himself. When the United States Supreme Court dissolved the Duke trust in 1911, Reynolds again assumed control of his company and made plans for his assault on the tobacco industry.

"Watch me and see if I don't give Buck Duke hell," he said.

The Rise of the Ruling Class

The pattern of civic management that would rule the city for 100 years began to form, as business leaders coalesced in the 1880s into an elite class that dominated the civic, economic, and political affairs of Winston. Their goal was to create an environment that was good for business. They assumed that it also would be good for the town.

Merchants and manufacturers founded a waterworks and an electric company because ample water and electric power were important to business expansion. They pushed for a rail connection to Martinsville in order to tap a prime bright-leaf growing region.

Reynolds and other tobacco manufacturers,

together with some of the town's leading merchants and professionals, formed the Forsyth Immigration Service in the mid-1880s. The idea was to recruit farmers to settle in the county and grow tobacco for the factories. From 1869 to 1889, the number of farms in the county rose by almost two-thirds, and the tobacco crop increased 20 times.

Businessmen exercised great control over the town's politics. They served on the town council and on the executive committee of the Democratic Party. They were appointed magistrates and elected mayor.

They also started using the term *Twin City* in their advertising and promotions in the 1880s, thus setting the stage for the official unification of the two towns.

Dates to Remember

West End Graded School

1866   The first local bank, First National Bank of Salem, opens. Salem Female Academy is chartered as a college.

1871   J. W. Goslen begins publishing the *Union Republican*.

1872   Thomas J. Brown opens the first permanent tobacco warehouse in the county, and Hamilton Scales starts the first tobacco factory.

1873   The Northwest North Carolina Railroad is extended from Greensboro to Winston, fueling the growth of the town. Pleasant and John Hanes move from Davie County to start a tobacco factory.

1874   R. J. Reynolds rides into town from Virginia. He opens his first tobacco factory a year later.

1879   The first attempt to consolidate Winston and Salem fails after voters in Winston turn back the proposal by a vote of nearly three to one. Wachovia National Bank is organized with $100,000 in capital.

1880   F & H Fries Company builds a new mill at the site of the old Salem Manufacturing factory at what is now Brookstown Mill. The company moves all its cotton milling there under the name Arista Cotton Mill. Arista Mills Company is formed in 1903 by the merger of Arista and Southside Cotton Mills. Arista abandons the Brookstown plant in 1927 and moves all its milling to the Southside factory on Goldfloss Street. Arista Mills enters data processing in 1956 and ends textile production in 1970.

1882   Winston's first volunteer fire company, Steamer Number 1, forms. Its members begin receiving pay—$10 a month—in 1886.

1884   The city's first public school for whites, West End Graded School, opens. The first black school, Depot Street School, opens three years later.

1885   The Twin City Club is built at Fourth and Marshall streets. The chamber of commerce, first known as the Winston Board of Trade, is incorporated. The *Twin City Daily*—the first of the daily newspapers—is published.

1887   The first electric streetlights—all 37 of them—usher in a new age. The first public hospital opens in a leased building on Liberty Street.

1888   The charter for the YMCA is drawn up. Members meet in various buildings until 1908, when a handsome four-story stone building opens at Fourth and Cherry streets.

1889   The Roanoke and Southern Railroad connects Winston with important markets in southwestern Virginia.

1890   The area's first telephones and electric streetcars go into service. R. J. Reynolds Tobacco Company is incorporated.

1892   Slater Industrial Academy, now Winston-Salem State University, opens to educate blacks. The Hotel Zinzendorf, less than two years old, is destroyed in a magnificent fire on Thanksgiving Day.

1893   Wachovia Loan and Trust, the first trust company in the state, opens in a former Chinese laundry. The first city hall is completed on the corner of Main and Fourth streets.

1895   A race riot is sparked by the fatal shooting of a police officer by a black man. The militia fires into a crowd of 300 to 500 blacks, killing an unknown number.

1897   The old courthouse is replaced by a Romanesque building that some say looks like a church. Sheriff E. T. Kapp has the county's first "long-distance" phone service, thanks to a line linking his house in Bethania with his office in Winston. The *Winston-Salem Journal* starts publication.

1898   Fries Manufacturing and Power Company begins the South's first long-distance transmission of electric power when its hydroelectric plant on the Yadkin River sends electricity the dozen miles to Winston's homes and businesses. The company's power plant, at what is now Idols Dam near Clemmons, is later bought by Duke Power Company and remains in operation today.

1900   John W. Hanes starts Shamrock Mills, which manufactures infants' hose and men's socks. It is incorporated 14 years later and renamed Hanes Hosiery. Nissen Park, the community's first formal park, opens in Waughtown.

P. H. Hanes Knitting Company's first factory on Sixth and Church streets

The Photograph Collection,
Winston-Salem/Forsyth County Public Library

1901   P. H. Hanes Knitting Company is organized.

1902   Slater Hospital, the first black hospital in the city, opens in Columbian Heights. It closes two years later because of financial problems, reopens in 1905, and closes permanently in 1912.

1904   The greatest disaster in Winston's history occurs on November 2, when a wall of the town's reservoir collapses. The torrent wipes away eight houses and kills nine people.

1905   Associated Charities, Winston-Salem's first organized private charity, is started.

1906   Carnegie Public Library, the city's first, opens on the corner of Third and Cherry streets. A post office is built at Liberty and Fifth streets; the present building on the site serves as the post office from 1914 until it is closed in 1991. Winston-Salem Mutual Life Insurance Company is organized by black leaders.

The Carnegie Library

The Photograph Collection, Winston-Salem/Forsyth County Public Library

1907   R. J. Reynolds introduces Prince Albert pipe tobacco, which turns his company into an international success.

1908   Cars begin appearing in Winston.

1910   The Winston-Salem Southbound Railroad is completed to Wadesboro. Connecting the Norfolk and Western and Atlantic Coast Line railways, the 89-mile-long railroad puts Winston on the main line. The Methodist Children's Home opens on the site of Davis Military School.

1911   Wachovia National Bank merges with Wachovia Loan and Trust to form Wachovia Bank and Trust Company.

1912   Segregation becomes complete when Winston passes ordinances against blacks living on the same street with whites.

Names to Know

Simon Green Atkins
The founder of black education in Winston, Atkins was born in Chatham County. He came to Winston in 1890 to become principal of Depot Street School. He founded Columbian Heights and opened Slater Industrial Academy—now Winston-Salem State University—in 1892; he was also Slater's first principal. The first modern high school for blacks opened in Winston-Salem in 1931 and was named for Atkins. He died three years later.

George H. Black
He came to Winston in 1889 from Liberty and took a job at the old Hedgecock Brickyard, where he learned the ancient art of brickmaking. Black opened his own brickyard in the 1920s and became known for his high-quality bricks. His handiwork can be seen in Salem College Library, Baptist Hospital, Old Salem, and more than 15 banks and homes in town. Black became a national celebrity in 1971 when Charles Kuralt featured him on one of his "On the Road" television programs. That led to a goodwill mission to Guyana, where Black, then in his 80s, taught the craft to villagers. He was honored by President Richard Nixon at a White House reception and was given a George Washington Medal of Honor by the Freedom Foundation. Black died in 1980.

John Henry Boner

Old Salem, Inc.

John Henry Boner
He was Salem's most brilliant, most famous, and most tragic literary figure of the last half of the 19th century. A poet who escaped serving in the Civil War, Boner became a Republican after the war, which turned many of his neighbors against him. He took jobs in Raleigh and then Washington and in 1883 published his first volume of poetry, *Whispering Pines*. Many of its 65 poems yearned for North Carolina and Salem. The themes were repeated, perhaps with a bit more melancholy, in 1901 in *Some New Poems*. Boner died in 1903 at his home in New York, where a colleague organized a memorial fund to ship him home. Finally, on December 11, 1904, the poet came home and was buried in God's Acre. The inscription on his grave reads, "That gentlest of minstrels who caught his music from the whispering pines."

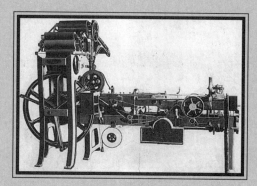

The cigarette machine developed by William Cyrus Briggs in the 1890s

North Carolina Collection, UNC Library at Chapel Hill

William C. Briggs
He arrived in Winston in 1892 from Fayetteville, where he had designed a cigarette machine. With financial backing from Winston and Salem's most prominent businessmen, Briggs started the Winston Cigarette Machine Company, building machines in a workshop on First and Chestnut streets. He teamed with William Shaffner in 1897 to start Briggs-Shaffner Company, which made cigarette-packing machines. Both enterprises helped revolutionize the cigarette industry.

Israel L. Clement
The popular Clement became the first black elected to the Winston Town Commissioners in 1881. He was the first of at least eight blacks elected to the commission before Jim Crow laws made it difficult for African-Americans to vote and hold public office. Clement died near the end of his one-year term.

Oscar Benjamin Eaton
A longtime mayor of Winston, Eaton became the city's first popularly elected mayor in 1909. Before then, mayors had been elected by the aldermen. Eaton also was the first mayor of the merged Winston-Salem.

Francis Henry Fries

The son of Francis L. Fries, he was called "Colonel" to distinguish him from his father. A graduate of Davidson College, Fries worked in the mills owned by his family. At the urging of R. J. Reynolds and other town leaders, he built a 122-mile railroad to Roanoke that linked Winston to markets in southwestern Virginia. He opened Wachovia Loan and Trust in 1893 and served as its president. The company merged with Wachovia National Bank in 1911, and Fries was the first president of Wachovia Bank and Trust Company.

Robert Broadnax Glenn

After moving to Winston from Danbury in 1886, Glenn, a lawyer, became active in civic affairs and played a leading role in founding the YMCA. A federal solicitor and federal district attorney under President Grover Cleveland, he was elected governor of North Carolina in 1905 and is best remembered for leading the state to prohibition. A teetotaler, Glenn was an ardent advocate of temperance and stumped the state eloquently pushing his cause. When statewide prohibition came in 1909, the two wholesale liquor houses and 12 saloons in his adopted hometown were closed. Glenn High School is named for him.

Robert Broadnax Glenn

North Carolina Division
of Archives and History

Albert B. Gorrell

A native of Greensboro, Gorrell grew up in Winston and was one of the town's most influential citizens in the late 19th century. A mayor, alderman, school commissioner, and merchant, he owned the largest tobacco warehouse in town. He died in 1898 while serving as mayor.

James A. Gray, Sr.

Born in Randolph County, Gray came to Winston as a child. He ran the store started by his father, Robert, was a town commissioner, and served on the city's first school board. He joined Wachovia National Bank when it started in 1879 and eventually worked his way up from assistant cashier to president. A high school,

now part of the North Carolina School of the Arts, was named in his honor in 1939.

Pleasant Henderson Hanes

Born on a farm in Davie County, Hanes moved to Winston in 1873 to start P. H. Hanes & Company with his brother, John, and Thomas J. Brown. The tobacco company soon was the largest in the city. Its factory on Chestnut Street was four stories high, had steam elevators and electric lights, and employed more than 300 people. The factory was destroyed by fire twice. Hanes sold the company in 1900 to R. J. Reynolds for $1 million. He used his share of the sale to buy land and start P. H. Hanes Knitting Company. In time, it became the largest producer of knitwear in the world. One of the city's great benefactors, Hanes donated 50 acres for the city park that bears his name. He also was a town commissioner and a member of the city's first school board. Hanes died in 1925 and is buried in Salem Cemetery.

Jacob L. Ludlow

A native of New Jersey, Ludlow came to Winston in 1886 and started a general engineering practice. He became Winston's first city engineer in 1889, designed its first sewer system, and directed its first street-paving program. He also drew the plats for the city's first major suburbs—Columbian Heights, Washington Park, and West End. His house on Summit Avenue and West Fifth Street is now a bed-and-breakfast.

Richard Joshua Reynolds

He rode into Winston in 1874 and built a small tobacco factory the following year. R. J. Reynolds Tobacco Company became the largest tobacco manufacturer in the world and the major force in Winston-Salem.

Calvin H. Wiley

He was one of the most notable figures in North Carolina during the 19th century. Born in Guilford County, Wiley was elected to the legislature in 1850 and became a champion of public education. He was appointed the state's first school superintendent, a post he filled until the legislature abolished the office in 1866. Wiley moved to Winston in 1874 and was elected chairman of the city's first school board in 1883. Under his guidance, instruction and hours were standardized and the system expanded. He died of typhoid fever on January 11, 1887. A middle school is named in his honor.

*The end of World War I was reason enough
to hold a parade through the streets of Winston.*

———

The Photograph Collection, Winston-Salem/Forsyth County Public Library

"A City Made of Two Parts"

Voters legally confirmed what had become a fact of historical development when they approved the consolidation of Winston and Salem in 1913. The hyphen was added, and a "new" city was born.

Its name was carried across the world on each pack of Camel cigarettes and each pair of Hanes underwear. Introduced that year, both products started a boom that rivaled the fantastic growth of the 1880s. The city became the South's second-leading industrial center, after Richmond, and its population more than tripled in 20 years. For a time, it was even the largest city in North Carolina.

Those were heady days which saw the city expand outward and its skyline climb upward. Everyone, it seemed, was doing well, most particularly R. J. Reynolds Tobacco Company. As Winston-Salem's largest employer and biggest taxpayer, the company took control of the city's destiny. Few decisions were made or civic projects undertaken without the company's approval and support. The theocracy that had guided Salem through its early years was replaced by an oligarchy of industrialists and bankers headed by the men who sat in the Reynolds boardroom.

The Depression defused the boom. Though it fared better than most cities, Winston-Salem would never again see triple-digit population growth and unbridled industrial expansion. Its heyday was over.

When in Rome . . .

Outsiders who visited Winston-Salem in the 1920s and 1930s came away with the impression that the city was the biggest and best-run company town in the South.

There is a story, supposedly true, about the state highway commissioner, who came to Winston-Salem in the late 1920s for a meeting at the Hotel Robert E. Lee. He sat down with the mayor and the men who wielded the real power: the city's tobacco and textile manufacturers and bankers.

The highway commissioner lit a cigarette that wasn't made in Winston-Salem, and a hush settled on the room. Someone finally slid a pack of Camels across the table and told the commissioner that he would be expected to smoke them while in town.

The state man stood up and began to undress.

"What in the world are you doing, man?" one of the astonished city representatives asked.

"I just remembered," the commissioner replied, "I don't have Hanes underwear on either."

Adding the Hyphen

Robert Gray, a perceptive man who bought the first lot in Winston in 1849, foresaw the day that the two towns a mile apart would be united. "I speak of Winston and Salem as one place. . . . Would that I could speak of them under one name," Gray said in a speech in 1876. "They are one in identity of interest and future. . . . I hail the coming day [from] which shall rise one united town."

So did others. Three years after Gray's speech, the town boards in Salem and Winston appointed a special committee to study consolidating the two towns. The committee

liked the idea and recommended that the united halves be named the "City of Salem." The charter was approved by the boards and ratified by the General Assembly. Salem voters endorsed the charter overwhelmingly, but people in Winston, fearing the loss of identity, turned it down almost three to one.

When the vote was taken, Salem was the larger and more influential of the two towns. It had a long and storied history and had provided the land and much of the leadership for Winston's founding. But the days when it could control the direction its stepchild took were coming to a close. As it grew and honed its industrial muscle, Winston began to overshadow its parent. It took control of Salem's destiny.

Instead of dictating the name of a new town, Salem found itself fighting to keep its name on the map in the 1890s. Twice during the decade, postal authorities proposed closing the Salem branch office and consolidating it with the office in Winston, to be known as the Winston branch. Each time, Salem residents dispatched their mayor, Henry E. Fries, to Washington to plead their case. Fries saved the post office in 1891, but the best he could come back with in 1899 was an assurance that the con-

solidated office would be known as the Winston-Salem branch. Many people had been referring to the two towns by that name for some time, but the hyphen took on permanence when it started appearing in postmarks.

By 1913, almost everyone considered the two towns one. For many in Salem, the old congregational town had lost its identity and was merely a quiet residential suburb south of bustling Winston. It was only natural that the union be legalized.

The General Assembly ratified a consolidation act and charter on January 27, 1913, and voters from each town approved the unification on March 18. On May 6, they elected Oscar B. Eaton, who had been Winston's mayor for 10 years, the first mayor of the combined city. Salem, 147 years old, became one of four voting wards.

The union seemed so natural four years later that no one remembered it had ever been otherwise, noted Bishop Edward Rondthaler, the pastor of the Salem congregation. "A city made of two parts, long separate, but now so harmoniously welded together as to forget that they ever lived and wrought apart," he wrote. "Our one Winston-Salem, God bless her."

Above and on opposite page:
Smokestacks and water towers stab at the sky in Winston-Salem's tobacco district during the 1920s. The intersection in the middle of the picture is West Second Street and Patterson Avenue. R. J. Reynolds Tobacco factories dominate the left side of the picture. Most are still there. S. J. Nissen Company, on the corner of Second and Patterson, did a steady business repairing Reynolds's wagons. The building now houses county offices.

Courtesy of Frank Tursi

The State's Largest City

The consolidation created a city of about 30,000 people, but no one wanted to stop there. The city's motto after the union was "Fifty-Fifteen." Translation: 50,000 people by 1915. For a while, even that fantastic goal seemed within reach.

Thousands of people moved into the city each year. Most came to work at R. J. Reynolds Tobacco Company or in the textile mills owned by Hanes Hosiery and P. H. Hanes Knitting Company. Those three companies employed 60 percent of the city's workers by 1940.

Reynolds, the city's largest employer since the turn of the century, introduced Camel cigarettes seven months after the unification vote. The cigarettes became the most popular brand in the world and propelled Reynolds to the top

of the tobacco industry. One statistic is sufficient to illustrate the might of Reynolds: it imported so much Turkish tobacco and French cigarette paper for Camels that Winston-Salem—more than 200 miles from the ocean—was made a port of entry by the United States Customs Service. By 1916, the city was the eighth-largest port of entry in the country.

For Hanes, the road to success was paved with underwear. Business was so good that the company, begun in a plant on Sixth and Church streets in 1901, built a spinning mill nine years later outside of town on South Stratford Road. Past the mill, the pavement gave way to a dirt path that wound through the woods to Clemmons.

Since its inception, the company had made men's underwear for other manufacturers, but it began producing garments under its own label in 1913. Pleasant Henderson Hanes, the company's founder, liked to flip up his cane and point proudly to the Hanes label sewn on each garment. It read, "We guarantee Hanes Underwear absolutely—every thread, stitch,

A composite shows the growth of R. J. Reynolds Tobacco Company from 1875 to 1916.

North Carolina Division of Archives and History

and button. We guarantee to return your money or give you a new garment if a seam breaks."

America's entry into World War I in 1917 spurred the city's tobacco and textile industries to greater growth. Production of Camels almost doubled from the previous year, to 12 billion, as Reynolds was determined that no doughboy should go without them. "In the tobacco industry, 1917 is the greatest year the city has seen," Bishop Rondthaler reported.

Hanes, which had built a new plant in 1914 at Sixth and Main streets, made thousands of undershirts for the army and had to add another cotton mill on Stratford Road.

New plants and increased production meant more and more workers. "Investors are swarming into the city like bees," a newspaper columnist wrote in 1920. "They know something

good when they see it, and Winston-Salem is on the way up."

When they came around for the 1920 count, the United States census takers found 48,395 people living in Winston-Salem, more than double the population of 1910. The total was enough to put Winston-Salem ahead of Charlotte as the state's largest city. Newspapers trumpeted the accomplishment with headlines in doomsday-sized type, but the celebration was short-lived. Charlotte reclaimed the top spot within a few years.

Still, Winston-Salem's industrial prowess remained unchallenged. By 1930, it produced more tobacco products than any other city in the world, more men's knit underwear that any other place in the country, and more knit and woolen goods and wagons than any other Southern city.

Hanes, the village built by P. H. Hanes Knitting Company in 1910 had its own railroad station, school and ballfields.

———

The Photograph Collection,
Winston-Salem/Forsyth County Public Library

Neat, small mill houses surrounded the giant mill on South Stratford Road.

———

The Photograph Collection,
Winston-Salem/Forsyth County Public Library

By 1920, P. H. Hanes Knitting Company had a new plant on Sixth and Main streets, center, and a cotton mill and a spinning mill in Hanes.

———

The Photograph Collection, Winston-Salem/Forsyth County Public Library

Wooden hogsheads of tobacco are loaded onto trucks for shipment from a R. J. Reynolds Tobacco Company warehouse to the company's factories. This picture was taken around 1920.

Courtesy of Frank Tursi

One City, Two Towns

From consolidation to the Depression—there has never been another period quite like it in Winston-Salem's history. For 16 years, it was the liveliest, most vibrant, and most boisterous city in the South. Financial success will do that to a place. Corporate profits were at an all-time high, and people worked contentedly in factories or busily built their own businesses. The good times rubbed off on everyone, black and white.

Segregation forced the races to live side by side, but separately. They worked in the same factories, but they went home to different neighborhoods, where they worshiped in their own churches, shopped in their own stores, and were cared for by their own doctors and dentists.

In that respect, Winston-Salem was no different from other Southern cities of the day. It departed from the norm by allowing its black citizens to share in some of the city's success. By 1920, about 40 percent of the city's population was black, a percentage that hasn't changed very much up to the present. Many of the new arrivals aspired to more than being a "mule" in a tobacco factory. A business directory published in the middle of the Depression listed 45 black-owned cafes and 25 black barbershops.

C. B. Cash and his son Artie had a popular shop on Third Street that catered to a mostly white clientele. Black grocers such as Thomas Hooper on Seventh Street and Patterson Avenue were the backbone of their community because they extended credit to their customers between paychecks. Teachers and principals in the black public schools also were admired and respected. Edward E. Hill, a teacher at Oak Grove School who later became principal of Carver School, picked up his students in his car and drove them to school. He fed them sandwiches and pinto beans that he cooked on his classroom's potbelly stove.

Fred M. Fitch, who opened one of the first black funeral homes in town, worked tirelessly to get streets and sidewalks paved in black neighborhoods. Despite his efforts, most remained unpaved in the 1920s. Black-owned buses, called jitneys, plowed through the mud to provide transportation in the black neighborhoods. George Dillahunt's "Lightning Express" was one of the favorites.

A more organized transportation system for blacks was started in 1926, when 12 jitney owners formed Safe Bus Company. Considered the largest black-owned transportation company in the world, Safe Bus served blacks for almost 50 years before being bought by the Winston-Salem Transit Authority in the early 1970s.

Blacks could ride the bus to the Lafayette Theater on Fourth Street or the Lincoln Theater on Church. They could take it up Patterson Avenue to Pythian Hall to catch a performance of Bethel Smith and his choral group. The Smith Choral Club, with 34 singers, was the most popular of the black choral groups in the city during the 1920s and 1930s.

Whites, of course, had their own movie theaters: the Hollywood and the Colonial on Liberty Street, the Carolina on Fourth, and the State Auditorium on Fifth and Liberty. The State was built in 1917 on the former site of the Elks Auditorium, which had burned a year earlier. With its 1,800 seats, the State was the city's major performance hall until R. J. Reynolds Auditorium opened in 1924. It and the Carolina had separate galleries for black customers.

The dances on New Year's Eve and Easter Monday at the Twin City Club were the social events of the year for the teenage children

Jitneys rumbled through the mud to provide transportation in black neighborhoods.

The Photograph Collection, Winston-Salem/Forsyth County Public Library

of the city's most prominent residents. The club's three-story building at Fourth and Marshall streets had a wide porch facing Fourth. Its rocking chairs were the favorite perches for serious girl-watching.

"When a girl went to her first dance there, it was inlieu [*sic*] of making her debut," Nancy Stockton Martin remembered. "Chaperons sat in straight chairs around the wall, and the young people were supposed to go around the circle shaking hands with each and every chaperon. The first time I went to a dance there I was shaking so that my date asked if I was sick."

For serious business dealings, no place matched the lobby of the Wachovia Building— now the BB&T Building—on Main and Third

streets. By the 1930s, Wachovia Bank and Trust Company was among the largest banks in the South. Business was conducted on "The Platform," a raised floor around the wall of the lobby where the bank officers sat. There was no retreating into offices.

Archie K. Davis, a bank officer at the time, remembered the disadvantages. "Dirt was just rampant," said Davis, who later became the bank's chairman and senior vice president. "I remember when I got on The Platform in the summertime, we'd have to open those huge windows behind us, and the smoke from Reynolds Tobacco would just pour in there. You'd go down there with a lovely linen suit that morning and you'd be as dirty as you could be by that afternoon."

Right:

A group of jitney drivers organized Safe Bus Company.

Below:

Duke Power Company bought the city's fading streetcars in 1935 and replaced them with buses the following year. The company served the central city and the white suburbs, while Safe Bus Company provided service to black neighborhoods. Duke sold its franchise to Safe Bus in 1968. The city's transit authority bought Safe Bus four years later.

The Photograph Collection,
Winston-Salem/Forsyth County
Public Library

Jitney drivers were known for their courteousness.

The Photograph Collection, Winston-Salem/Forsyth County Public Library

Top:
U. S. Reynolds, center, and the faculty of Depot Street School in 1918

Bottom:
The 1921 graduating class at Depot Street School

Joseph Bradshaw Collection

The students at Oak Street School in 1920

Joseph Bradshaw Collection

The junior girls basketball team at Columbia Heights High School

Joseph Bradshaw Collection

"The Terribilist Thing I Every Seen"

The worst riot in Winston-Salem's history began innocently enough—with an evening stroll to the neighborhood store.

Jim and Cora Childress left their house north of Winston-Salem on Saturday, November 16, 1918, and began the half-mile walk to Pulliam's store. Mrs. Childress later estimated that it was about seven o'clock when she and her husband reached the Southern Railway trestle over what is now Inverness Street. A black man stepped out of the shadows and pointed a shiny pistol at the couple.

"We were much too frightened to make any outcry," Mrs. Childress told the sheriff. "It happened so suddenly that we were completely dazed."

The man forced the white couple down a deep gully beside the railroad tracks, where he shot and wounded Childress, raped his wife, and robbed her of $2.25.

Mrs. Childress gave the sheriff a murky description of her assailant but said she was sure she could identify him. Deputies chased a few suspects in the vicinity that night but didn't catch anyone.

Winston-Salem police stopped Russell High on Sunday afternoon on the corner of Fourth and Depot streets. They arrested him for carrying a concealed weapon. High, a black man from Durham, had just moved to town. Since arriving, he had "borne a good reputation, had been industrious, and had spent the greater part of the time in his room," Police Chief James A. Thomas later told the newspapers.

After an investigation, the police were convinced that High had nothing to do with the attack on the Childresses. Word of his arrest spread around town, though, and whites gathered in front of city hall, which contained the jail. The crowd got uglier as it got larger.

A procession of town officials, preachers, and business leaders urged the crowd to disperse. Even Mrs. Childress told the people to go home. She had seen the prisoner, she told them, and he wasn't the man who had attacked her and her husband.

"We want that nigger!" the newspaper reported some in the mob responding. "We want to lynch him!"

Racial tensions in Winston-Salem were high, as they were in many cities after World War I. Resentment came to a head when whites returned from the war and found blacks holding jobs normally reserved for whites. Blacks supported the war as strongly as whites, and they thought they deserved good job opportunities and living conditions. In 1919 alone, 25 race riots—mostly by whites—rocked the nation's cities. More than 70 blacks were lynched in the United States after the war.

The growing black population in Winston-Salem heightened tensions in the city. Black neighborhoods such as Columbian Heights expanded after World War I, encroaching on the predominantly white neighborhoods in East Winston. The Ku Klux Klan, which enjoyed a resurgence after the war, marched through the neighborhoods.

It was against such a backdrop that Mayor Ralph W. Gorrell viewed the mob, which was estimated to be between 2,000 and 3,000 people, and decided to call in the Home Guard. Made up of men too young, too old, or too sick to fight in the war, the militia joined the police in blocking the steps to city hall.

The mob broke through and rushed into the lobby and down to the cellblocks. Shots rang out. The bullets, presumably meant for High, hit one of the mob instead. Police and the Home Guard pushed the people out the building.

About six that evening, firemen were ordered to turn their hoses on the crowd. More shots were fired. Robert Young went down and became the riot's first fatality. A former policeman and fireman, Young was a shoe salesman who was helping his former colleagues handle the hoses.

The shooting became widespread, with most people firing aimlessly in the air. Thirteen-year-old Rachel Levi was watching from a second-story window when a stray bullet found her. She died instantly.

Members of the mob broke into downtown stores, stole guns, and headed down Fourth Street toward the black neighborhoods. The sight of the approaching mob was vivid in the memory of a black woman who later, at age 81, told her story to college students during an oral history project in 1975. "And so I look up and saw those gang of folk coming," she said. "They had these swords and guns and things. It scared me so bad I just flew. I flew back into the house and I didn't know what in the world was happening. I knew this riot was here, but I didn't know it was coming after me. I be living here in Winston-Salem every since I was 15 years old and that's just about the terribilist thing I every seen."

Desultory firing continued until three o'clock Monday morning.

Federal troops and militia from Charlotte, Greensboro, and Raleigh patrolled the streets at dawn, and a tank was stationed at the courthouse square. Though there was no more violence, some troops remained in Winston-Salem for a week.

An exact count of casualties was either never made or no longer exists. Some researchers estimate that five or six people were killed and 15 to 20 wounded; others put the death toll as high as 23. Most of the victims were black, though a white man is known to have been shot and killed by a mob of blacks. Unsubstantiated stories persisted for decades in black neighborhoods that hundreds of black bodies were stuffed into culverts or put in boxcars and shipped out of town.

Embarrassed by the violence, citizens of both races demanded that those who had taken part be brought to justice. Several people were arrested and convicted of murder, attempted lynching, or inciting a riot. The man who started it all—the Childresses' attacker—was never found.

Russell High was spirited out of town early Monday morning to a jail in Raleigh. He served time for his weapons violation and was never seen in Winston-Salem again.

The violence was deplorable, but as Bishop Edward Rondthaler, pastor of the Salem congregation, noted in the church's annual memorabilia, the better angels of the city's nature responded: "The man was not lynched. Every part of our city administration from the mayor down, and including our own Home Guard, stood up to the duty to which they were so suddenly called; the moral sense of the community, both black and white, completely steadied the city after its first surprise was over; there has been such a close judicial sifting and such severe penalties have been inflicted as will leave their salutary impression on the dangerous boys and men of the city and all the neighborhood around."

The Forsyth Savings and Trust Company catered to black customers. It became a casualty of the Depression.

Joseph Bradshaw Collection

Outward and Upward

The city's affluence showed itself in a building boom that produced some of grandest homes and commercial buildings in Winston-Salem. The wealthy abandoned their Victorian mansions on West Fifth Street for the secluded enclaves of Country Club Estates and Buena Vista. R. J. Reynolds set the tone in 1917 when he moved his family to a house that was in keeping with his status as the richest man in the state, who paid $66,000 in state taxes, or about twice as much as any other North Carolinian. Reynolda, more than 1,000 acres on the city's outskirts, had the feel of a self-sustaining feudal estate. Surrounding the 60-room mansion were barns, a school, a post office, a chapel, a blacksmith shop, and a greenhouse.

Reynolds's brother William left town in 1921 for a 1,117-acre estate on the Yadkin River that he called Tanglewood. Bowman Gray, Sr., another Reynolds executive, began building a rambling Norman Revival mansion across from Reynolda. The Depression slowed construction, and Graylyn wasn't completed until 1932.

For the less affluent, there was always Ardmore. Advertisements began appearing in the newspapers in 1914 enticing prospective homebuyers to a suburb where they could purchase "the country home in the city." During the next 22 years, at least a house a week was built in Ardmore, named after a well-known suburb in Philadelphia. The original section included the area west of Sunset Drive and south of First Street and bounded on the west by Hawthorne Road and Queen Street. It was composed mainly of farmland bought from William Ebert and John Nading for

The intersection of Academy and Fenimore streets in Ardmore in 1939

The Photograph Collection, Winston-Salem/Forsyth County Public Library

The home of U. S. Reynolds, a school principal, was among the many fine homes on East 14th Street in the 1920s.

———

Joseph Bradshaw Collection

$60,000, or about $120 an acre. Twenty-four years later, a quarter-acre lot sold for about $1,200. Homes in Ardmore now routinely fetch more than $100,000.

Houses sprang up in Granville and around Reynolda in 1915. Crafton Heights, Melrose, West Highlands, Buena Vista, Westover, and Westview followed. Development spread to the north and south in the 1920s with Montview, Forest Hills, Bon Air, Konnoak Hills, and Alta Vista, believed to be the first restricted black suburb in the country.

Most affluent blacks still lived around Winston-Salem Teachers College in Columbian Heights or on East 14th Street. Rufus S. Hairston, who owned a drugstore at Third and Liberty streets, built a high-ceilinged home on East 14th in the mid-1930s. His neighbors included U. S. Reynolds, the respected principal of Depot Street School; Bishop Linwood W. Kyles of the A.M.E. Zion Church; Jeff Hairston, one of the founders of Safe Bus Company; and George Washington Hill, a founder of Winston-Salem Mutual Life Insurance Company.

Traditional housing patterns began to change between the world wars, as the burgeoning black population spread north and east from historic black neighborhoods. What is now predominantly black East Winston was a white neighborhood at the turn of the century, with white families living along East Third, East Fourth, and East Fifth streets. The construction of City Hospital, Skyland School, Union Station, and Bowman Gray Stadium in the area reflected the stability of the white neighborhood.

Blacks built houses on the fringes of East Winston after World War I, which caused friction. A black woman moved into a house on the corner of Woodland Avenue and East Eighth Street, then a white section. She was burned out. It wasn't until 1941, when Jasper Carpenter became the first black to buy a house around City Hospital, that the white exodus from East Winston began. Within two years, the area was entirely black.

The transformation of Reynoldstown was just as complete. R. J. Reynolds Tobacco Company had bought 84 acres along Cameron Avenue in East Winston in 1917 and built 180 houses that it sold at cost to white employees. Within 20 years, Reynoldstown turned into a predominantly black neighborhood.

Not all the buildings of the period were grand. There was the huge post office at Fifth and Liberty streets, built in 1914 to replace a much prettier building that was only eight years old. The third Forsyth County Courthouse, opened in 1926, is drab compared to the beautiful Romanesque courthouse it replaced.

Most of the new buildings downtown reached for the sky. The use of reinforced concrete introduced *skyscraper* into the language, and Winston-Salem became one of many cities captivated with the notion of having the tallest building around. The Wachovia Building, at seven stories, was the tallest when Winston and Salem merged. It lost the distinction when the eight-story O'Hanlon Building went up in 1915, but gained a tie when a floor was added to the bank in 1918. Next came the 12-story Hotel Robert E. Lee in 1921 and then the 18-story Nissen Building—now the First Union Building—in 1926.

The race was over when R. J. Reynolds Tobacco Company completed its 22-story head-quarters building in 1929. The graceful and elegant skyscraper was a fitting end to a period of frenzied building. It cost almost $3 million and won national acclaim for its architect, Shreve & Lamb, which used the structure as a model when it designed New York's Empire State Building.

The O'Hanlon Building on Fourth and Liberty streets was the city's first skyscraper when it was built in 1915.

The Photograph Collection, Winston-Salem/Forsyth County Public Library

Richard and Katharine Reynolds spent most of their married life in a big Victorian house on West Fifth Street, where the Main Branch of the public library is now.

The Photograph Collection, Winston-Salem/Forsyth County Public Library

Top:

Katharine holds Smith in this picture taken at the Fifth Street house about 1912. On the ground with R. J. Reynolds are, from left, Mary; Nancy; Katharine's nephew Jim Dunn; and Richard, Jr.

Left:

Nancy, Mary, Richard, Jr., and Smith with R. J. Reynolds.

———

Reynolda House Museum of American Art

A proud pappa with Smith on the porch at Fifth Street

Reynolda House Museum of American Art

R. J. Reynolds takes his children Smith, Nancy, and Mary for a sleigh ride on Fifth Street about 1913. The horses pulling the sleigh are Prince, on the left, and Albert.

North Carolina Baptist Collection, Wake Forest University

The children growing up, about 1917: Mary, Smith, Nancy, and Richard, Jr.

Reynolda House Museum of American Art

A family portrait, about 1915
Mary, R. J. Reynolds, Nancy, Katharine, Richard, Jr., and Smith

Reynolda House Museum of American Art

The Good Women Behind the Men

Katharine and Kate Reynolds could have taken it easy. As the wives of two of Winston-Salem's richest men, they could have retired to the isolation of their country estates to ride their horses and host grand parties. Instead, they did more for Winston-Salem than any other women in the city's history.

They were their husbands's consciences, pushing for better wages and working conditions for factory employees. They started hospitals, built schools and an elegant auditorium, and left behind a charitable foundation that has helped thousands of North Carolina's needy.

Of the two, Katharine Smith Reynolds was the more energetic. She was 25 when she married R. J. Reynolds in 1905. He was by then a successful and rich businessman almost 30 years older than his bride.

Reynolds had known his wife since she was a child. He and her father, Zachary Taylor Smith, were cousins who had grown up together in Virginia. Reynolds often visited Smith at his home in Mount Airy and teased the young Katharine that he would one day marry her.

After graduating from college with a degree in English literature, Miss Smith took a job as Reynolds's secretary and won a $1,000 prize in a company-sponsored contest. Reynolds said later that he married her to get his money back.

He got his money's worth. Katharine urged her husband, whom she always called "Mr. Reynolds," to shorten his employees' workweek and to improve conditions in his factories by providing lunchrooms, a medical department, and a day nursery. Reynolds, a good man who gave freely of his time and money to worthwhile community projects, didn't need much prodding. He granted each of his wife's wishes.

Katharine and her sister-in-law, Kate Bitting Reynolds, constantly stressed the need for safe housing for the young girls who moved to Winston-Salem during World War I to work in the Reynolds factories. Just before he died in 1918, R. J. Reynolds bought the Plaza Hotel, at Chestnut and Third streets, and remodeled it. It was named the Reynolds Inn. The first girls moved in September 21.

Even Reynolda, the 1,000-acre family estate that Katharine planned, had a higher purpose than merely being the home of a rich family. It was a model farm where she taught local farmers the most current methods of scientific, diversified farming. Employees lived in a village on the estate and had their own schools and churches. While Reynolda was being built, Katharine offered evening classes to workers who wanted to learn to read and write.

After her husband's death, Katharine gave the city land atop Silver Hill, north of downtown, for a new public high school. She also built the community an auditorium on adjacent property. All she asked was that the buildings be named after her late husband.

Kate Bitting Reynolds, 14 years older than her sister-in-law, shared the same commitment to bettering the city. A native of Yadkin County, Miss Bitting moved to Winston as a child. She married William N. Reynolds, R.J.R.'s younger brother, in 1889 and became a leader in civic affairs.

Kate Reynolds contributed to numerous projects and helped start City Hospital, Winston-Salem's first modern hospital. She and her husband also gave the city $200,000 to build a modern hospital for blacks. The result was the Kate Bitting Reynolds Memorial Hospital, affectionately called the "Katie B.," which opened in 1938. It served blacks until 1970, when patients were moved 100 yards to the new Reynolds Memorial Hospital. The Katie B. was demolished three years later.

When she died in 1946, Kate Reynolds left $5 million in perpetual trust for the needy. The Kate B. Reynolds Health Care Trust has contributed millions of dollars over the years to provide health care for the state's poor.

The R. J. Reynolds High School complex overlooks Hanes Park in the 1920s.
The high school gym is in the foreground, and R. J. Reynolds Auditorium sits atop Silver Hill.

The Photograph Collection, Winston-Salem/Forsyth County Public Library

Construction on Reynolda took almost eight years.

Reynolda House was Katharine Reynolds's doing. She bought the land, hired the architect and builders, and made most of the decisions. "She could read a blueprint like an engineer," said an employee. The name of the 1,000-acre estate tells who the boss was. "Reynolda" was thought to be the feminine form of Reynolds. Charles Barton Keen, an architect from Philadelphia, designed the house, and Thomas Sears planned the grounds and gardens. Katharine started buying the land in 1909, and construction on the 60-room main house took almost eight years. The family moved in just before Christmas in 1917. The estate included a farm, church, school, and village for the employees.

A sweeping drive led to the front of the house.

The "lake porch" in the back overlooked manmade Lake Katharine.

The chauffeur and the family limousine

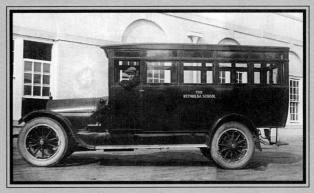

The Reynolda school bus and driver

The Mysterious Death of Z. Smith Reynolds

Questions surround the short life of Zachary Smith Reynolds. What if his parents hadn't died while he was so young and had given him some direction? What could he have accomplished if he had followed his famous father's example and applied his talents to hard work rather than fretting them away? What if he had lived beyond his 20 years?

What happened—or didn't happen—that night at Reynolda in the early 1930s is all anyone remembers, or knows, about Z. Smith Reynolds. His life has been defined by his tragic and mysterious death.

The youngest child of R. J. Reynolds, Smith was seven when his father died and barely a teenager when his mother, Katharine, passed away. He was brought up by his uncle Will Reynolds and his aunt Kate, a childless couple who probably had their hands full with Smith and his brother and two sisters.

An indifferent student, Smith quit school as a teenager to take up flying. He became quite good at it. During the last year of his life, Smith flew solo from London to Hong Kong, and the flight log reveals that he could be disciplined, cool-headed, and capable of making decisions expected of more experienced pilots. Had he displayed the same qualities on the ground, Smith could have accomplished great things.

He was instead fickle and immature. At 18, he married Anne Cannon, the daughter of the towel baron, then divorced her within a year. "She liked big parties and I like little parties," Smith said, summing up their differences.

Six days after the divorce, he married Libby Holman, a 25-year-old singer who had catapulted to top billing on Broadway after her hit song "Moanin' Low" in 1929. At a time when soup lines wound through the streets of Manhattan, Holman was making $2,500 a week.

Smith didn't care about the money, of course. He had $17 million coming from his father's estate when he turned 21. He had seen Holman perform and was taken with her sensuous good looks. Infatuated, he asked her to marry him while he was still married to Anne Cannon. Smith reportedly told Holman he would kill himself if she continued to refuse.

Holman finally accepted, and the two were married November 29, 1931, by a justice of the peace in Monroe, Michigan. She gave up her stage career to become the baroness of Reynolda.

Parties became the couple's trademark, and the one they threw on Tuesday, July 5, 1932, was typical. The guest list included Smith's friends from Winston-Salem and actress Blanche Yurka. They drank, swam in the pool, and drank some more. All the guests left by midnight except Yurka and Ab Walker, one of Smith's closest friends.

Walker said he was downstairs about one o'clock Wednesday morning when he heard a muffled shot from the second floor. A drunken Libby staggered to the balcony and screamed, "Smith's killed himself!" Walker said he rushed upstairs to find Smith sprawled on a bed with a bullet wound in his right temple. Libby and Walker took Smith to Baptist Hospital, where he died about four hours later.

His death was initially ruled a suicide, but a coroner's inquest a few days later decided that Smith had died "at the hands of a party or parties unknown." In August, a grand jury indicted Libby for murder and Walker as an accomplice.

The shooting, still the most sensational in Winston-Salem's history, attracted reporters from all over the country. It had all the elements of a juicy story: a young tobacco heir, a beautiful show girl, mysterious circumstances, conflicting evidence.

It went on for weeks. Soon, stories began to appear about drunken orgies at Reynolda, Smith's impotence, and Libby's alleged affair with Ab Walker.

"The Reynolds family," one reporter later said, "was taking a beating."

Will Reynolds wrote the district attorney that the family would be "relieved" if the charges were dropped. The district attorney complied, citing lack of evidence, and no trial was ever held.

Something positive did come from the tragedy. After a protracted lawsuit over Smith's estate, his siblings used their share, about $7.5 million, to start the Z. Smith Reynolds Foundation, which has been a force for good throughout the South.

"The Salem Conscience, the Winston Purse"

Built at Main and Fourth streets on the site of the first city hall, the Reynolds Building also was, according to Clement Eaton, "a symbol of the victory of the great tobacco company whom my father fought in vain against [in] its take-over of city government." Eaton's father, Oscar, was Winston-Salem's first mayor.

Such symbolism wasn't lost on a historian who visited Winston-Salem in the 1930s for a book he was writing on the tobacco industry. "Granted the right topography and the right orientation, Winston-Salem folks, whether factory hands in East Winston or executives in Buena Vista, go to sleep with its floodlighted tower in their bedroom windows, [and] awake to see it shining in the morning sun," Leonard Rapport wrote in *People in Tobacco*.

By the time of Rapport's visit, a maxim had developed in Winston-Salem: Nothing was done in town unless it was first approved on the 19th floor of the Reynolds Building. That referred specifically to the company's executive offices and generically to a system of civic management controlled by R. J. Reynolds Tobacco Company and the other industrialists and bankers in town.

Old-timers, a touch of nostalgia in their voices, now call it "the paternalistic oligarchy," referring to the Grays, Reynoldses, and Haneses—the families that built the factories, employed most of the people, and ran the city.

The families were headed by men like James A. Gray, Jr., who had definite ideas about how things should be done, ideas that weren't restricted to his company. Gray, who became president of Reynolds in 1934, personi-

The Reynolds Building, completed in 1929, marked an opulent end to a decade of frenzied construction.

———

The Photograph Collection,
Winston-Salem/Forsyth County Public Library

fied the Winston-Salem of his day: he was industrious, pious, honest, sober, thrifty. His grandfather had been one of the town's first settlers; his father had run its major bank; and he followed his brother Bowman as president of its biggest employer. James A. Gray knew Winston-Salem because he and his family had helped shape it.

"Nothing happened in this community that Mr. Gray didn't catch," said Chester Davis, a former agent with the Federal Bureau of Investigation who wrote about the city for the

Winston-Salem Journal for 30 years. "I don't think there was any man who believed he had the good of Winston-Salem in his heart more than he did."

The youngest child of James and Aurelia Gray, "Jamie," as he was called by his brothers and sisters, grew up in the family's big Victorian house on Second and Cherry streets, completed in 1885. He played ball in the yard with his friend Norman Stockton, who lived across the street, and picked the luscious blackheart cherries that grew in the trees that gave Cherry Street its name.

After graduating from the University of North Carolina, Gray worked at Wachovia National Bank, where his father was president. There, he caught the eye of R. J. Reynolds, who admired the young man's sound business judgment. A dying Reynolds picked Gray to run his company's finances, and Gray left Wachovia in 1919 to become a vice president at Reynolds.

At the time of Gray's arrival, the company was riding the popularity of Prince Albert smoking tobacco and Camel cigarettes to the top of the tobacco industry. It employed more than 10,000 people.

The company was also the top taxpayer in the state. By the time Gray became president, R. J. Reynolds Tobacco Company was consid-

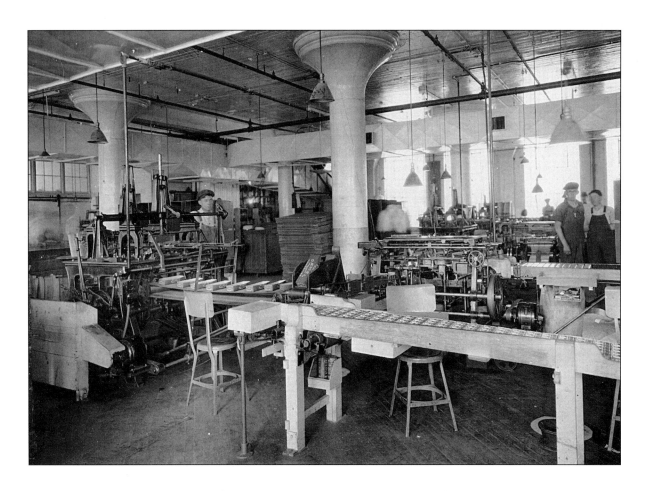

Machines in factory No. 12 churn out Camel cigarettes, about 1920.

Joseph Bradshaw Collection

ered one of the most profitable corporations in the world. It made two-thirds of all the cigarettes in the state, paid a fourth of the city's property taxes, and contributed $1 of every $2.50 in state income taxes.

The company that employs the most people and pays the most taxes generally wields the most clout. That unwritten rule of civics certainly applied to R. J. Reynolds Tobacco Company. "The Reynolds company without a doubt controlled Winston-Salem," said the late Reverend Kenneth R. Williams, a chancellor of Winston-Salem State University who grew up in the shadows of the Reynolds smokestacks. "Anyone who says otherwise just doesn't know what the situation was."

Reynolds executives directed the extralegal power structure of manufacturers and bankers that had developed since the 1890s. Nothing was done in town without their support, leadership, and, usually, money.

"Oh, they dominated government," Charles B. Wade, Jr., a retired Reynolds senior vice president, said of company executives, "but they never dominated it selfishly."

Between 1913 and 1940, more than half of the 59 men who served on the Winston-Salem Board of Aldermen came from the city's tobacco or textile factories or its banks. Others from those industries were elected mayor or sent to Congress or the state legislature. Holding public office was one way to ensure a friendly climate for expanding industrial empires.

James Gray followed the pattern. He served in the North Carolina Senate from 1917 to 1920 and did a strange thing for a fiscally conservative man of money: he co-sponsored the amendment to the state constitution that provided for a state income tax. Gray said later that he did it because the state needed money to improve its schools and roads.

Sitting in the president's chair of R. J. Reynolds Tobacco Company gave Gray more power than the city's mayor, but he never let that change him. Change was not something that Gray took to easily. As he had done since his first day at the company, Gray continued to walk the few blocks from the house on Cherry Street to work each morning. A friendly, open man, he stopped to talk with the people he met along the way.

Gray seems to have been a man who felt that certain things were done certain ways. For instance, he didn't follow the other moneyed men who left the city for country estates. Gray stayed downtown. Remaining in the house where he was born, he said late in life, was his proudest accomplishment.

Every city has wealthy families that bestow their generosity on its citizens, but not many cities have relied so heavily on the wealth and leadership of a few. One only has to trace the histories of Kate Bitting Reynolds Memorial Hospital, P. H. Hanes Park, Bowman Gray School of Medicine, R. J. Reynolds Auditorium, Smith Reynolds Airport, Tanglewood Park, Graylyn Conference Center, and Reynolda House Museum of Art to understand what those families have meant to Winston-Salem. Outsiders have always viewed such gifts suspiciously, wondering what the city had to give in return. A writer from *Forbes* magazine summed it up in an article about Winston-Salem in 1957: "Townspeople, for their part, view Reynolds with a mixture of gratitude and misgiving. They appreciate Reynolds's generosity, but distrust the motives."

Such cynicism ignores Winston-Salem's long history of caring and giving. The founding Moravians put great emphasis on good works and devotion to the community. James Gray and the other tobacco and textile barons grew up in that history and continued its legacy. They combined what Chester Davis termed in one of his articles "the Salem conscience and the Winston purse."

The Conquering Camels

Less than five months after Winston and Salem were joined by a hyphen, an event occurred that ensured the success and growth of the new city. Camels arrived.

R. J. Reynolds Tobacco Company introduced its Camel cigarettes on October 19, 1913. The brand's immense popularity made Reynolds the leading tobacco company in the world and Winston-Salem the leading producer of tobacco products. That meant jobs and prosperity for the company and the town.

R. J. Reynolds, the company's founder and president, was reluctant to enter the cigarette market. He had made his fortune on chewing tobacco and Prince Albert smoking tobacco. Unlike cigarettes, neither required sophisticated machinery and skilled workers.

A savvy businessman, Reynolds couldn't ignore the trends, though. Most people still rolled their own cigarettes and disliked the manufactured brands, but cigarette smoking was becoming more popular and would one day overtake chewing.

Never a man to risk everything on one roll of the dice, Reynolds decided to make four brands of cigarettes, each using a different blend of tobacco. Only Camels survived. They were a mixture of domestic burley and bright tobacco, with Turkish leaf added for taste and aroma, along with a generous amount of sweetener. Most cigarette brands were made of straight Turkish tobacco, and Camels are credited with being the first truly American cigarette.

To appeal to American smokers' taste for Turkish tobacco, Reynolds chose a name that evoked images of the desert. The pack's design, with its temples, pyramids, and oasis, also was very Middle Eastern. The first pack looked pretty much like the current pack, except that the original camel was a pathetic-looking dromedary with one hump, short, pointed ears, and a drooping neck.

Distressed by the image of the sickly creature on his cigarette pack, Reynolds sent his secretary, Roy Haberkern, to Barnum & Bailey Circus when it came to town in the fall of 1913. Haberkern searched the menageries for a suitable animal and found a two-humped camel and a dromedary. The animal boss, a disagreeable fellow named Patterson, refused to allow them to be photographed. Haberkern reminded Patterson that R. J. Reynolds always closed his factories for the circus but could keep them open. Patterson relented, and the pictures were taken. The camel behaved, but the dromedary was unwilling to hold still. Patterson slapped it on the nose, and Old Joe raised its tail, threw back its head, and closed its eyes. The unwilling Old Joe thus became the most famous dromedary in the world.

Cigarettes were marketed regionally at the time, and each section of the country had its favorite. Camels were the first brand to be sold nationally, starting with teaser ads in magazines and newspapers warning, "The Camels Are Coming."

They came and they conquered. About 1.1 million were made that first year. More than 18 billion were produced in 1921, when half the cigarettes smoked in the United States were Camels. A few years later, the company turned out 30 billion Camels. The cigarettes were so successful that competitors spread rumors that workers in Reynolds's cigarette room had leprosy or syphilis.

Part of the brand's success stemmed from aggressive and imaginative advertising. The idea for one of the most famous advertising slogans in history came in 1918, when a foursome of golfers ran out of cigarettes. One of the men said to Martin Reddington, who handled outdoor ads for Reynolds, "I'd walk a mile for a Camel." The slogan first appeared on a billboard in June 1921.

"Teaser" ads for Camel cigarettes ran on consecutive weeks when the brand was introduced in 1913.

R. J. Reynolds Tobacco Company

Third Street, between Liberty and Cherry streets, 1910
The original First Presbyterian Church is at the head of Third Street. Winston High
School, which burned down in 1923, is next door on the right. The YMCA building is
next door on Cherry and Fourth streets.

———

Courtesy of Frank Tursi

The freshest vegetables and the latest gossip were available
at the City Market, which opened on North Cherry Street in 1925.
The building, on the left, now houses the city's visitors center and an elementary school.

The Photograph Collection, Winston-Salem/Forsyth County Public Library

The YMCA, old Winston
High School, and the
Presbyterian Church
crowd Cherry Street.

The Photograph Collection,
Winston-Salem/Forsyth
County Public Library

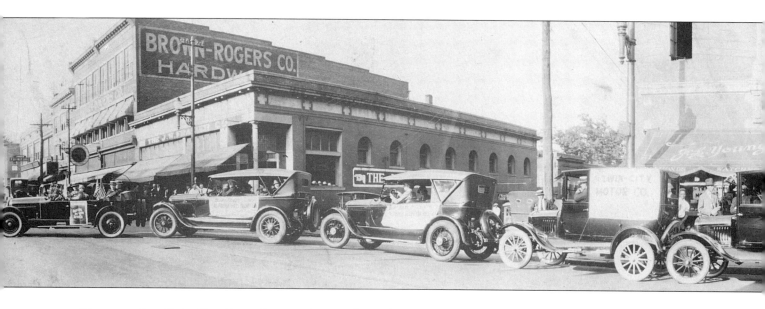

These cars from Twin-City Motor Company line up along Liberty Street to promote the movie Hunting Big Game in Africa With a Gun & Camera *that was playing at* The Auditorium Building. *The view in this circa 1920 photograph is looking toward the intersection of West Fifth and Liberty streets. Only four buildings pictured here still remain: Rominger Furniture at 423 South Liberty, the old Brown-Rogers building, the building to the left of it, and the Jones Furniture building. A parking deck has replaced all the buildings from Young Jewelers to Rominger's.*

Courtesy of Frank Tursi

The Amuzu

Moviegoers in the 1920s had a variety of theaters to choose from.

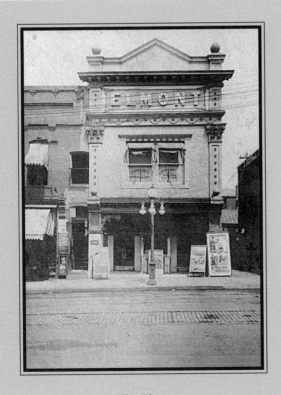

The Elmont

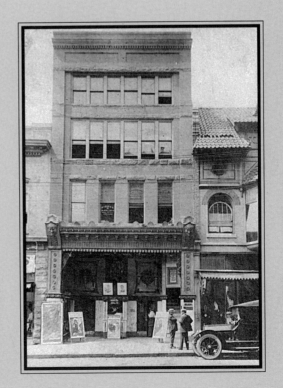

The Pilot

Winston Steamer Company No. 1 was formally organized on February 11, 1882.

The Photograph Collection, Winston-Salem/Forsyth County Public Library

The Brethren of Salem took early precautions against fires. The Moravian Church had numerous rules aimed at preventing fires, and fire inspectors were appointed in the 1770s to examine buildings and note anything that seemed dangerous. In 1785, the village bought two fire engines from Germany and bought a third from Philadelphia in 1832. The first organized company of volunteers, the Salem Vigilant Fire Company, was organized in 1856. By the 1890s, the town had a hook and ladder company and regular fire drills were held in Salem Square.

Winston was a little slower to act. W. F. Keith, representing a group of citizens, appeared before the town commissioners in 1882 to propose that the city form a volunteer fire company with new equipment and uniforms provided by the commissioners. Winston Steamer Company No. 1 was formally organized in 1882.

Horses were used to pull the engines until 1912, when the Winston department paid $9,000 for a "One Type 12 Triple Combination Motor Car" made by the LaFrance Fire Engine Company. The Winston and Salem departments merged the following year when the two cities consolidated.

Top:
Salem's hook and ladder company

Bottom:
The Brown-Rogers Hardware Store on Main and Fourth streets burned in 1912.

———

The Photograph Collection, Winston-Salem/Forsyth County Public Library

The State Sunday School Convention poses outside the First Presbyterian Church on Cherry Street. The picture probably was taken in 1923, the year Winston High School burned. The school is the derelict building next to the church. The YMCA is on the far right, and fashionable houses line Cherry Street to the left.

Courtesy of Frank Tursi

Mr. Stroud, the photographer, was kept busy on this day in the 1920s taking pictures of various members of this church.

Courtesy of Frank Tursi

The author purchased about 2,000 photographs at an auction when a photography studio went out of business in 1991. Most were family snapshots taken in Winston-Salem during the 1930s. Those who took the pictures either forgot them or didn't have the money to pick them up. A sampling is offered here.

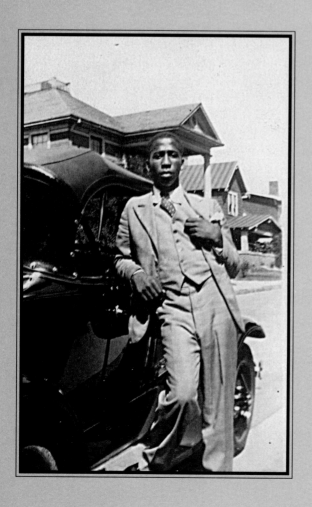

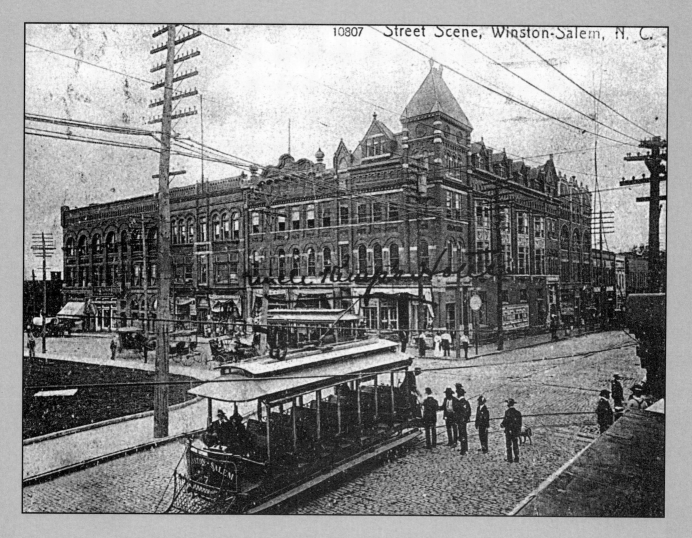

The Phoenix Hotel on Fourth and Liberty streets

———

North Carolina Collection, UNC Library at Chapel Hill

Winston-Salem had some fine hotels during its history. The Fountain between Second and Third streets, was originally called the Central. Captain R. W. Belo bought it, put a fountain out front, and renamed it. Its quiet atmosphere made it popular with businessmen.

The Phoenix Hotel on Fourth and Liberty streets, was built in the 1890s. Each of its 72 rooms had steam heat and running water. It was torn down in 1928 for the present Pepper Building.

The corner of Main and Third streets was the site of numerous hotels. The Merchants Hotel became known as the Hotel Jones, when J. L. Jones bought it. R. J. Reynolds lived there during his early years in Winston. The hotel was popular when the circus came to town because the elevated porch was a fine place to watch the circus parade.

One of the city's grandest hotels, the Zinzendorf, was built on the site of the Jones in 1906. A predecessor of the same name burned in 1892. The new Zinzendorf had 120 rooms, each with a telephone and hot and cold running water. Thirty rooms had their own baths. The lobby was sumptuous with a flowing fountain and a terrazzo floor, and the dining room was spacious. A victim of urban renewal, the hotel was torn down in 1970 and the Federal Building was built in its place.

The Fountain
between Second and Third streets

The Photograph Collection,
Winston-Salem/Forsyth County
Public Library

Hotel Jones

The Photograph Collection,
Winston-Salem/Forsyth County
Public Library

The Zinzendorf

The Photograph Collection,
Winston-Salem/Forsyth County
Public Library

The trees are thick and large in this view of Salem Square, circa 1925. The Main Hall of Salem College is in the background.

Courtesy of Frank Tursi

Children from the Methodist Children's Home return from an outing.

The Photograph Collection, Winston-Salem/Forsyth County Public Library

The Sunday School class at St. Philip's Moravian Church, about 1934

Courtesy of William Melvin Oates

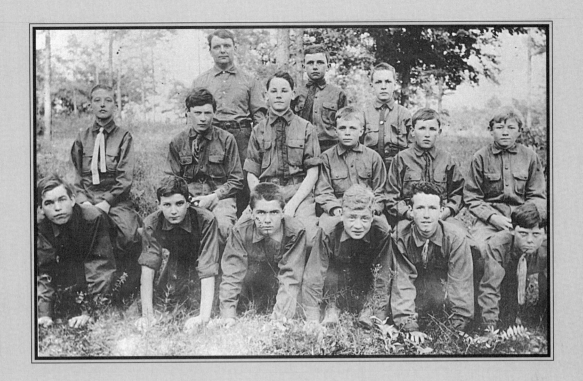

This may be the first Boy Scout Troop in Winston-Salem.

The Moravian Archives of the Southern Province, Winston-Salem

Students in the library at R. J. Reynolds High School

The Photograph Collection, Winston-Salem/Forsyth County Public Library

That must be "Railroad" Jones waving to the camera in this photograph of his oil company on South Main Street taken in the 1920s. He was strategically located between Buick and Cadillac dealerships.

Courtesy of Frank Tursi

The Bubble Bursts

The banks didn't go under in Winston-Salem during the Depression, but the city almost did. It had to be bailed out by its rich friends.

During the 1920s, North Carolina started building what became the largest state road system in the country. Winston-Salem got caught up in the frenzy. Usually frugal in such matters, the city began paving streets and sidewalks where no one lived. Winston-Salem had about 12 miles of paved roads in 1915, when the most common form of transportation was still horse and buggy. By 1929, it had more than 130 miles of paved streets. And it was all financed with bonds.

After the stock market crashed in 1929, Winston-Salem's revenue dropped precipitously. Strapped property owners knew that the city would take five years to foreclose on their property if they didn't pay their taxes, but that banks would foreclose immediately. So they paid their mortgages and let their taxes ride.

The city responded by firing workers and cutting pay. It reduced its budget by more than $1 million by 1933 and cut its tax rate five cents. Winston-Salem seemed ready to weather the crisis until those street bonds came due.

Mayor George W. Coan, Jr., reported to the aldermen in the spring of that year that Winston-Salem had $1.5 million in bonds to pay and no money. No bank would lend the city the money, so Coan went hat in hand to the city's most prominent citizens, who financed the debt. R. J. Reynolds Tobacco Company even paid its property taxes in advance.

Winston-Salem fared better than most cities during the Depression. It had one of the lowest unemployment rates in the South, and the Federal Reserve Board listed it among the top 10 cities in the country in business activity. At

Men were kept busy during the Depression building roads.

———

The Photograph Collection,
Winston-Salem/Forsyth County Public Library

a time when jobs and money were scarce, the city ranked second in the state in retail sales.

Like many cities, Winston-Salem used a number of innovative employment programs. A cleanup campaign put scores of people to work repairing houses and schools. Unemployed men fixed parks and playgrounds and surfaced roads. Companies started a "Share-a-Job Plan" that split jobs between two people, both working half what they would in normal times. The most popular program sent hundreds of homeless families to work old farms in the county. The family of Bowman Gray, Sr., donated money to the city that allowed it to get a grant from the federal Works Progress Administration. The grant was used to put hundreds of men to work building Bowman Gray Stadium, the city's first municipal arena. It opened in 1939.

The Depression ended the most frenzied period in Winston-Salem's history. No longer would population growth exceed 50 percent. The once-boisterous city settled into middle age.

Christmastime along West Fourth Street in the late 1930s

The Photograph Collection, Winston-Salem/Forsyth County Public Library

Dates to Remember

1913   Winston and Salem are consolidated. R. J. Reynolds Tobacco Company begins producing Camel cigarettes. Hanes underwear hits the market when P. H. Hanes Knitting Company makes underwear under its own label for the first time.

1914   City Hospital, Winston-Salem's first modern hospital, opens. A $240,000 bequest to the city by R. J. Reynolds leads to the construction of a wing for black patients in 1922 and another wing two years later.

1915   The eight-story O'Hanlon Building opens, becoming the city's tallest. The first sewage treatment plant is built.

1917   To supply drinking water for its growing population, the city builds a dam along Salem Creek, and Salem Lake is created. A filter plant is added eight years later.

1918   Five or six people are killed when a mob of about 3,000 whites storms the jail in city hall in an attempt to lynch a black man they think raped a white woman.

1919   The Winston-Salem Foundation, the South's second-oldest community foundation, is started. Maynard Field, the first municipal airport in the South, opens east of the city. It is replaced by Miller Airport in 1927.

1923   North Carolina Baptist Hospital opens after citizens raise $140,000 for the building fund. Security Life and Trust Company—now Integon Corporation—moves its headquarters from Greensboro. The Community Chest of Forsyth County, the forerunner of the United Way, is organized; it raises $36,000 for 20 health and welfare organizations.

1924   R. J. Reynolds Auditorium is dedicated. Hanes Dye and Finishing Company is organized.

1926   The Romanesque courthouse is replaced by the present structure; wings are added in 1960. Safe Bus Company is founded by a group of independent black bus owners.

1929   The Reynolds Building opens, marking an end to a decade of frenzied building that changes the city's skyline. During the 1920s, many of the city's grandest buildings are completed: the Hotel Robert E. Lee (1921), city hall (1926), the Nissen Building (1926), the Pepper Building (1928), and the Carolina Apartments (1929), now the Stevens Center for the Performing Arts .

1930   WSJS Radio, the city's first station, goes on the air on Good Friday; the choir of St. Paul's Episcopal Church presents a program of religious music.

1931   The state's first modern high school for blacks opens in Winston-Salem and is named, fittingly, for Simon Green Atkins.

1932   Z. Smith Reynolds, the youngest child of R. J. Reynolds, dies in a mysterious shooting at Reynolda, his home.

1935   Eastern Airlines begins commercial air service to Miller Airport. The service is discontinued after eight months because of poor facilities. It is reestablished permanently in 1941. Brown Derby Hat Works, the only black-owned hat maker in the state, opens on Patterson Avenue.

1938   Kate Bitting Reynolds Memorial Hospital opens for black patients.

1939   Bowman Gray Stadium is dedicated.

Football always drew a crowd to Bowman Gray Stadium, which opened in 1939.

The Photograph Collection, Winston-Salem/Forsyth County Public Library

Names to Know

Adelaide Fries was the city's most respected historian.

Adelaide Lisette Fries
She was probably the city's most devoted and respected historian. A graduate of Salem College, Dr. Fries published a brief local history, *Forsyth County*, in 1896 when she was only 27 years old. She quickly followed that up with histories of Salem College, the Moravians in Georgia, and Moravian funeral chorales. She then spent most of the remainder of her life compiling the fascinating *Records of the Moravians of North Carolina*, an invaluable collection of journals, letters, and other records of Bethabara, Bethania, and Salem. The first volume was published in 1922 and the most recent in 1969. Dr. Fries also published *Forsyth: A County on the March*, the first modern history of the city and county. She died in 1949, the year the book was published.

Bowman Gray, Sr.
The eldest son of James A. Gray, Sr., went to work at R. J. Reynolds Tobacco Company in 1895 as a traveling salesman. Twenty-nine years later, he was president of the company, the first of three members of his family to hold that position. His son once said that his father had two interests in life: the company and his family. In 1932, Gray donated his house and land on West Fifth Street to Centenary Methodist Church for its new building and moved his family to Graylyn, a huge, stone Norman Revival house on 87 acres west of Winston-Salem. A frequent contributor to orphanages and hospitals, Gray quietly paid to educate the children of friends who had lost money during the Depression. He died in 1935 and left Wake Forest College $750,000 worth of RJR stock to establish a four-year medical school in Winston-Salem; Bowman Gray School of Medicine opened in 1941. Gray's family partially financed the construction of Bowman Gray Stadium, which opened in 1939, and it gave Graylyn to Wake Forest in 1946. The university uses the house as a conference center.

James A. Gray, Jr.
The youngest child of James A. Gray, Sr., Gray followed in his father's footsteps. After graduating from the University of North Carolina, he became a clerk at Wachovia National Bank, which his father had helped start. A vice president of the bank by 1919, Gray resigned to become a vice president of R. J. Reynolds Tobacco Company, eventually becoming its president. A friendly man, Gray was proud that he never left the family house on North Cherry Street. He gave almost $3 million to colleges and charitable institutions across the state during his lifetime. Gray died in 1952 at age 63.

Pleasant Huber Hanes, Sr.
He took over P. H. Hanes Knitting Company when his father, Pleasant Henderson Hanes, died in 1925. Hanes led the company during its great expansion. Abrupt and forceful, he was a born salesman and could be very persuasive. He helped raise $1.5 million to move Wake Forest College to Winston-Salem, and he played an important role in raising more than $1 million for Bowman Gray School of Medicine. He died in 1967 and is buried in the family

plot in Salem Cemetery.

Robert M. Hanes
He joined Wachovia Bank and Trust Company in 1920 and became its president in 1931. Hanes held the position for the next 25 years, directing the bank's expansion. He doubled the number of cities in the state that had branch offices and increased deposits from $40 million to $400 million. The son of John Wesley and Anna Hanes, he served in both the North Carolina House of Representatives and Senate. Offered the presidencies of the New York Stock Exchange and the Chase Manhattan Bank of New York, then the largest bank in the United States, Hanes decided to stay at Wachovia. He died in 1959. The first building in Research Triangle Park was named in his honor.

Kate Bitting Reynolds
One of Winston-Salem's early civic leaders and the wife of William N. Reynolds, she fought for better hospitals and health care. She and her husband gave the city $200,000 to build a modern hospital for blacks. She died in 1946 and left $5 million in perpetual trust for the needy.

Katharine Smith Reynolds
The wife of R. J. Reynolds, Katharine was one of Winston-Salem's great benefactors. She persuaded her husband to improve working conditions in his plants. She also planned the family's Reynolda estate and established schools there for company employees. She gave the city land to build a high school and an elegant auditorium in honor of her late husband. She died in 1924.

William N. Reynolds
A younger brother of R. J. Reynolds, he came to Winston during his summer breaks at Trinity College—now Duke University—to work in the tobacco company his brother had started. He joined the company permanently in 1883 and assumed the presidency when R. J. Reynolds died in 1918. He and his wife, Kate, lived for a long time in a mansion on West Fifth Street before moving to a 1,100-acre estate on the Yadkin River called Tanglewood. "Mr. Will" retired in 1942 and devoted his time to raising and training champion trotter horses. A philanthropist who donated money to schools and churches, Reynolds died in 1951 and gave his country home to Forsyth County to be used as a public park. His estate of $14 million went into a trust for the benefit of the Z. Smith Reynolds Foundation and now provides about 60 percent of the foundation's income. Reynolds Coliseum on the campus of North Carolina State University in Raleigh is named in his honor.

Z. Smith Reynolds
The youngest child of R. J. and Katharine Reynolds, Smith was a pioneer aviator who flew from England to Hong Kong in 1931–32, the last year of his life. His mysterious death at Reynolda attracted worldwide attention. His brother and two sisters used their share of his estate, $7.5 million, to establish a charitable foundation that bears his name. One of its first grants went to modernize Winston-Salem's airport, which was renamed in honor of Z. Smith Reynolds.

Ernie Shore
The city's "Mr. Baseball," Ernest Grady Shore was born in Yadkin County in 1891. He starred as a pitcher at Guilford College, where he caught the eye of New York Giant scouts. He made his debut for the Giants in 1912 and pitched for eight seasons in the major leagues. Most of those years were spent with the Boston Red Sox, where Shore roomed with Babe Ruth. He is best remembered for pitching a perfect game in 1917 after relieving Ruth, the starting pitcher, who was thrown out of the game after walking the first batter and arguing with the umpire. Shore came to Winston-Salem after retiring in 1920 and was elected sheriff in 1936. A popular man described as gentle, unassuming, and fair, Shore served as sheriff until he retired in 1970. In the 1950s, he led a committee that raised $200,000 to build a new baseball park. The stadium was dedicated in 1956 and named for Shore.

A circus parade down Fourth Street

The Photograph Collection, Winston-Salem/Forsyth County Public Library

Remaking the City

The austerity demanded by 10 years of the Depression and four years of war scarred Winston-Salem. The city was unkempt, shabby, and unattractive when World War II ended. The downtown streets were a cluttered mess of choked traffic. Festering slums, where sewage pooled to the surface, riddled many black neighborhoods. The city's hospital was antiquated, its school system crowded, and its library a disgrace.

So Winston-Salem set out to remake itself. During the next 30 years, expressways and parkways crisscrossed the city to relieve traffic congestion. A medical school and modern hospitals made the city a leader in health care. The luring of Wake Forest College gave Winston-Salem a college of the first order. The city polished its tarnished reputation as a cultural center by landing the North Carolina School of the Arts and turning the deteriorating Salem neighborhood into a museum of national renown.

The years also saw the city's wall of provincialism crack, as new industries, headed by Western Electric, came to town. They brought the first sizable influx of outsiders to the city since tenant farmers from South Carolina had rolled into Winston on boxcars 50 years earlier. The new people brought with them new ideas that invigorated the city.

After the war, the industrialists and bankers loosened their grip on the reins of government. Marshall Kurfees, the perennial outsider, drove home the point in 1949 when he became the first man not anointed by the ruling class to become mayor.

Blacks unionized R. J. Reynolds Tobacco Company and thus found their political voice. They swelled the voting rolls, elected the first black aldermen in the 20th century, and began to demand better living conditions and more representation in city government.

A new city started to take shape.

When he stopped running, Marshall Kurfees turned out to be one of
the ablest mayors the city has ever had.

———

The Photograph Collection, Winston-Salem/Forsyth County Public Library

The Man Who Liked to Run

Marshall Kurfees was the runningest man ever seen in Winston-Salem. He always seemed to be running for some elective office, and he always seemed to be losing. He one time pulled out of a mayoral race, causing a newspaper wit to wonder in print if "Marsh" withdrew because he wanted to run in the Kentucky Derby instead.

This hankering for public office began back in 1934, when Kurfees ran for the state legislature. He drank a bit in those days and ran on the "wet" ticket in the middle of Prohibition. To prove that a man could find a bottle of bootleg booze in town, Kurfees stayed drunk for three days and was finally arrested after lying down in front of a car and refusing to move. He got all of 389 votes that year.

But Kurfees wasn't dissuaded. One of his favorite sayings was "Get up where you fell down." Though he kept running and losing, there Kurfees was in 1949, a candidate for mayor. His opponent in the Democratic primary was incumbent George D. Lentz. In those days, the Republican Party offered candidates every two years merely to keep up the appearance of a two-party system. The winner of the Democratic primary could begin moving his furniture into the mayor's office.

No one gave Kurfees much of a chance, except for Kurfees himself, and maybe his wife, Mabel. Lentz had the backing of R. J. Reynolds Tobacco Company, the Hanes companies, and everyone else who mattered in the city. The candidates anointed by the establishment always won; elections made the choices legal.

Reynolds opposed Kurfees throughout the campaign. So did the Hanes companies and Wachovia Bank and Trust Company. He was too flamboyant, too outspoken, they thought. Not mayoral material.

Kurfees was surprised, then, when he received a telephone call from James A. Gray, Jr., the chairman of Reynolds, on the night before the primary. Gray had asked Kurfees not to run some months earlier.

"Marsh, let me be the first to congratulate you on being elected mayor," Gray said.

An astonished Kurfees mumbled a thanks,

Marshall Kurfees hams it up with Earline King, left, and other performers in the Arts Follies.

then asked "Mr. Gray" if he wasn't being a bit premature.

"Oh, you're going to win," Gray replied, "and I would like to meet with you after the election."

Kurfees beat Lentz and trounced his Republican opponent in the general election, winning even the precinct that included Buena Vista for the first time in his life. After eight failures, he had finally won something.

He and Gray had their meeting. The company, Gray told the new mayor, had nothing against Kurfees personally, and he hoped that they could work together. They did for the next 12 years, as Kurfees went on to dominate city hall like no mayor before him.

Kurfees's election was a turning point in city affairs, the first hint that the oligarchy of businessmen and bankers that had ruled the city for 70 years was weakening. Kurfees was the first mayor who wasn't one of its hand-picked candidates. Though he reached an accommodation with the powers that were and had their support in later elections, Kurfees proved that someone could actually win an election in Winston-Salem without having friends in the companies' boardrooms.

He also proved everyone wrong. Amiable and hardworking, Kurfees became the city's first full-time mayor and one of its ablest. He was unusual among politicians because he believed campaign promises should actually be kept. Soon after taking office, Kurfees set out to fulfill a promise he had made to voters by persuading the General Assembly to allow city residents to vote on liquor stores. The resulting ABC stores were derisively called "Kurfees drugstores."

During Kurfees's tenure, major roads were built, slums were cleared, and blacks began to find their place in government.

It's the little things, though, that define a person's character.

A woman on Chatham Road called Kurfees one day to complain that her basement had flooded after the city had cut down trees in her area. Kurfees rushed to the woman's house, donned hip boots, and helped her bail water.

He felt sorry for the tobacco farmers who crowded into the city. They often parked their trucks outside the warehouses and answered nature's call wherever it was convenient. The least the city could do was provide them with a bathroom, Kurfees said. He had one built for them beside the Pepper Warehouse on Trade Street. Relieved farmers came to call it the "Kurfees Crapper."

When he finally retired, a great many people found, to their complete astonishment, that Marshall Kurfees had done a pretty good job.

Winston-Salem
at War

Anyone who wanted a job could find one in Winston-Salem during World War II. P. H. Hanes Knitting Company made more than 38 million garments for the armed forces. R. J. Reynolds Tobacco Company worked around the clock to produce billions of cigarettes for servicemen. The company's foil division made aluminum strips, called "windows," that were dropped by Allied planes to jam enemy radar. In 1943, National Carbon Company opened a plant to make batteries, and Allied Aviation made weapons.

The United States Army Air Force's Office of Flying Safety moved its headquarters from Washington to Winston-Salem in 1942. Its 600 officers and men investigated air force airplane accidents. They took over the Nissen Building on Fourth and Cherry streets and built a hangar, an operations building, and barracks at the recently completed Smith Reynolds Airport. National Guardsmen patrolled the airport, where young Tom Davis and his fledgling Piedmont Aviation Services were busy training hundreds of military pilots.

The county's Selective Service Board sent 13,333 men into the armed services. Hundreds more, including 34 women, volunteered. Any man who could fight was in uniform, from 18-year-old boys to 50-year-old grandfathers. Not since the Civil War had the city sent so many men to war.

Those who stayed home did their part by working in essential war industries, buying war bonds, volunteering as air-raid wardens, planting "victory gardens," and enduring rationing without complaint. The federal government placed strict controls on luxuries and many necessities, such as gasoline and food. Other items became scarce as factories retooled to meet the war's gigantic demand.

American tobacco companies increased production by 48 percent from 1940 to 1946. Lacking the manpower to meet the demand, R. J. Reynolds Tobacco Company obtained permission from the government to use German prisoners of war. About 250 men from Field Marshal Erwin Rommel's Afrika Korps were sent to Winston-Salem in 1945. Shed 112, a Reynolds storage building that still stands on the corner of Reynolds Boulevard and Indiana Avenue, was converted into a barracks. The prisoners helped make cigarettes in the Number 1 and Number 2 leaf houses. They were shipped back to Germany in 1946.

Some of the former prisoners wrote to the people they had befriended in Winston-Salem. "Shure your [sic] remember this little black haired boy Karlheinz Kroll, who worked with me in your shift," one wrote from Germany soon after the war. "He is working as a construction worker for . . . about 20 cents one hour your currency. . . . Kroll and his mother are living in one room, no stove, no coals, and nearly no food. I think he is too proud to beg for himself, so I do it because I am his friend and I cannot help him otherwise." The Germans' friends in Winston-Salem sent packages of food.

Winston-Salem celebrated the end of the war in 1945 and joyfully welcomed its men home. Three hundred and one did not return.

Pressmen at Twin-City Sentinel *examine the edition that everyone was waiting for.*

The Photograph Collection, Winston-Salem/Forsyth County Public Library

The Shabby and Shopworn City

The servicemen came back to a city that was dirty and frayed. Years of belt-tightening during the Depression and inattention during the war had left an accumulated obsolescence that was frightening. Most of the city's public services, from the library to the sewage plant, were too small or too old. A crosstown car ride meant bouncing over potholes and negotiating traffic jams along the city's narrow streets.

There wasn't even a decent place to eat in 1945. The Hotel Robert E. Lee, the city's showcase, was so unsanitary that the Office of Flying Safety declared it off-limits. Health officials worried about the rats that scurried through the streets at night.

Hotel Robert E. Lee

The Photograph Collection,
Winston-Salem/Forsyth County Public Library

Clearly, it was time for change. City manager John Gold, a proponent of urban expressways, teamed with Mayor Kurfees to push for the parkways and highways that are so familiar to modern Winston-Salem commuters.

A highway to route the traffic off downtown streets was the first priority. Some argued that the road should circle the city, while others, led by Kurfees, favored a more direct route to encourage downtown development. Kurfees prevailed when the city secured cheap right of way through a downtown slum.

The city signed a contract with the state in 1952 to build the East-West Expressway, a limited-access highway that would carry local traffic through town. Construction on the first section, from Main Street west to the city limits, began two years later.

In what certainly was a terrible blunder, federal highway officials acceded to the city's wishes in 1957 and agreed to include the expressway in the interstate highway system. They had planned to build an interstate south of town, but city officials protested. Downtown, they feared, would wilt if traffic were routed away from it. Though not being built to interstate standards, the East-West Expressway was included in the new Interstate 40.

On January 6, 1958, Kurfees cut the ribbon and Joe Bailey threw the switch that bathed the first three-mile section of the expressway in an orange glow. When completed two years later, the six-mile, $16-million highway became part of an interstate that would eventually connect Wilmington, North Carolina, to Barstow, California.

It was with much fanfare that the city ushered in the new age that day in 1958. Dignitaries gathered under the highway bridge over Cloverdale Avenue. Spotlights supplied by the fire department stabbed at the darkening sky. J. Melville Broughton, Jr., representing the State Highway Commission, spoke glowingly of North Carolina's first limited-access highway.

After Kurfees broke out the scissors and Bailey, the outdoor lighting manager for General Electric Company, hit the switch to the streetlights, everyone headed to Forsyth Country Club for speeches and supper.

The new road unclogged downtown streets—the first leg cut crosstown driving time by 15 minutes—but it also reflected the city's boastful personality. Unlike the highway bypasses that later skirted the more demure cities of Greensboro and Raleigh, this road boldly went through the middle of town.

Enough concrete was poured on the first section, the newspaper reported, to provide everyone in town with an eight-by-10-foot porch, and enough steel was used to build 5,000 automobiles. An editorial writer couldn't contain himself. "This is a beautiful strip of roadway," he wrote, "a unique one in this section of the country and one which gives every promise of serving the purpose for which it was intended. Clipping along at 45 miles an hour, hampered neither by stop lights nor intersections, we may even grow to take its convenience for granted."

A highway official was more to the point and closer to the truth. "This is not a roadway for beginners," he warned.

The road was obsolete from the day it opened. Within two years, its design capacity of about 35,000 vehicles a day was exceeded. By 1973, some 62,000 cars and trucks used the road each day. It was the busiest in the state and one of the deadliest. The short access ramps and the serpentine section over Hawthorne Road were the scenes of hundreds of accidents and numerous fatalities.

In 1992, federal highway officials did what they had planned all along, opening Interstate 40 Bypass south of the city, at a cost of $191 million. The old road finally became what planners had envisioned more than 40 years earlier: a local crosstown expressway.

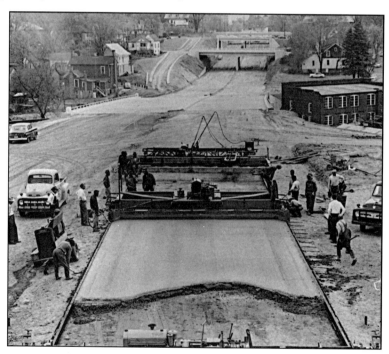

Workers begin paving the first section of the East-West Expressway.

The Photograph Collection, Winston-Salem/Forsyth County Public Library

The Making of Hawthorne Curve

Steel beams span Hawthorne Road as the infamous Hawthorne Curve takes shape.

The Photograph Collection, Winston-Salem/Forsyth County Public Library

The first section of Winston-Salem's grand East-West Expressway through downtown opened in January 1958. Within months, a new term entered the local lexicon—*Hawthorne Curve*. It would come to stand for danger and death.

Seen from the air, it's an elegant thing—a two-mile viaduct between Stratford Road and Peters Creek Parkway. It includes a six-percent grade as it climbs for a mile to the top of Cloverdale Hill, where it ends in a sweeping 10-degree curve. Those features make negotiating the curve hazardous and at times fatal. Before Interstate 40 Bypass opened in 1992, easing traffic on the downtown expressway, the curve was the scene of hundreds of accidents. Its injury rate was nearly twice the average for interstate highways in the state, making Hawthorne Curve one of the most dangerous sections of roadway in North Carolina.

Soon after the highway opened, the curve was labeled a deathtrap, and the finger-pointing began. How could such a thing happen? Who was responsible? Marshall Kurfees was a convenient target. The mayor when the expressway was built, Kurfees had pushed for the road to be routed through downtown. He had made sure that it avoided politically important friends who owned businesses on Hawthorne Road and First Street. That was the rumor, anyway, and a newspaper editor fond of alliteration coined a term to fit it: *Kurfees Curve*.

Kurfees spent much of the rest of his life denying he had anything to do with the curve's design. "It

was the engineers," he said in 1990. "I had about as much to do with it as you did."

The facts seem to support him. To make the proposed six-mile expressway more palatable to state and federal highway planners, Winston-Salem bought much of the right of way. The city had committed more than $1 million to the project when it faced its toughest decision: what to do with the business district at the intersection of Hawthorne and First, the city's first western shopping area. Buying the property would have cost $500,000 and probably would have killed the project. Routing the highway that way would have been akin to building a road through Hanes Mall. To save the highway, the city chose a cheaper route along a curving creek. Town Steak House was the only business that had to be moved.

In defense of parsimonious city officials, no one expected the curve to be subjected to the heavy traffic of an interstate highway. It was designed as part of a local road. Federal officials added the East-West Expressway into their plans for Interstate 40 in 1957, while the expressway was under construction.

Over the years, state highway officials installed flashing warning lights and better guardrails on the curve, but the death toll mounted. It fell only after the new bypass opened. Now that fewer drivers travel the curve, the North Carolina Department of Transportation plans to replace it with a straighter road.

*Cherry Street, looking north from Fourth Street,
showing the Union Bus Station and
the Hotel Robert E. Lee*

The Photograph Collection,
Winston-Salem/Forsyth County Public Library

Slums like these shanties on East Second Street didn't exist, according to the Winston-Salem aldermen.

The Photograph Collection, Winston-Salem/Forsyth County Public Library

Clearing the Slums

What slums?

That was the board of aldermen's reply to Richard J. Reynolds, Jr., who ran unopposed for mayor in 1940 with a promise to clean up the city's slums. After his election, the aldermen issued a report that concluded there were no slums in Winston-Salem. The official verdict prevented the city from receiving federal money for slum clearance.

Reynolds, the only surviving son of the tobacco company's founder, knew better. He had pictures made of black neighborhoods where sewage bubbled to the surface, of rental houses owned by politicians and city officials that had red condemnation notices tacked to the doors. One block of tenements with 32 families had one cold-water spigot and three toilets, two of which were stopped up. Reynolds presented his evidence to federal officials, who gave him money for the first federal housing project in North Carolina. With the money, Reynolds built 338 housing units.

World War II interrupted the work, but Marshall Kurfees and succeeding mayors continued it under the general heading of "urban renewal." The City County Planning Board, formed in 1948, drew up a master plan that included redeveloping the blighted inner city left behind as residents continued to move to the suburbs. Those residents soon were joined by downtown businesses lured to the shopping centers that began sprouting on the city's outskirts after the first, Thruway Shopping Center, opened in 1955.

The Redevelopment Commission, organized in 1951, used federal money and private donations to build low-cost housing and provide space for small businesses to relocate downtown. A project in East Winston removed 2,500 substandard houses and replaced them with $13 million of new construction, including a new hospital for blacks.

Plans to reconstruct a 35-block section of the city's core took shape after a report in 1959 showed that less than half the buildings in the central business district were adequate. More than $100 million in public and private money was invested during the next 15 years. Included in the new construction were some of the city's major buildings: the M. C. Benton Convention Center, the Hall of Justice, and the Wachovia Building, which at 30 stories is one of Winston-Salem's most conspicuous landmarks.

The tearing down and building up had profound, and sometimes negative, effects on the city's black neighborhoods. Whole neighborhoods were demolished, for instance, to make room for expansion at R. J. Reynolds Tobacco Company and Winston-Salem State University. Roads such as Interstate 40, U.S. 52, Univer-sity Parkway, and Peters Creek Parkway were routed through black neighborhoods, destroying large sections of them and setting the boundaries that now define them. Though sincere in its attempt to improve blighted areas, urban renewal disrupted entire neighborhoods and destroyed many of the city's black historical landmarks. More than 600 acres of houses were razed in the early 1960s, and 4,000 families were moved from their homes, some into federal housing projects. Areas such as East Winston, Happy Hills, and Kimberly Park were redeveloped with little regard for the stable, even prosperous, housing areas in those neighborhoods.

Richard J. Reynolds, Jr., center, flanked by Bowman Gray, Jr., left, and an unidentified man.

The Photograph Collection, Winston-Salem/Forsyth County Public Library

*The black business district
along Church and Third streets was demolished
by urban renewal.*

The Photograph Collection,
Winston-Salem/Forsyth County Public Library

Students at Kimberly Park School in 1941
The school burned down in the 1960s and was replaced by the current school.

Joseph Bradshaw Collection

The May Day pageant at Columbia Heights Elementary School in 1947

Joseph Bradshaw Collection

*The J. C. Cleanup Gang ready to do battle with weeds and grime.
The adult leaders from left are Frank Wade, O. A. Brown, and Clark Brown.*

———

Joseph Bradshaw Collection

Harding's Camel City Orchestra raises the roof at Pythian Hall.

Joseph Bradshaw Collection

Saving Old Salem

The old Moravian village wasn't a slum, but it had deteriorated badly by 1947, when a grocer announced plans to build a supermarket in the middle of Salem. Residents howled in protest, and Mayor George Lentz formed the Citizens Committee for the Preservation of Historic Salem. Following its recommendation, the city established the Old and Historic Salem District and banned new construction in the area.

Moravians and non-Moravians, historians and businessmen formed Old Salem, Inc., a nonprofit corporation chartered by the state in 1950. The corporation envisioned spending about $2.5 million to restore eight to 10 historically important buildings. It figured to have the job done by 1966, Salem's bicentennial. The mission gradually broadened, and Old Salem underwent a long-term transformation into a living museum. Using state and local money and private donations, Old Salem, Inc., has restored or reconstructed more than 60 buildings and demolished more than 100 that didn't conform with the museum's 1766-to-1856 time period. Aided by the ample and meticulous records left by the Moravians, the corporation turned the old village into one of the most authentic historical restorations in the country and one of the state's top tourist attractions.

Attendance bottomed out in the 1980s, and Old Salem began losing money. After all, once you've been through the Single Brothers House and visited Winkler Bakery, what else is there? The energetic Hobie Cawood took over the presidency of Old Salem, Inc., in 1991 and immediately shook the cobwebs off the staid museum. He brought in actors to play George Washington and Ben Franklin and opened a kiosk at Hanes Mall where shoppers can buy Moravian cookies and freshly baked bread. Cawood struck a deal with a furniture company for an Old Salem line of chairs and dressers. The result: Old Salem started turning a profit again. Attendance rose to a record 158,115 in 1992.

Hospitals and a College

Like Salem, City Hospital had seen better days when the war ended. Built in 1914, the city's only public hospital for whites was so obsolete that it was one of the major postwar issues.

The old hospital's roots went back to 1887. Thirty-one of Winston-Salem's most prominent women had formed the Twin-City Hospital Association that year. They raised a little money and rented the old Martin Grogan house on Liberty Street. Doctors donated their services, and the mayors of Salem and Winston pledged $12 a month for rent, equipment, and upkeep. The little hospital soon was overrun with patients, and the association moved to a larger building on Brookstown Avenue. Funds were so meager that doctors had to bring their own equipment.

Winston voters approved bonds for a modern hospital in 1912, and City Hospital was completed on East Fourth Street two years later. Separate wings for black and white patients were added in the 1920s after R. J. Reynolds willed $240,000 to the hospital. Blacks got their own hospital, Kate Bitting Reynolds Memorial Hospital, in 1938, when Kate and Will Reynolds gave the city $200,000 to build it.

There things stood until 1959, when voters

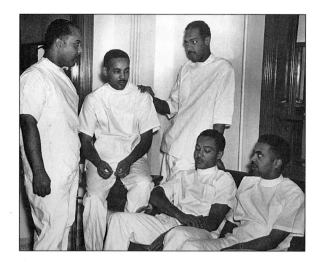

passed a bond referendum to build a modern hospital on 77 acres along Silas Creek Parkway. Blacks were promised a new hospital if they would support the referendum. Forsyth Memorial Hospital opened in 1964, and Reynolds Memorial Hospital for blacks followed six years later. Black patients were transferred to Forsyth Memorial in 1972, and Reynolds Memorial was turned into a family health center, Reynolds Health Center.

Across town, another major hospital was taking shape, thanks in large part to tobacco money. On a single day in 1921, citizens had raised $140,000 toward a building fund established by the North Carolina Baptist State Convention, which wanted to build a hospital in Winston-Salem. North Carolina Baptist Hospital opened two years later on a small hill in an area known as "the wilds of Ardmore."

Before he died in 1935, Bowman Gray, Sr., the president of R. J. Reynolds Tobacco Company, established a fund in his will that consisted of about 14,000 shares of company stock. Four years after his death, the entire fund, worth about $750,000, was offered to Wake Forest College to expand its two-year medical school to a full-fledged four-year program. There was one catch: the medical school had to move from the Raleigh area to Winston-Salem.

The college trustees accepted the offer, and Baptist Hospital agreed to be the school's teaching arm. The medical school, named in honor of its chief benefactor, moved to Winston-Salem in 1941, and classes began the following year.

By the late 1940s, Winston-Salem could boast of major corporations, a growing medical center, an arts council, and dozens of other amenities. However, there was one thing it didn't have that all first-rate cities did: a major college. So the city's leaders decided to buy one. Bearing gifts of Reynolds money and Reynolds land, they approached the trustees of Wake Forest College in 1946. This time, the Z. Smith Reynolds Foundation offered them a $10.7-million endowment if they would move their school to Winston-Salem.

The trustees considered the offer carefully. Wake Forest, founded in 1834, had strong ties with its hometown of the same name, and it had achieved a considerable scholastic reputation under the influence of the Baptists. The North Carolina Baptist State Convention met in special session on July 30, 1946, and accepted the offer with the stipulations that the school retain its name and remain under the control of the convention.

Charles and Mary Reynolds Babcock gave the school a 320-acre tract that was part of the Reynolds estate. Local citizens raised $1.6 million toward the school's building fund of $6 million. Baptist churches, the college's alumni, and the Z. Smith Reynolds Foundation provided the rest of the money.

President Harry Truman, the country's leading Baptist layman, turned over the first spade of dirt at the groundbreaking on October 15, 1951. Classes began five years later.

Top:
Nurses stand in front of the Twin City Hospital on Brookstown Avenue.

Bottom:
The condition of City Hospital built in 1914, was a major issue after World War II.

Baptist Hospital began with a building in the "wilds of Ardmore."

———

The Photograph Collection, Winston-Salem/Forsyth County Public Library

Workers at R. J. Reynolds Tobacco Company go on strike.

The Winston-Salem Journal

"I Shall Not Be Moved"

Thousands of blacks crowded onto the grounds of Woodland Avenue School to call for a strike against R. J. Reynolds Tobacco Company. It was April 27, 1947, the day blacks in Winston-Salem stepped out of the shadows.

For almost 50 years, they had been virtually ignored by the white majority. They had helped build the city, but most couldn't vote, and none could hold public office. They had to sit unseen in the balcony or in the back of the bus. Most restaurants wouldn't serve them; most hotels wouldn't let them in. It was a time of segregation and stereotypes, when a man couldn't drink from a water fountain because of the color of his skin.

Glenn Jones, who was at the school that day, signaled the beginning of the end to all that. Like almost everyone else there, Jones belonged to Local 22 of the Tobacco Workers International Union, which had organized workers at Reynolds in 1944. The union and the company had been haggling over a new contract for almost nine weeks. It was time to make the company take notice, Jones told the crowd. It was time to strike. Ford Hunt seconded the motion, and almost everyone approved. Someone in the crowd started singing a black spiritual from the 1930s. Soon, everyone picked it up.

> I shall not, I shall not be moved,
> I shall not, I shall not be moved,
> Just like a tree planted by the water,
> I shall not be moved.
> When my cross is heavy,
> I shall not be moved.

The strike started on May 1 and lasted for 38 days. It unified blacks in the city for the first time. The white power structure was shocked that blacks could be so organized. Rallies were held almost every Sunday at Shiloh Baptist Church, where the Reverend Robert Pitts, considered the greatest pulpit orator in the city, inspired the crowd. Drives sponsored by the union swelled the number of blacks on the voter rolls from 300 to 3,000.

Published allegations that Communists had infiltrated the union's top leadership broke the back of the strike. The union, discredited and harried by federal investigators who saw Reds everywhere, gradually lost its power and was decertified in 1951.

The union had served its purpose. Black voters in 1947 put the Reverend Kenneth R. Williams on the board of aldermen, making him the first black elected to the board in the 20th century. Blacks soon won seats on the school board and were appointed to public positions. Schools were integrated, and Jim Crow toppled.

"The purpose of the union was to try and get blacks organized and registered to vote," explained William E. Rice, a Winston-Salem native who joined the union picket lines as a high-school student. "Through that effort, we got the first alderman and eventually blacks on the school board and what have you. It was through that arena that blacks became more visible."

African-Americans fared better in Winston-Salem then they did in most Southern cities. R. J. Reynolds Tobacco Company provided steady employment to thousands of blacks, which gave them a relatively high economic standing. A no-frills, but good, black public-school system and Winston-Salem Teachers College encouraged blacks to get an education. So it's not surprising that a study published in 1966 ranked Winston-Salem blacks in the top five economically, socially, and educationally among blacks in Southern cities.

Winston-Salem also had a few progressive

politicians who weren't afraid to champion black causes. The tone was set by Mayor Marshall Kurfees, who appointed blacks to city boards and encouraged slum clearance when such things were considered traitorous by white politicians.

Maybe, then, it's easy to see why there were some anxious moments but no violence when Gwendolyn Y. Bailey entered Reynolds High School in 1957 to become the first black in a white public school in the city. Someone had scrawled "Black Nigger" on Hawthorne Road in front of the school, and a black dummy had been hanged in effigy from the flagpole, but they were removed before Miss Bailey arrived. The late Claude "Pop" Joyner, the school's principal, made it clear to students and teachers that he would stand for no racial incidents.

Integration of all schools in the county continued slowly through the 1960s. By 1969, 45 of the 66 schools in the system were integrated to some degree. A federal judge forced the desegregation of all schools in 1971 by requiring busing to achieve racial balance.

Racial violence did erupt in Winston-Salem in the late 1960s, as it did in dozens of the nation's cities. The worst of the three incidents—and the only one that could be termed a riot—occurred between November 2 and November 5, 1967. Blacks went on a rampage of burning and looting after a black man, James Eller, was killed in a struggle with police. The rioters set about 100 fires and did about $750,000 in damage. The diplomacy of Mayor M. C. "Red" Benton and the appearance of 1,000 National Guardsmen restored order.

Gwendolyn Bailey, left, enters R. J. Reynolds High School accompanied by two reporters.

The Photograph Collection, Winston-Salem/Forsyth County Public Library

A Turkey for Truman

*John Carter, a longtime house steward for the Reynolds family, and his wife pose
with the turkey in the butler's pantry minutes before it was served to President Truman.*

Joseph Bradshaw Collection

The turkey was ready for the president, and John and Marjorie Carter couldn't have been prouder.

The date was October 15, 1951, and President Harry S. Truman was in Winston-Salem for the ground-breaking of Wake Forest College. Before the shoveling and the speech-making, Truman and 50 of the city's most illustrious residents ate lunch at Reynolda House, the home of Charles and Mary Reynolds Babcock.

It was quite a feast: ham, roast beef, peppers stuffed with corn, pickled peaches, whipped potatoes, string beans, peas, cherry tarts, and ice cream. But the big turkey stole the show. Carter always remembered the day and ranked it as the proudest of his life.

Carter, known as "Mr. Reynolda," had been working for the family for almost 50 years when this picture was taken. He and his wife lived in a modest house on West Seventh Street. At Christmas, Carter hauled in the biggest tree he could find and strung it with lights, and music played from outdoor speakers. People lined the street to watch and listen. He always said he would like the tree to be lighted after his death.

He died in 1955, three weeks before Christmas. Babcock brought the tree that year and made sure it was lighted.

"His death is an irreplaceable loss to Reynolda," Babcock said. "I have never known a man of higher integrity."

The Coffee Pot

The Mickeys, of course, liked to include the coffee pot in the pictures of their business.

Collection of Old Salem

Photographers liked to include the coffee pot in their postcard views of the city, as one did in this shot of Main Street in 1907.

North Carolina Division of Archives and History

In 1858, Julius Mickey and his brother Samuel placed a giant tin coffee pot outside their tinsmith shop on South Main Street as a sort of advertising sign. Through the years, the old pot became a favorite of photographers. So many pictures were made of it that the coffee pot became the unofficial symbol for Winston-Salem.

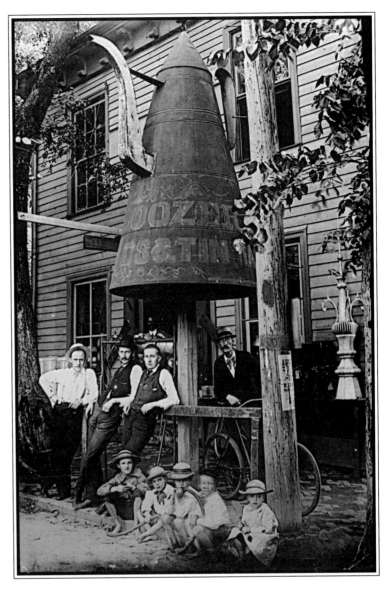

right:

Plumber L. B. Brickenstein, the adult on the left, owned the pot when this photograph was taken in the late 1890s.

below:

Not even the cherished coffee pot could stand in the way of progress, though. It was moved to its present location on Main Street when the East-West Expressway was built in 1960.

The Photograph Collection,
Winston-Salem/Forsyth County
Public Library

Over the years, equipment for firefighting became more modern.

The Photograph Collection, Winston-Salem/Forsyth County Public Library

The city's first all-black fire company was organized in 1950. One of those firefighters, Lester Ervin, was promoted to head the department in 1980 and became the first black fire chief in the state.

Winston-Salem Fire Department

A fire on North Trade Street on November 22, 1964

Winston-Salem Fire Department

Fourth and Liberty streets at Christmas

The Photograph Collection, Winston-Salem/Forsyth County Public Library

A City of the Arts

The Salem Orchestra

The Moravian Archives
of the Southern Province,
Winston-Salem

Virginia Lee Comer panned Winston-Salem's cultural life in 1943. It came as a stinging rebuke to a city that had long prided itself on its artistic heritage. Her harsh critique pricked the city's pride and spurred its leaders into taking actions that have earned Winston-Salem a national reputation as, in the words of one magazine in the early 1980s, "the culturopolis of the South."

A consultant for the Junior League, Comer issued a series of reports that noted the city's lack of art exhibits and art instruction in the high schools. The Little Theater reached a limited audience, she reported, and the city's only museum—the Wachovia Historical Museum—opened only on special occasions. In a state known for its poor libraries, Winston-Salem "stands on the bottom of the list," Comer wrote.

All in all, it was a horrible review for a city that traced its cultural roots to the 1750s, when the Moravians brought their love of music and language to the backwoods of North Carolina. By the late 1800s, the people of Winston and Salem could boast of a classical music society and an orchestra. The Little Theater and the Carnegie Library were formed in the first decade of 20th century. A downtown opera house drew standing-room-only audiences, and the Civic Music Association booked nationally known musicians at R. J. Reynolds Auditorium.

Comer's review, though, served notice that the artistic accomplishments of the past weren't enough. The city had to enliven its old cultural offerings and provide new ones that reached larger audiences. In 1946, the Winston-Salem Civic Orchestra—now the Winston-Salem Piedmont Triad Symphony—and an operetta association were formed.

An organization was needed to coordinate the effort. Twenty-nine people, headed by May Coan Mountcastle, met in August 1949 and formed Arts Council, Inc., the first such organization in the country. The idea was to create a group that could be a clearinghouse for the programming, scheduling, and fund-raising efforts of its members. Eight cultural groups joined that first year. An annual musical revue called the Arts Follies was started in 1952 to raise money for the council's members. The follies, which continued until 1958, netted about $17,000 that first year. The Arts Council of Winston-Salem and Forsyth County now counts about 40 arts and cultural organizations among its members, with yearly fund-raising goals of $1.5 million or more.

The city's leading citizens got together again in 1956 and started the Winston-Salem Gallery of Contemporary Arts in an old piano warehouse. It was the first gallery where local artists could exhibit and sell their work. The gallery moved to Old Salem in 1960 and got a new name in 1974, Southeastern Center for Contemporary Art. The only regional museum of its kind in the United States, SECCA now is in the remodeled home of James G. Hanes off Reynolda Road.

Other art museums and galleries followed, including the Museum of Early Southern Decorative Arts in Old Salem, the Delta Fine Arts Center, Piedmont Craftsmen, and the Sawtooth Center for Visual Design. The most stunning is certainly Reynolda House Museum of American Art, in the rambling 60-room home of R. J. Reynolds. Barbara Lassiter, Reynolds's granddaughter, assembled a wonderful collection of works by American artists— Gilbert Stuart, John Singleton Copley, Thomas Cole, Thomas Hart Benton, Andrew Wyeth. The house opened as a museum in 1965.

To preserve the Moravians' love of music, the Moravian Music Foundation was organized in 1956 to catalog, edit, arrange, and make available music of the Moravians in Wachovia, as well as 18th- and 19th-century music related to the Moravians. The foundation has the best collection of Moravian and colonial American music in the country.

North Carolina School of the Arts solidified Winston-Salem's artistic reputation. The General Assembly appropriated $325,000 in 1964 to start the school. Many cities wanted it. The final contenders were Winston-Salem, Raleigh, Durham, Greensboro, and Hillsborough. Winston-Salem offered the buildings and the 22-acre campus of James A. Gray High School.

Governor Terry Sanford's advisory committee visited the city on April 28, 1964. Early that morning, Smith Bagley and a corps of campaigners began soliciting pledges to raise $900,000 for dormitories. By five o'clock that afternoon, they had $214,729. They achieved their entire goal by the end of the next day. Sanford announced on April 30 that Winston-Salem would get the school. The only one of its kind in the country, the school opened in 1965, offering high-school and college courses in the performing arts.

The school's downtown theater, the Roger L. Stevens Center for the Performing Arts, opened in 1983 amid high expectations. The $13-million renovation of the Carolina Theater on Marshall and Fourth streets was supposed to encourage the redevelopment of downtown. Supporters predicted that the theater would trigger $100 million worth of additional projects that would turn downtown into an arts center. But except for a restaurant in the theater's lobby and a few in the remodeled Woolworth Building next door, the Stevens Center did little to turn the declining fortunes of the city's center.

The theater itself, though, has been a rousing success. Tastefully remodeled, the old Carolina Theater is the city's cultural Parthenon. It struggled its first few years because the arts school, which controls bookings, was too selective in what it allowed to play in the theater and just didn't use it enough. Under a new school administration, the Stevens Center has flourished. It stays booked most of the year with school productions; a Something for Everyone Series, which offers everything from children's sing-alongs to bluegrass bands; and the immensely popular Broadway Preview Series, which brings professional plays to the theater before they hit Broadway.

Some of the country's top black artists perform at the Stevens Center and at other theaters in town during the National Black Theater Festival. Begun in 1989, the festival is held every two years and offers a week-long series of theatrical productions and workshops. The North Carolina Black Repertory Theater oversees the festival. Founded in Winston-Salem in 1979, the organization is the state's foremost black theater ensemble.

The Stevens Center's rise, unfortunately, has been at the expense of Reynolds Auditorium, the once-elegant theater that a grateful Katharine Smith Reynolds gave to the city. After it opened in 1924, Reynolds was the city's main theater. Such national celebrities as Harry Houdini, Will Rogers, and Lily Pons performed on its ample stage.

The auditorium fell into the hands of the school system when city and county schools were consolidated in 1963. Strapped for money, school administrators neglected to properly maintain the building, which fell into sad disrepair. With the opening of the Stevens Center, Reynolds was relegated to being a glorified high-school auditorium for adjacent R. J. Reynolds High School.

Newspaper stories about the building's condition in the early 1990s forced school administrators to appoint a citizens' committee to study how best to use Reynolds. The committee recommended a credible plan to restore Reynolds as a community auditorium. Not wanting to give up control of the building, the school board rejected the plan in 1993 and endorsed a more limited concept presented by school officials. Because their plan depends on school bonds and private contributions, the auditorium's future is uncertain.

The Dixie Classic Fair was smaller in the 1950s.

The Photograph Collection, Winston-Salem/Forsyth County Public Library

Auto races at Bowman Gray Stadium

The Photograph Collection, Winston-Salem/Forsyth County Public Library

Up until the early part of the 20th century, the number of people attending the service at God's Acre in Salem was small.

On Easter morning the sound of brass instruments awakens the residents of Winston-Salem and beckons them to join in a tradition that started in Germany in 1732. The Easter Sunrise Service first was held in Salem 41 years later. Up until the early part of the 20th century, the number of people attending the service at God's Acre in Salem was small. It began to attract large crowds from all over the state in the 1920s and was first broadcast locally on the radio beginning in 1930. The first national broadcast was held 11 years later.

Opposite page:
By the 1960s, people filled the streets of Salem on Easter dawn to celebrate the risen Lord.

The Wall
Begins to Crumble

The Winston-Salem of 1960 was far different from the city that had emerged from World War II. It was larger, for one thing, with a population that topped 100,000 for the first time. It was younger, thanks to a baby boom that dropped the median age to 27.4. And it was slightly richer. The 1950s had been the best of times for the middle class, with the median income in Winston-Salem rising to $6,738, which was second in the state to Charlotte.

A closer look at the city's numbers reveals an odd statistic. The percentage of residents native to North Carolina dropped in the 1950s. North Carolinians had always made up more than 90 percent of Winston-Salem's population. Their percentage fell nearly 10 points by 1960. For the first time since the city's early days, outsiders were moving to town.

Unlike many large Southern cities, Winston-Salem grew from within. All of its major companies began in the city, grew there, and remained there. Their leaders were homegrown men who had very definite ideas about their town. It wasn't until World War II that operations like the Office of Flying Safety and Bowman Gray School of Medicine brought a sizable transfusion of new talents and viewpoints. Major trucking companies such as McLean, Pilot, and Hennis continued the trend by moving their headquarters to Winston-Salem before 1950. A regional office of the Veterans Administration and companies like Bassick-Sack and Duplan came to town after the war, bringing new people with them.

None, though, compared with Western Electric Company, which opened a radio works in the old Chatham Mills plant in 1946. The company was the first major corporation to move to Winston-Salem. Later known as AT&T, it opened two large manufacturing plants that employed thousands of people, and it transferred executives and managers from other plants throughout the country. The infusion of new blood invigorated a city that had become known for its stubborn provincialism.

More large companies followed during the 1960s and 1970s: Varco-Pruden, Westinghouse, Amp, Joseph A. Schlitz Brewing Company. The development of Wake Forest College added considerable leaven to the mix.

The "Big Four"—R. J. Reynolds Tobacco Company, P. H. Hanes Knitting Company, Hanes Hosiery, and Wachovia Bank and Trust Company—continued to exert their influence on Winston-Salem.

By 1960, Reynolds employed one out of every five of the city's workers. It had done well during the war and the decade of prosperity that followed. But with the sweet smell of tobacco hanging over the city in 1954 came a hint of trouble. Scientists began linking smoking to lung cancer that year. Bowman Gray, Jr., the company's president, started the line of defense that the tobacco industry has clung to ever since: there was nothing to it, said Gray, a four-pack-a-day man.

But just in case, Reynolds introduced its first filtered brands, Winstons and Salems, in the mid-1950s. By 1966, Winstons were the top-selling cigarette in the country, and Salems weren't far behind. The popularity of those brands and the old standby—Prince Albert pipe tobacco—made Reynolds the country's leading tobacco company in 1958, a position it had lost to American Tobacco Company in 1941. Reynolds had sales of more than $1 billion, and its profit margins were the highest in the industry. Its stock was considered the bluest of the blue chips. There is a story about a young boy who rushed to the tree on Christmas morning. He ignored the train set and the shiny new bike and turned away disappointed. "What, no Reynolds Common A?" he said.

The company began diversifying in the 1960s. RJR Foods, a subsidiary started in 1963, acquired food brands like Hawaiian Punch and Chun King. Sea-Land Service was added to the company in 1969, as was American Independent Oil Company—Aminoil—in 1970. A new parent company, R. J. Reynolds Industries, Inc., also was created that year. It had sales of $4 billion in 1975 and employed 33,600 people worldwide.

Hanes Hosiery was the largest maker of seamless hosiery in the world by the end of the 1940s. P. H. Hanes Knitting Company continued its dominance of the underwear business. The two companies merged in 1965 to become Hanes Corporation.

Wachovia Bank and Trust Company, under the leadership of president John F. Watlington, became the first bank in the Southeast to reach $1 billion in deposits.

In 1937, the city had 97 factories that turned out $349 million in products. Ten years later, 250 factories produced $1 billion in goods. Aside from tobacco and textiles, products included electronic equipment, furniture, batteries, air conditioners, industrial machinery, mattresses, wagons, paint, swimming suits, toys, and chemicals.

South of Richmond and east of the Mississippi, there wasn't another industrial center like Winston-Salem. It produced seven times more than any other city in the Carolinas. There seemed to be no end in sight for "the City of Industry."

A City with a Heart

Many cities boast more people than Winston-Salem. Many can claim more buildings and more parks, more schools and restaurants and theaters. Few have more heart.

Since the first Moravians arrived in 1753 and tended to their sick neighbors, Winston-Salem always has been known as a caring place. The brothers and sisters of Salem took it as an article of faith to look out for one another. More than a century later, Annie Grogan, who became known as the "mother of charity," rode her buggy through the streets of Winston to collect for Associated Charities, the city's first organized private charity. Her legacy lives on. The modern Winston-Salem has led the country in per capita giving to the United Way.

The city's largess is the stuff of legend. Smith Bagley and R. Philip Hanes, Jr., raised nearly $1 million in two days in 1964 to bring North Carolina School of the Arts to Winston-Salem. Dale Gramley and Henry Kamm had no problem collecting $225,000 at one luncheon to ensure that the North Carolina Governor's School for gifted students came to the city. A campaign to expand Baptist Hospital and Bowman Gray School of Medicine once raised $7 million, and Old Salem, Inc., achieved half its goal in a recent fund-raiser before the campaign officially began. Winston-Salem's largest industries and most prominent citizens have left land and money to build parks, schools, churches, libraries, museums, and auditoriums.

Some of them established charitable foundations that are now among the 10 largest in the state. The Kate B. Reynolds Health Care Trust, the Z. Smith Reynolds Foundation, the Mary Reynolds Babcock Foundation, and the Winston-Salem Foundation have almost $700 million in combined assets. They give millions of dollars each year to the needy and to various worthwhile projects throughout the South. The city and Forsyth County are home to 49 charitable foundations in all. In North Carolina, only Charlotte and Mecklenburg County, with 130 foundations, have more.

A view of Winston-Salem during the construction of the Wachovia Building

The Photograph Collection, Winston-Salem/Forsyth County Public Library

Dates to Remember

1941 Wake Forest College's two-year medical school moves to Winston-Salem and becomes Bowman Gray School of Medicine.

1942 A new terminal at the airport is completed with a gift from the Reynolds family, and the airport is renamed for Z. Smith Reynolds. Workers at Reynolds and other tobacco plants organize a union.

1943 Malcolm P. McLean begins Winston-Salem's tradition as a trucking center when he moves the headquarters of McLean Trucking to the city. Pilot Freight Carriers and Hennis Freight Lines establish headquarters in the city before 1950. For years, they are the "big three" among the 40 trucking companies with headquarters in Winston-Salem.

1945 Oscar Morris, the city's first black police officer, is sworn in.

1946 Western Electric opens its radio works in the old Chatham Mills plant. Later known as AT&T, the company subsequently opens major manufacturing plants on Old Lexington Road and Reynolda Road. The North Carolina Baptist State Convention agrees to move Wake Forest College to Winston-Salem.

1947 Unionized workers, mostly black, strike R. J. Reynolds Tobacco Company for 38 days. Winston-Salem hires its first city manager, C. E. Perkins.

1948 Piedmont Airlines, based in Winston-Salem, begins commercial passenger service with a flight from Wilmington to Cincinnati. The airline carries about 40,000 passengers to 22 cities the first year.

1949 The Winston-Salem Arts Council begins. It is the first permanent organization of its kind in the country. Marshall Kurfees is elected mayor of Winston-Salem.

1950 Old Salem, Inc., is chartered to rescue the old Moravian village. WAAA, the state's first black radio station, begins broadcasting.

1951 President Harry Truman presides over groundbreaking ceremonies for the new campus of Wake Forest College. The school moves from its site near Raleigh five years later.

1953 WSJS-TV, the city's first television station, goes on the air. The Forsyth County Jail opens on Church Street, replacing a jail built in 1908.

1954 R. J. Reynolds Tobacco Company introduces Winstons, which become the best-selling cigarette brand in the country. Salems are introduced in 1956 and become the top menthol cigarette.

1955 War Memorial Auditorium opens. So does Thruway Shopping Center, the city's first.

1956 Ernie Shore Field opens.

1957 Gwendolyn Y. Bailey begins the slow process of integrating the public schools when she enrolls at all-white R. J. Reynolds High School. It is 14 years before the school system is completely desegregated.

1958 The first section of the East-West Expressway, now Interstate 40 Business, opens.

1959 Winston-Salem wins the first of its two All-America City awards. The second comes in 1964.

1960 Winston-Salem/Forsyth County Industrial Center opens. Its name is changed three years later to Forsyth Technical Institute. The name is later changed to Forsyth Technical Community College.

1961 R. J. Reynolds Tobacco Company opens Whitaker Park, the largest and most modern cigarette factory in the world.

1963 Voters approve the consolidation of city and county schools, creating the second-largest school system in the state.

1964 Forsyth Memorial Hospital opens.

Some of Piedmont Airlines' first pilots pose in front of one of the airline's DC-3s.

The Photograph Collection, Winston-Salem/Forsyth County Public Library

1965   North Carolina School of the Arts opens in old Gray High School. Two companies started by members of the same family—P. H. Hanes Knitting Company and Hanes Hosiery—merge to form Hanes Corporation. Reynolda House opens as a museum of American art.

1966   Winston-Salem's tallest and most conspicuous landmark, the 30-story Wachovia Building, is completed. At the time, it is the tallest building in the Southeast. Bobbie B. Bircham and Lillian Bonner, the city's first female police officers, are sworn in.

1967   Blacks riot after a black man is killed by police. Stores are burned and looted, but no one is seriously injured. These riots are the most serious of three racial disturbances of the late 1960s. The others occur in 1969.

1969   M. C. Benton Convention Center opens. Joseph A. Schlitz Brewing Company opens a brewery south of Winston-Salem. The company is bought by Stroh's Brewing Company in 1982. Stroh's is bought by Coors Brewing Company in 1989.

Names to Know

Charles and Mary Reynolds Babcock

A graceful and compassionate man, Babcock was an investment broker who married Mary Reynolds, one of R. J. Reynolds's daughters. They were two of the city's great philanthropists. They provided the land for the Wake Forest College campus and were two of the guiding lights behind the restoration of Old Salem. Babcock had a hand in many other projects, including Meals on Wheels and the restoration of Bethabara. The Mary Reynolds Babcock Foundation gave Wake Forest University $2 million in 1968 to establish the Babcock Graduate School of Management.

Gwendolyn Y. Bailey

She was 15 that fall day in 1957 when she entered Reynolds High School and became the first black student to attend an all-white county school. She graduated two years later and attended Winston-Salem Teachers College. She now is a teacher and minister in Maryland.

Archie K. Davis

Davis personifies Winston-Salem's dedication to service. A city native who became senior vice president and chairman of Wachovia Bank and Trust Company, Davis spent a lifetime working for his city and state. Research Triangle Park and the National Humanities Center would not be what they are today without Davis's prodigious fund-raising talents. Old Salem, Inc., the Moravian Archives, Salem College, and his beloved University of North Carolina all have benefited from Davis's touch. American presidents appointed him to commissions looking into government waste and the future of the South, and governors called him whenever they needed money raised for a good cause. Like his hometown, Davis always was quick to respond. "If you don't want me to do anything for the state, don't ask. It's that simple; it really is," said Davis, who retired from Wachovia in 1974. "It's almost a life of debt as far as I'm concerned because of what this state has meant to me and my family. You owe a powerful debt. You can't live long enough when you think about it."

Thomas H. Davis

A Winston-Salem native who had been flying since he was 16, Davis teamed with Lewin McGinnis in 1940 to start Piedmont Aviation, Inc. They began by selling and servicing small aircraft at Miller Airport. Davis bought out his partner in 1942. Five years later, he received a license to fly commercial flights to small cities and towns in the region that the national airlines missed. Piedmont Airlines began the next year with six DC-3s and 12 pilots. When Davis retired as the company's president in 1983, Piedmont employed 12,500 people, and its routes covered the country. USAir bought Piedmont in 1987.

Edward O. Diggs

A Winston-Salem native, Diggs was working as a mail clerk in Greensboro in 1951 when he applied to the medical school at the University of North Carolina. He was accepted and became the first black to attend the university. He went on to a successful practice in Washington.

Archie K. Davis

The Photograph Collection, Winston-Salem/Forsyth County Public Library

Archie Elledge

"Mr. Arch" was the most colorful and controversial alderman Winston-Salem has ever had. He served for 16 years until his death in 1966. His was the style of the old-time Populist. "The little man," "the working man," and "the taxpayer" appeared frequently in his public vocabulary. Tough and gentle by turns, Elledge would rear back in his padded chair in the council chambers, his coat unbuttoned, a rosebud in his lapel, a bow tie around his neck. "My dad used to say, 'Say what you mean and mean what you say,'" he would chide speakers and other aldermen. He often was at odds with Mayor Marshall Kurfees, the two exchanging barbs at meetings and in the newspaper. Elledge exerted influence on every major decision of city government during his tenure. He was a leader in the effort to expand and improve the city's water and sewer systems and was influential in bringing about the rerouting of the East-West Expressway, now Interstate 40 Business, to avoid splitting a residential neighborhood. Because of Elledge's leadership in getting bonds passed for a new sewer plant, Kurfees named it after him in 1965. Some considered it a back-handed compliment, but Elledge was proud of the honor.

John M. Gold

He was city manager of Winston-Salem for 21 years, until his death in 1972. A proponent of urban expressways, Gold had a hand in planning the East-West Expressway, the North-South Expressway—now U.S. 52—and the city's parkway system. The section of U.S. 52 through Winston-Salem was named in his honor in 1975.

Bowman Gray, Jr.

Gray followed in his father's footsteps at R. J. Reynolds Tobacco Company. He started as a salesman in 1930 and was president and chairman of the board by 1959. Gray urged the company to produce its first filtered brand, Winston, in 1954 to counter the emerging evidence of smoking's ill effects on health. He personally chose the tobacco blend for Winston—number 736—out of the 250 blends that the company tested. When Gray died in 1969, R. J. Reynolds Tobacco Company was considered the best-managed tobacco company in the country.

Gordon Gray

Unlike his brother Bowman Gray, Jr., and the other members of his family, Gray didn't enter the tobacco business. He practiced law in New York and Winston-Salem before buying the *Winston-Salem Journal*, the *Twin-City Sentinel*, and WSJS Radio. He was among the first Southern newspaper publishers to hire black reporters. Like so many members of the city's prominent families, Gray ran for public office. He was elected to the state senate in 1939, 1941, and 1947, running unopposed. After resigning his senate seat in 1942 to volunteer as a private in the army, he began what must have been one of the most meteoric careers in military history. Commissioned a second lieutenant, Gray joined General Omar Bradley's 12th Army Group in Europe as an intelligence officer. He was discharged a captain in 1945. Two years later, Gray

was appointed assistant secretary of the army by President Harry Truman. He became secretary of the army in 1949. Bradley, his former boss, was his chief of staff. Gray resigned a year later to become president of North Carolina's Consolidated University System but continued to take government assignments. He helped form the country's Cold War strategy as director of the Psychological Strategy Board. He resigned his university job to become assistant secretary of defense under President Dwight Eisenhower. Gray died in 1982.

Pleasant Huber Hanes, Jr.

It was often said about Hanes that he didn't want to own all the land in Forsyth County, just the land next to his. When he saw a nice piece of property, Hanes bought it. "Then he'd send for the bulldozer," a friend once said. The result was Stratford Road. That may be an exaggeration, but Hanes did develop much of the commercial district that sprawls along Stratford Road across what were once the vast holdings of the Hanes family. In 1970, he sold 108 acres of Burke Farm, which had belonged to his grandfather, Pleasant Henderson Hanes, to Sears, Roebuck & Company. From the one-time cornfields rose the bricks and mortar that would bear his name—Hanes Mall. But Hanes did more than unleash bulldozers to lay bare

Gordon Gray talks to employees at the Winston-Salem Journal.

The Photograph Collection,
Winston-Salem/Forsyth County Public Library

the Piedmont's red clay. He was a caring man who fought to preserve Pilot Mountain, and he made city beautification an article of faith. Hanes once offered to install clutter-free traffic lights at an intersection on Main Street just to prove to the city that it could be done. He took over the running of P. H. Hanes Knitting Company from his father and approved the merger with Hanes Hosiery in 1965. He was the first president of the resulting Hanes Corporation. Hanes died in 1974.

Velma Hopkins

A native of Asheville, Hopkins moved to Winston-Salem as a child. She took a job in the stemming room at R. J. Reynolds Tobacco Company and became chairman of a committee that organized a union at Reynolds in the 1940s. Hopkins remained a tireless and aggressive proponent of civil rights.

Lawrence Joel is honored with a parade after winning the Medal of Honor.

The Photograph Collection,
Winston-Salem/Forsyth County Public Library

Lawrence Joel

Winston-Salem's only Medal of Honor winner, Joel, who grew up in East Winston, was a medic in the army's 82nd Airborne Division during the Vietnam War. He was cited for conspicuous gallantry in 1965 when his unit was ambushed by 700 Vietcong north of Saigon. Wounded twice, Joel bandaged himself and continued to help the wounded in his unit until they were evacuated. He was credited with saving at least 13 wounded soldiers. President Lyndon Johnson gave Joel the medal in 1967. Joel died in 1984. After much debate filled with racial overtones, the city named its new coliseum for him in 1986. The coliseum opened three years later.

Marshall Kurfees

Mayor for 16 years, Kurfees was the first man elected to the office who didn't have the backing of the city's business leaders. An able, hardworking mayor, Kurfees improved the city's roads and hospitals and appointed blacks to city boards.

Carl W. Matthews

On February 8, 1960, a week after the historic lunch-counter sit-in in Greensboro, Matthews took a seat at the lunch counter of the S. H. Kress store in downtown Winston-Salem. The store manager closed the counter rather than serve him. Matthews subsequently led 21 people to the Kress store on North Liberty Street on February 23. They were arrested and charged with trespassing.

Robert Neilson

Some would say that Bob Neilson was the father of modern Winston-Salem. He worked for the city's public-works department for 50 years. As a young engineer, Neilson staked a city reservoir on Salem Creek in 1917, and as the head of the department for 12 years, he saw to the laying of miles of water pipe. Almost 300 miles of streets were paved during Neilson's time, and private privies were replaced by a modern sewer system. He retired in the 1970s and wrote a two-volume history of Winston-Salem's government. In 1963, a new water-treatment plant was named for Neilson.

Richard J. Reynolds, Jr.

Reynolds bore little resemblance to his famous father. An often-married international playboy who tended to be a maverick and a loner, he ran unopposed for mayor in 1940 and promptly annexed the city's rich—including himself—who had built large estates outside town to avoid the higher taxes. As mayor, he sided with cabdrivers in their strike against management, explaining that he knew what it was like to drive a cab, having done so after running away from home as a teenager. He also was a seaman on a freighter and the pilot of a sightseeing plane in New York. One thing he never did was become an executive in the tobacco company his father founded. "They seem to be getting along all right without me," he once explained. Often overlooked are Reynolds's contributions to the city. He gave the family's homesite on West Fifth Street to the county for the main branch of the library and made sizable donations to Baptist Hospital, the YWCA, and the Wachovia Historical Society. He died in Switzerland in 1964.

Carl H. Russell, Sr.

The most prominent black politician in the city in the 1960s and 1970s, Russell was elected to the board of aldermen in 1961. He remained on the board for 16 years and was noted for his efforts to improve housing, education, and medical care for blacks. The flamboyant, cigar-chomping Russell ran for mayor in 1977 and finished first in the Democratic primary. Lacking a majority of the vote, he was forced into a runoff with Wayne A. Corpening, who won the runoff and the general election. In 1966, Russell became the city's first black mayor pro tem, a position he held for eight years. He had a long history of delinquent taxes and faced legal action by the city. "I think it's more important to keep my children in college than to pay my taxes on time," said Russell, the father of 10. He also was a successful businessman, having started Russell Funeral Home in 1939. He died in 1987, but not before seeing the city honor his services by naming a community center for him at Helen W. Nichols Park.

John C. Whitaker

"Mr. John" joined R. J. Reynolds Tobacco Company in 1913 and was an operator on the first machine that made Camel cigarettes. He was made president of the company in 1948 and chairman of the board four years later. The most beloved of the company's executives, Whitaker liked to brag that he could walk through the factories and know everyone by their first name. The company named its huge manufacturing plant for him in 1958. Forsyth Memorial Hospital named its rehabilitation center after him in honor of his support. Whitaker died in 1978.

Kenneth R. Williams

Reared in Winston-Salem and educated in Boston, the Reverend Williams was the chancellor of Winston-Salem State University for 16 years, starting in 1961. In 1947, he became the first black elected to the board of aldermen in the 20th century.

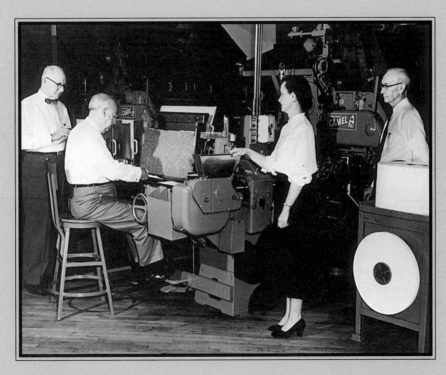

John C. Whitaker, the president of R. J. Reynolds Tobacco Company, shows employees how to run a cigarete machine. Whitaker started with the company in 1913, operating the first machines that made Camels.

The Photograph Collection, Winston-Salem/Forsyth County Public Library

Looking east on Fourth Street about 1970

———

The Photograph Collection, Winston-Salem/Forsyth County Public Library

The End and a New Beginning

Cities, like people, evolve and grow and, yes, die. The countryside is littered with the carcasses of once-grand places abandoned by their people because of economic turmoil or the routing of a railroad or some great natural disaster.

Winston-Salem could have been such a place. If not for its will, the city could have folded up and become a sad footnote in the history of the 1980s, a time of unfettered economic expansion that shook Winston-Salem to its very soul.

Buyouts, mergers, bankruptcies, and foreign competition claimed its venerable companies one by one: Hanes Corporation, McLean Trucking, Piedmont Airlines, AT&T. Each jolt was harder than the preceding one. The biggest came in 1987. RJR Nabisco, Inc., the giant corporation that had grown from the "little red factory" on Depot Street, announced that it was shedding more than 100 years of tradition by moving its headquarters to Atlanta. The company that had nurtured Winston-Salem, that had helped build hospitals and schools, that had provided so much of the city's leadership and identity was simply leaving town. It was a dagger to Winston-Salem's proud heart.

"The Move," as it became known, was a turning point, more important to Winston-Salem than the sorry spectacle that followed—the bidding war that reduced a great company to a mere object of greed. The Move served notice that the stability of the old days and the leadership of the old guard were gone.

The uncertainty and fear that gripped Winston-Salem in 1989 were played out in a bitter and divisive mayoral race that year. It pitted a candidate supported by what was left of the old power structure against Martha S. Wood, an alderman who campaigned for a more diversified and open government. Her election marked the opening of a new chapter in the city's history.

That chapter is still being written, but it's clear that Winston-Salem is no longer the company town it once was. Its economy is more diversified and no longer as reliant on the strength of a few large manufacturers. Neither does the city depend totally on them for guidance. For the first time in Winston-Salem's history, its future is being charted outside corporate boardrooms.

There are problems still, such as crime and race relations, and finding leadership to replace what was lost has not been easy, but Winston-Salem emerged from the crucible of the 1980s a better place. Instead of dying, it evolved and is better prepared to meet the challenges of a new millennium.

The Most Hated Man in Town

Bucolic.

It's a nice word for describing a shepherd tending his flock or a picturesque farmhouse in a mountain valley. And maybe F. Ross Johnson didn't mean much by it when he used the word to describe Winston-Salem, but it earned him the lasting enmity of an entire city.

Johnson is the outsider who ruined R. J. Reynolds Tobacco Company. Ask anyone who lived in Winston-Salem during the 1980s and that's what he or she will tell you. He's remembered for spending the money of a company known for its frugality on fleets of white limos and shiny jets, on Rolls Royces and Rolex watches, on homes in Palm Beach and fashionable apartments in New York. He's remembered for disdaining 112 years of tradition by moving the company headquarters to Atlanta. But most of all, Johnson is remembered for calling proud Winston-Salem *bucolic*.

It was 1987, and Johnson was describing to a reporter of the *Atlanta Constitution* why he moved the headquarters of RJR Nabisco, Inc., the company that had been formed after the merger of R. J. Reynolds Industries, Inc., and Nabisco Brands, Inc., in 1985. The new company, he said, had to attract young, highly specialized professionals. "You find them [in Atlanta] because that's where they want to live. They have a distinct lifestyle," said Johnson, the company's president and chief executive officer. "They are interested in the arts, or they are interested in education. They look for, not only their own style of living, but for peers like themselves. You're not going to find that in a Winston-Salem or a Greensboro."

That snub was bad enough for a city that prided itself on its cultural heritage and on being the home of Wake Forest University. Johnson, though, wasn't done. Winston-Salem, he said, was just too "bucolic."

Johnson immediately became the man Winston-Salem loved to hate. Bumper stickers that said "Honk If You're Bucolic" became hot items. Cartoons showing Johnson scaling the Reynolds Building King Kong–style started appearing on company bulletin boards all over town. A retired factory worker who had become a major stockholder reminded Johnson in a letter, "We built the foundations for this company while you were still in knee pants."

Such vitriol surprised Johnson. Moving the corporate headquarters involved only a couple of hundred people, and Johnson made up for the loss by relocating the Planters LifeSavers division to Winston-Salem. To a rootless man like Johnson, tradition meant little. He was part of the nomadic breed of executives that came to power in the 1980s, men not bound by history or company or loyalty. Increase the price of the stock to make the shareholders wealthy—that was his goal, even if it meant selling age-old brands, adding new businesses, and firing employees whose fathers and grandfathers had worked for the company. Deals and yields were his life. To stand still, he said, was to fail. In tradition-bound, staid Winston-Salem, such a man was like a Formula One racecar puttering around Bowman Gray Stadium.

A native of Manitoba, Johnson did not escape the wilds of the Canadian provinces to settle back quietly. He could have done that in Toronto, where he worked for pressed-suit General Electric. Johnson got a master's in business administration while in Toronto, but his career at GE was going nowhere. After 13 years, he left, moving among small Canadian companies and acquiring a reputation as a man who thumbed his nose at authority and organization.

In 1971, Johnson was 40 years old and still had not run his own company. His chance came when he was made president of the Canadian arm of Standard Brands, a solid but unexciting American food company best known for Fleischmann's Margarine and Chase & Sanborn Coffee. Johnson made the most of the opportunity. Within two years, he was running the company's international operations, and by 1976, he was the chief operating officer of the entire company. Four months later, Johnson became the chief executive after orchestrating the ouster of his boss.

Standard Brands had always been conservative with its money, but Johnson loosened the purse strings. He tripled his salary and gave hefty raises to the other executives. He bought a company jet, a company Jaguar, and a company box at Madison Square Garden in New York. Breezy and likable, Johnson started paling around with sports personalities such as Don Meredith and Frank Gifford.

Underneath the loose exterior was a good businessman, though. Johnson made Standard attractive to Nabisco, the food giant. The two companies merged in 1981, with Johnson as the number-two man in the renamed Nabisco Brands, Inc. He was running the company in three years.

When R. J. Reynolds Industries came calling, Johnson held out for the number-two spot in the new company. Eager to strike the deal, J. Tylee Wilson, Reynolds's president and chief executive officer, acceded. Reynolds bought Nabisco for $4.9 billion, which at the time was the largest corporate acquisition outside the oil industry.

Within a year, Johnson had Wilson's job. He immediately purged the executive ranks of longtime Reynolds employees and replaced them with Nabisco people. "Looks as if someone may have underestimated the cookie monster's appetite," the *Winston-Salem Journal* frowned in an editorial.

Because of tobacco's high profit margins, Reynolds churned out $1 billion in profit a year. That was real money, and Johnson was just the man to milk the cash cow. Bryan Burrough and John Helyar summed it up best in *Barbarians at the Gate*, their book about the RJR Nabisco buyout: "Out went the Moravian: Make way for the bacchanalian."

James A. Gray, Jr., one of Johnson's predecessors in the president's chair, had prided himself on walking to work each day. Johnson preferred Jaguars and Rolls Royces. Gray's brother, Bowman, another Reynolds president, had left money to start a medical school. Johnson's idea of benevolence was organizing a pro-am golf tournament. He jetted off each weekend in a company plane to the company house in Palm Springs or his own houses in Florida and New York. The carpet in his office in Atlanta was said to cost $200 a yard.

Such free spending shocked the sensibilities of the folks back in Winston-Salem, a city Johnson tried to avoid. He did return to play in the Vantage Pro-Am golf tournament, arriving in a helicopter and accompanied by a bodyguard—another first for a Reynolds executive. But there was no protection from the invective that rained down on Johnson from the gallery. Not even his playing partner, the popular Arnold Palmer, was spared. "Nice drive, Arnie!" someone hollered. "Too bad you have to play with that son of a bitch."

Economic Turmoil

Winston-Salem entered the 1980s with about 130,000 people, which was less than the population 10 years earlier. It marked the first time in the city's history that its population declined. Residents during the 1970s continued the trend that had started in earnest 20 years earlier. They fled the city and its higher taxes for suburbs like Clemmons and Kernersville or subdivisions just outside the city. Winston-Salem, one of the least aggressive cities in the state when it came to annexation, didn't extend its borders to reclaim them.

Its economy, though, remained the envy of other cities its size. It was the home of R. J. Reynolds Tobacco Company and Piedmont Airlines. Sara Lee Corporation, which bought Hanes Corporation in 1979, was among the state's textile leaders. AT&T employed more than 3,000 people making telephone transmis-

sion equipment, and the city was the center of the trucking industry in the Southeast.

Unrestrained free enterprise and a dislike of government regulations marked the 1980s. Corporations went on a borrowing binge, piling on mountains of debt—much of it to buy or merge with other companies. The threat of cheap foreign competition forced many companies to reorganize, closing plants and firing workers.

These forces first claimed the city's trucking industry. The deregulation of the trucking industry in 1980 allowed thousands of small companies to start hauling freight. Prices fell, and many companies couldn't compete. Spector Red Ball, which owned Winston-Salem's Hennis Freight Lines, declared bankruptcy in 1982. McLean Trucking followed four years later. Pilot Freight Carriers—the last of the "big three"—closed its terminal in Kernersville in 1989.

In contrast, high-flying Piedmont Airlines became a victim of its own success. In 1948, its first year, the small regional airline had carried 40,000 passengers to 22 cities that other airlines bypassed. By the mid-1980s, Piedmont was flying millions of passengers all over the country. Its financial success, solid reputation, and attractive routes appealed to USAir, which wanted to expand. It bought Piedmont for $1.59 billion in November 1987. The last Piedmont flight landed at South Bend, Indiana, shortly before midnight on Friday, August 4, 1989. The next day, the airline became part of USAir.

Only four of Piedmont's original 40 officers remained with the new airline, and many mid-level managers and clerical workers refused transfers to lesser jobs and quit in frustration. USAir made up for the job losses by transferring its accounting and computing departments to Winston-Salem. Though the city gained about 100 jobs overall, many were low-paying clerical positions that didn't offset the loss of the executives at Piedmont's headquarters. USAir also built a shop to repair landing gear at Smith Reynolds Airport that added about 100 more jobs.

No similar compensation accompanied the closing of AT&T's giant plant on Lexington Road. The company announced in 1988 that the plant, with its 3,300 jobs, would shut down. Deregulation had come in January 1984 in the wake of an out-of-court settlement of a suit brought by the United States Justice Department. The settlement ended AT&T's monopoly of long-distance telephone service and forced the company to splinter into 22 regional telephone companies.

AT&T was left with three core businesses, including Networks Systems on Lexington Road. For years, the company had essentially sold equipment to itself without worrying much about cost. After the settlement, independent telephone companies were free to buy from the most competitive suppliers, which were in Japan and not on Lexington Road.

The Decline of RJR

In the mid-1950s, R. J. Reynolds Tobacco Company was the top cigarette maker in the world, a fantastically successful hometown company ruled by homegrown men. Within 30 years, it became a flashy international conglomerate run by strangers who flew to golf tournaments in helicopters. In the process, Reynolds lost its standing as the country's top tobacco company.

The stage was set for the company's decline in the early 1950s, when the first scientific studies linking cigarette smoking to lung cancer and heart disease were published. Cigarette sales declined seven percent in two years, but then began to rise again. Having seen the future, however, Reynolds executives embarked on a diversification campaign that would prove disastrous to the company's core tobacco business.

The company's link to its founder was broken in 1969 with the death of its president, Bowman Gray, Jr. The reins of power passed to a string of successors who acted as if they were in charge of something other than a tobacco company. They acquired companies that made soft drinks, wine, pineapple chunks, fried chicken, Chinese food. Tobacco became just one of the many products of R. J. Reynolds Industries, Inc. Though it provided most of the company's profits, the tobacco business was neglected and its manufacturing equipment allowed to get old.

Philip Morris USA, a relatively minor cigarette maker in the 1950s, took a different course. Instead of trying to find new products to sell in a shrinking domestic market, the company entered into joint deals with foreign tobacco companies. Riding the popularity of its Marlboro brand, Philip Morris became the top cigarette manufacturer in the world in 1972, though Reynolds still claimed the top spot in the country.

J. Paul Sticht became president of Reynolds the following year and its chief executive officer by the end of the decade. The first outsider to head the company, Sticht tried to stave off the upstart competitor. He started an international tobacco division in 1975 and embarked on a $2-billion modernization of the company's aging tobacco plants that included the construction of a huge manufacturing plant in Tobaccoville, in northern Forsyth County. The plant began production in 1986.

Convinced that Reynolds needed new blood with new ideas to beat Philip Morris, Sticht remade the company's corporate structure. He replaced tobacco executives with outsiders who knew little about selling cigarettes. Philip Morris overtook Reynolds as the nation's top cigarette manufacturer in 1983.

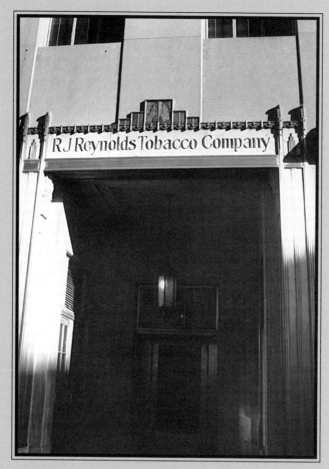

The company that
R. J. Reynolds started in
a small factory on Depot
street was transformed in
the 1980s.

The Greater Winston-Salem
Chamber of Commerce

The Humble Nouveau Riches

Neat rows of little 40-year-old houses lined the quiet residential street. Old cars and trucks were parked in the driveways. Inside, cross-stitched homilies about family and home hung on the walls and color pictures of smiling grandchildren graced the mantels.

Winston-Salem's new Millionaire's Row looked much like hundreds of other neighborhoods in town. But in that Southside neighborhood, four retired employees of R. J. Reynolds Tobacco Company lived within two blocks of each other. Each had worked for the company for at least 30 years, accumulating a sizable amount of company stock. And each had become fantastically wealthy in 1989 after the takeover of RJR Nabisco, Inc.

The thousands of stockholders who were forced to sell their stock all shared in the $2.5 billion that flowed into Winston-Salem in early 1989. As the Wall Street equivalent of lottery winners, the RJR shareholders captured the fancy of the country's major newspapers and magazines. Hordes of reporters descended on Winston-Salem. They came looking for millionaires in bib overalls driving shiny Cadillacs, for country bumpkins so overjoyed with their good fortune that they lavishly spent their new wealth on big cars, fancy homes, and exotic vacations.

The reporters were shocked to learn that these people weren't happy at all, even though they had doubled their wealth in less then six weeks. Instead of praising F. Ross Johnson for making them rich, the local shareholders took delight in a song that a Winston-Salem stockbroker had recorded. Sung to the tune of "Frosty the Snowman," the chorus went,

> F. Rossie the snowman had a triple comma dream,
> You can have the skim milk and I'll make do with cream.
> Hey all you bucolics, here's a deal that's really sweet.
> You take title to the chaff and I'll haul off the wheat.

"You have to remember," the stockbroker told one of the reporters. "Reynolds isn't a stock; it's a religion."

The majority of the company's stockholders had worked most of their lives at Reynolds, putting a little away each month for company stock. They had planned to hold onto it, maybe using it to buy a home or put the children through college or cushion their retirement. Having come through the Depression, they had always been conservative with their money. Just because they suddenly had more of it than they had ever dreamed possible was no reason to change. Treasury notes and certificates of deposit, not Cadillacs and beach houses, were the hottest sellers after the buyout.

Mrs. C., one of those Southside millionaires, was typical. There's no need to use her full name. Money matters are, after all, rather personal, and she has been badgered by salesmen and quick-buck artists. Mrs. C. was 78 in 1989, having retired from Reynolds after 38 years. She had bought her first shares of company stock on May 25, 1937. Mrs. C. knew the exact date because she recorded each stock purchase in a frayed notebook. She sold it all for $94 a share, or almost double what it had been worth a few months earlier. "Let's just say that I made several million dollars," she said.

She had no intention of moving out of the corner brick house that she and her late husband had built in 1959. Nor did she plan to trade in her three-year-old Chevrolet. She spent $3,500 on new carpet and put the rest of her money in treasury notes. "I'm just an old, plain everyday person, one of those Old Salem people," said Mrs. C., who had grown up in Salem. "I don't even feel no different. Let me tell you, honey, I always drove a Chevrolet, and I'm not going to change."

Her neighbors, Mr. and Mrs. P., had also built their house in the late 1950s. Dolls sat in small chairs that Mr. P. had made in his basement workshop for the five grandchildren. A framed saying Mrs. P. had cross-stitched hung on a wall. Home, it said, is "where you share and love and grow." The house was their home. They had raised three children there, grown old together there. They had no desire to move. "This isn't Buena Vista, but we like it here," Mrs. P. said.

That's the way it was all over town, to the chagrin of car dealers, boat salesmen, and real-estate brokers. A study by economists at the University of North Carolina later confirmed what everyone in town knew: there was no orgy of spending in Winston-Salem after the buyout, except for certificates of deposit.

Charitable foundations and churches were the exceptions. They did well after the buyout, as stockholders sought to lessen their tax burden by donating money or shares. The Winston-Salem Foundation received $1 million in company stock in two days, and the United Way of Forsyth County received about $100,000 in pledges in a fund-raiser aimed at Reynolds shareholders.

Some of the money came in handy in settling old grudges, like the one Mr. L. had against the *Winston-Salem Journal*. A longtime Reynolds employee, Mr. L. made about $800,000 from his stock, but no, he didn't want to talk to the *Journal* reporter about it. He had once submitted an article for publication, only to have it rejected by the paper's managing editor, Joe Goodman.

"You tell that ———— Joe Goodman that if I want to get a ———— article in the ———— *Winston-Salem Journal*, I'll buy a ———— page," said Mr. L., who wasn't kidding. "I'm rich now, you know."

Bringing Down the General

The local businessmen needed a name for the hotel they planned to build in Winston-Salem. "The Forsyth" seemed to be gaining favor, until Pleas Hanes, a Civil War veteran, suggested the General Robert E. Lee. What could be more fitting than to name a city's grandest hotel after the South's finest gentleman? Hanes asked. No one disagreed.

In the fall of 1921, the Hotel Robert E. Lee opened for business on the corner of Fifth and Marshall streets. For the next 51 years, it was the city's premier hotel. General Dwight D. Eisenhower stayed there. So did Vice President Hubert Humphrey. Every governor who served during the hotel's existence slept in one of its 350 rooms. The city danced the nights away on the Balinese Roof, the hotel's rooftop ballroom.

Time and changing lifestyles caught the hotel in the 1960s. Patrons preferred "motor courts" to the worn-down elegance of the Lee. The last guest checked out in February 1971.

At precisely 7:26 in the morning on March 26, 1972, the first of 300 explosive charges rocked the old hotel. It shuttered for a moment and then came down. In 8.5 seconds, 51 years of tradition was reduced to a four-story-high pile of rubble.

A new hotel was built on the site.

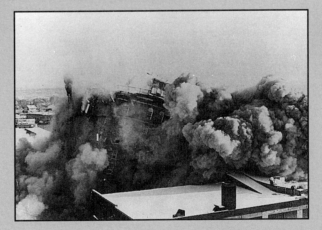

The Selling of RJR

To F. Ross Johnson, the price of RJR Nabisco stock was a report card. A high price meant the stockholders were making money and he was doing his job. Conversely, a low price meant the stockholders were unhappy, which could lead to his having to find another job. The price of the company's stock was never high enough to suit Johnson. Lesser food companies had worse years than RJR Nabisco, but their stock prices were higher. Johnson was convinced that the public's perception of tobacco was dragging down the price of his stock.

When the stock market crashed on October 19, 1987, RJR Nabisco stock, which had been trading in the mid-70s, fell to the low 40s, where it languished for weeks. Johnson began searching for a means to boost the price, such as buying another food company, entering joint ventures, or issuing different stock for food and tobacco.

The daring risk-taker took a bold approach. A year to the day after the crash, Johnson shocked Winston-Salem by announcing that he and a management team wanted to take the company private in a leveraged buyout. In such buyouts, which were in vogue on Wall Street during the go-go 1980s, some money is put down and the rest of the purchase price is financed, using the company as collateral. Costs are then slashed and assets sold off to satisfy the debt. Johnson offered the company's board of directors $75 a share, or about $17 billion.

Johnson's proposal had the result he knew it would: the company's stock, which had been selling for $56 a share, jumped $21 in one day. It also had an unexpected effect: it put the company, in the parlance of Wall Street, "in play." "The genie's out of the bottle," one company official warned Johnson, "and we'll never stuff it back again."

He was right. Wall Street investment bankers and lawyers salivated at the multimillion-dollar fees that such a buyout would generate. Others were motivated by ego, the desire to be part of what was sure to be the biggest business deal in history. The board received other offers, but the main competitors were Johnson's group and Kohlberg Kravis Roberts & Company, the New York investment firm that was the recognized leader in leveraged buyouts. It was headed by the cool and crafty Henry Kravis.

For six weeks, the two captured the nation's headlines and Winston-Salem's disgust as they put once-proud RJR Nabisco, the 19th largest corporation in America, on the auction block. Kravis finally won on November 30 with a bid of $109 a share, worth $25.4 billion. The offer was almost double the size of the previous largest takeover, and all but $5 billion of it was financed. RJR Nabisco was saddled with a debt that was more than the combined national debts of Bolivia, Uruguay, Costa Rica, and Honduras.

"It's just too big. We just don't understand it," noted Charles B. Wade, Jr., a retired company executive who had worked during the simpler days when companies existed to make things. "Here we are at the seat of the largest LBO in the world, and we just don't understand it."

The RJR Nabisco buyout came to symbolize the excesses of the 1980s, a freewheeling, freespending decade of feverish deal-making, mega-mergers, and insider trading. It was a time when, to paraphrase the sleazy Gordon Gecko in the hit movie *Wall Street*, greed was good. The RJR deal was the decade's opulent climax. Leveraged buyouts fell out of favor, and nothing like it was tried again.

Johnson resigned in February 1989, when Kravis officially took over the company. For his troubles, Johnson walked away with more than $60 million in RJR stock, bonuses, and pension payments. He also made the cover of *Time* magazine for its story on corporate greed.

As for RJR Nabisco, it became a shadow of its former self. More than 2,000 of the company's 12,000 jobs were cut when Kravis took over. With attention focused on repaying its massive debt, the company lost the leadership role it once enjoyed in the community. The days of company largess were over.

In the aftermath of the buyout, R. J. Reynolds Tobacco Company faced an even bigger threat: the rising public sentiment against smoking. People continued to light up even after the United States surgeon general issued the now-famous report on cigarettes' health effects in 1964. Evidence mounted in the 1980s about the effects of secondhand smoke on nonsmokers. Antismoking ordinances swept the country, and smokers were treated as social outcasts.

That sounded the death knell for the domestic cigarette market. Reynolds shipped a record 209 billion cigarettes in 1982, but by the end of the decade, the total was down to about 170 billion. Declining sales and the debt from the buyout forced more personnel cuts. In 1993, the company employed about 8,500 people, the lowest total in about 100 years.

An era that had begun in 1872 ended at midnight on June 29, 1990, when Reynolds workers completed their shift at Factory Number 12. That plant, the last of the dozens of tobacco factories that once dominated Winston-Salem's downtown, closed.

R. J. Reynolds, fighting the pancreatic cancer that would kill him in 1918, had surveyed his domain and been pleased. "I have written the book," the dying Reynolds said. "All you need to do is follow it." It didn't end the way he imagined.

Picking up the Pieces

The economic turmoil of the 1980s severely rocked Winston-Salem's confidence. Thousands of people lost their jobs, and many more feared pink slips with their next paycheck. An emotional debate on how to fix the city's ailing economy framed the mayoral election in 1989, probably the most divisive in the city's history.

Wayne Corpening, a popular, affable executive at First Wachovia Corporation, retired after 12 years in office. Republican Dee Smith, a businessman who had the support of the city's corporate leaders, ran against Democrat Martha S. Wood, an alderman who had made her reputation as a neighborhood activist. With the old power structure in shambles, the election became a means of gauging the direction the city would take.

The election degenerated into a bitter struggle that featured pamphlets linking Smith to the Ku Klux Klan and a billboard along Interstate 40 comparing Wood to Pinocchio. Backed by a loose coalition of blacks and neighborhood groups, and promising an open government, Wood won a narrow victory and became the city's first female mayor.

Winston-Salem turned a corner after the election. Cooperation became the new buzzword. City and county government worked with industry and the Greater Winston-Salem Chamber of Commerce to develop a strategy for economic development. Groups like Forsyth Community Development Council and Winston-Salem Business, Inc., formed to help attract new businesses.

Some stunning successes followed. New companies such as Lee Apparel, Siecor Corporation, Southern National Bank, and Pepsi-Cola opened plants, headquarters, or service centers. Existing companies expanded. James A. Gray's old bank, Wachovia, had merged with First Atlanta Corporation in 1985 to become First Wachovia, one of the 30 largest banks in the country; in 1992, it ended speculation that it might leave its home when it announced plans to build a new headquarters downtown.

Sara Lee Corporation, which had bought Hanes Corporation in 1979, expanded its textile operations and established four headquarters in Winston-Salem. It increased its employment in Forsyth County to almost 5,500 by the end of the 1980s.

Health care was by far the largest growth industry in the city during the decade. Led by Bowman Gray/Baptist Hospital Medical Center and Carolina Medicorp, Inc., which owns Forsyth Memorial Hospital, the industry came to employ almost 15,000 people, or about 10 percent of the county's work force. The medical center, with more than 8,000 employees, will certainly overtake R. J. Reynolds Tobacco Company as the city's leading employer sometime during the 1990s.

Despite citizens' angst over their city's economic condition, Winston-Salem ended up with more employers and jobs in 1990 then it had 10 years earlier. A profound change took place, however. Almost half the city's workers had at one time made something with their hands—socks, cigarettes, circuit boards. More than 13,000 factory jobs were lost in Forsyth County after 1980. They were replaced by lower-paying retail and service jobs. Though the city is still a manufacturing leader in the state, almost as many people work in stores as in factories. Service jobs—banking, legal work, health care, and the like—now make up the largest segment of the local economy.

Replacing jobs turned out to be the easy part. Finding civic leaders to fill the vacuum left when the oligarchy of businessmen collapsed has been more difficult. Winston-Salem has no

real history of governing itself. That task has always been done for it, first by the Moravian Church and then by the city's leading families and businessmen. It was a stable and efficient way of running things. Want a college? A family offered the land, others put up the money, and Wake Forest was a reality.

Democracy is messier. An issue as momentous as establishing a college now would be argued interminably by the board of aldermen. Committee reports and financial reports and environmental reports would follow. By the time it was all settled, Wake Forest would have moved to Charlotte.

That, of course, is an exaggeration, but the point is that self-government isn't easy. Winston-Salem has stumbled along this new path, but it is slowly finding its way. Groups such as Leadership Winston-Salem are tapping possible leaders of the future, and efforts at building partnerships with businesses and citizens' groups are making government more open and responsive.

Recent years have seen a good number of African-Americans appointed to city boards. Blacks now are regularly elected to the school board and the board of aldermen. The black middle class is healthier then it has ever been, and blacks have better educational and job opportunities.

Improving relations between the races remains the city's most intractable problem. A study of 1990 census figures shows that Winston-Salem has the most segregated housing pattern of all the state's large cities. Most whites live in the western part of town and most blacks in the eastern part.

Grievances against the police department led blacks to call for a citizens' board to review complaints. The issue was a daily topic around the city and split the aldermen along racial lines. The tie was broken by Mayor Wood, who voted for the board.

A black alderman complained about the city's

racial problems in a letter to the National Civic League, which was considering Winston-Salem for its 1993 All-America City award. The letter was credited with torpedoing the city's chances.

The city's rising crime rate—Winston-Salem had the greatest increase of violent crime of any large city in the state in 1993—is also a cause for concern.

Winston-Salem emerged from the 1980s a changed, but better, place.

The Greater Winston-Salem Chamber of Commerce

The solitude of Old Salem draws thousands of visitors a year.

The Greater Winston-Salem
Chamber of Commerce

Fresh fruit and vegetables are the main attractions at the City Market.

The Greater Winston-Salem
Chamber of Commerce

A Music at Sunset concert draws a crowd at Tanglewood Park.

———

The Photograph Collection, Winston-Salem/Forsyth County Public Library

Fiesta '93 showcased the culture of the city's growing Hispanic population.

———

The Greater Winston-Salem Chamber of Commerce

A morning mist engulfs fishermen at Salem Lake.

The Greater Winston-Salem Chamber of Commerce

Sunny days entice students at Wake Forest University to take a break from their studies.

The Greater Winston-Salem Chamber of Commerce

Looking to the Future

If he could take one of his walks down Winston-Salem's streets toward the close of the 20th century, James A. Gray, Jr., would immediately realize just how far the city he helped create has come. He would see a cleaner city, where black soot from R. J. Reynolds Tobacco Company's smokestacks no longer blankets the town. He would hear music tumbling from Winston Square and watch schoolchildren pile into the Stevens Center for a concert. He would marvel at the futuristic RJR Plaza and the green glass of Southern National Financial Center.

Gray would no longer know everyone he met along the way, but he would remember his old friend Archie Davis. The two would talk, Gray revealing his sadness at the demise of his tobacco company and his fears for the future of the city. Davis would comfort his friend. The city has survived, Davis would say. It was too good a city not to. The future is nothing to fear.

"We have an enviable past and an enviable character," Archie Davis has said. "I'm far from pessimistic, particularly if people handle the future as they have the past. We have great momentum."

Dates to Remember

1970   Hanes Corporation introduces L'eggs pantyhose.

1971   Tanglewood Park, near Clemmons, is integrated. The park, the former home of William N. Reynolds, opened in 1954 for whites only, according to the terms of Reynolds's will. Still a public park, Tanglewood now is run by a private corporation. Ernestine Wilson, the city's first female alderman, is elected. Under a court order, the school system approves an attendance plan that totally desegregates schools for the first time.

1972   John P. Bond III becomes the highest black in city government when he is promoted to deputy city manager. Many blacks move into high government positions in the following years, including Alexander R. Beaty, an assistant city manager, and Lester E. Ervin, who becomes the city's first black fire chief in 1980. The once-magnificent Hotel Robert E. Lee is demolished and a new hotel takes its place.

1974   The *Winston-Salem Chronicle*, a paper serving the city's black residents, begins publication.

1975   Hanes Mall opens, as does the Forsyth County Hall of Justice.

1976   The Federal Building opens.

1978   Mazie S. Woodruff becomes the first black elected to the Forsyth County Board of Commissioners.

1979   Consolidated Foods, the maker of Sara Lee products, buys Hanes Corporation.

1982   Hennis Freight Lines is the first of the city's "big three" trucking companies to become a casualty of the deregulation of the trucking industry when Spector Red Ball, its owner, declares bankruptcy. McLean Trucking goes bankrupt in 1986, and Pilot Freight Carriers shuts down three years later.

1983   North Carolina School of the Arts opens its downtown arts center, the Roger L. Stevens Center for the Performing Arts, in the remodeled Carolina Theater.

1985   R. J. Reynolds Industries, Inc., buys Nabisco Brands, Inc. The resulting company is named RJR Nabisco, Inc., the following year. Wachovia Corporation merges with First Atlanta Corporation to become First Wachovia Corporation, one of the 30 largest banks in the country.

1986   After much heated debate with racial overtones, the aldermen vote to name the new coliseum after Winston-Salem native Lawrence Joel, a black who won the Medal of Honor in Vietnam. The coliseum opens three years later. R. J. Reynolds Tobacco Company begins production at its huge plant in Tobaccoville.

1987   RJR Nabisco, Inc., shocks Winston-Salem by announcing that it will move its headquarters to Atlanta. Piedmont Airlines is bought by USAir for almost $1.6 billion; Piedmont disappears into USAir within two years. One Triad Park's blue glass building becomes the latest edition to the city's skyline.

1988   AT&T announces that it will close its giant plant on Lexington Road, costing the city about 3,300 jobs; by the end of 1989, only 400 people work in the plant. Wake Forest University hosts a presidential debate between Vice President George Bush and Democratic candidate Governor Michael Dukakis of Massachusetts.

1989   Kohlberg Kravis Roberts & Company buys RJR Nabisco, Inc. The $25-billion leveraged buyout is the largest in history and comes to symbolize the corporate greed of the 1980s. Martha S. Wood is elected the city's first female mayor.

1992   The long-awaited Interstate 40 Bypass opens south of Winston-Salem, easing congestion through downtown. The 24.4-mile section of road costs almost $191 million and takes five years to build. First Wachovia Corporation announces that it will build a 28-story headquarters building downtown. Construction starts in 1994.

1993   Southern National Corporation moves the headquarters of its North Carolina bank to One Triad Plaza. The building is renamed Southern National Financial Center. Pepsi-Cola announces that it will open a service center in Winston-Salem that will employ 1,000 people.

Names to Know

Maya Angelou
A woman of many talents, Angelou has been a singer, a dancer, an author, an actress, a playwright, and a teacher. A professor at Wake Forest University since 1982, Angelou is best known as a poet. She was chosen by President-elect Bill Clinton to recite a poem at his inauguration in 1993.

Beaufort Bailey
In 1974, Bailey became the first black elected to the school board. He lost in 1978 but won election to the board four years later. His loss in 1990 prompted the state legislature to adopt a district plan that ensures black representation on the school board.

Wayne A. Corpening
Probably no one was more loyal to Winston-Salem then Corpening. The city's mayor for 12 years starting in 1977, Corpening was an old-fashioned guy from Henderson County. Quiet and unassuming, he lived according to the plaque that sat on his desk: "There's no limit to what a man can do or where he can go if he doesn't mind who gets the credit." Without much fanfare or publicity, Corpening pushed for the completion of Interstate 40 Bypass, a new coliseum, a new sewer plant, and One Triad Plaza. The plaza at the building was named after Corpening.

John Ehle
Ehle is a writer whose books have won numerous prizes, including the Sir Walter Raleigh Award for fiction (five times) and the North Carolina Award for Literature. He has reached beyond his craft, however, to leave an indelible mark on North Carolina. As an assistant to Governor Terry Sanford in the mid-1960s, Ehle helped start the first state antipoverty program in the country, the North Carolina School of the Arts, the Governor's School for gifted children, and several other organizations and institutes. A former professor at the University of North Carolina at Chapel Hill, Ehle has lived in Winston-Salem with his wife, actress Rosemary Harris, since 1964.

Carl Eller
One of the Minnesota Vikings' famed "Fearsome Foursome," Eller starred for 15 years in the National Football League. He grew up in Winston-Salem and graduated from Atkins High School in 1960.

Clarence "Bighouse" Gaines
It was said that there were two things to fear at Winston-Salem State University: God and Bighouse. Gaines was athletic director and head basketball coach at the school for 47 years before retiring in 1993. He won more games during his career than any active basketball coach and is second on the list of lifetime victories. He has been inducted into the National Basketball Hall of Fame.

R. Philip Hanes, Jr.
Described as the father of the community arts movement, Hanes is credited with helping start 16 arts organizations in the United States and has served on the boards of 19 others. In Winston-Salem, the energetic Hanes helped found Piedmont Opera and the Southeastern Center for Contemporary Art. He was instrumental in raising money for North Carolina School of the Arts, the Roger L. Stevens Center for the Performing Arts, Winston Square, and the renovation of Brookstown Mill. Hanes, chairman emeritus of Hanes Companies, Inc., has received three presidential appointments to national arts boards and was given the National Medal of Arts by President George Bush in 1991. His personal contributions to the arts exceed $10 million. In 1993, Hanes gave Wake Forest University his home on Robinhood Road and his vast art collection.

Dr. Richard Janeway
He came to Bowman Gray School of Medicine in 1963 as a neurologist. After being named dean in 1971, Janeway remained at the helm for 23 years, the longest tenure of any medical-school dean in the country. By the time he retired as dean in 1994, the school and Baptist Hospital had joined to form a medical center that spread across Hawthorne Hill and was the second-largest employer in the city.

F. Ross Johnson
Probably the most disliked man in Winston-Salem, Johnson earned the lasting enmity of city residents when he kicked a century of tradition in the gut and moved the headquarters of RJR Nabisco, Inc., from Winston-Salem to Atlanta. Johnson dropped his bombshell only 15 days after becoming the company's chief executive officer in 1987. A year later, Johnson started a feeding frenzy when he formed a management team that offered to purchase the company in a leveraged buyout. A bidding war between Johnson's team and other suitors ended when Kohlberg Kravis Roberts & Company bought RJR Nabisco in the largest leveraged buyout in history. Johnson pocketed an estimated $61 million.

Annie Brown Kennedy
Kennedy was appointed to fill a vacancy in the North Carolina House of Representatives in 1979, becoming the first black woman to serve in the General Assembly. Defeated in 1980, Kennedy won two years later and served in the legislature until her retirement in 1994. In Raleigh, she was a passionate advocate for affirmative action, women's rights, and minority representation on local boards. An attorney since 1954, Kennedy was the first black female lawyer in Winston-Salem and the second in the state.

John G. Medlin, Jr.
Medlin built a reputation as one of the country's most respected bankers during his 17 years at the top of Wachovia Corporation. When Medlin became the bank's chief executive in 1977, Wachovia had assets of $3.3 billion and branches only in North Carolina. When he retired in 1994, the bank's assets had increased tenfold, and Wachovia had more than 500 branches in North Carolina and Georgia.

Paul M. Wiles
The baby-faced Wiles became president and chief executive officer of Carolina Medicorp, Inc., and Forsyth Memorial Hospital in 1984, when he was just 37. Under his leadership, the hospital ex-

panded to more than 1,200 beds and added a Women's Center, new operating rooms, a new intensive-care unit, and a technology building. CMI, the not-for-profit corporation that owns the hospital, became a far-flung medical empire under Wiles. It built a nursing home and an outpatient surgical center on hospital grounds and a medical complex in Kernersville. The company also bought Medical Park Hospital, across Hawthorne Road from Forsyth Memorial Hospital.

Louise G. Wilson
One of the city's most influential advocates for the poor, Wilson was the executive director of the Experiment of Self-Reliance for 17 years. A former teacher, she also worked tirelessly to register black voters.

Martha S. Wood
An alderman for eight years, Wood narrowly won election as the first female mayor of Winston-Salem in 1989, after a divisive campaign that alienated the city's businessmen. Her administration, stressing openness and diversity, symbolized the new direction of the city after the demise of the oligarchy of businessmen that once ran Winston-Salem.

Mazie S. Woodruff
The first black to serve on the county commissioners, Woodruff was elected in 1978. She lost her seat in 1986 and was reelected in 1990.

Bibliography

Books and Pamphlets

Beatty, Jerome, Jr. *Our 100th Anniversary, 1875–1975*. Winston-Salem: R.J. Reynolds Industries, Inc., 1975.

Burrough, Bryan, and John Helyar. *Barbarians at the Gate: The Fall of RJR Nabisco*. New York: HarperCollins, 1990.

Clewell, John Henry. *History of Wachovia in North Carolina*. New York: Doubleday, Page & Company, 1902.

Crews, C. Daniel, ed. and trans. *Bethania: A Fresh Look at Its Birth*. Winston-Salem: Archives of the Moravian Church, Southern Province, 1993.

Crow, Jeffrey J., and Mark A. Mathis, eds. *The Prehistory of North Carolina, An Archaeological Symposium*. Raleigh: North Carolina Division of Archives and History, 1983.

Crow, Jeffrey J., Paul D. Escott, and Flora J. Hatley. *A History of African-Americans in North Carolina*. Raleigh: North Carolina Division of Archives and History, 1992.

Davis, Chester. *Hidden Seed and Harvest: A History of the Moravians*. Winston-Salem: Wachovia Historical Society, 1959.

Foltz, Henry W. *Winston Fifty Years Ago*. Winston-Salem: privately published, 1926.

Forsyth Centennial Committee. *The First 100 Years: Program for Forsyth Centennial and Piedmont Festival, 1849–1949*. Winston-Salem: Forsyth Centennial Committee, 1949.

Fries, Adelaide L. *Forsyth: A County on the March*. Chapel Hill: University of North Carolina Press, 1949.

Fries, Adelaide L., J. Edwin Hendricks, and Thurman Wright. *Forsyth: The History of a County on the March*. Chapel Hill: University of North Carolina Press, 1976.

Fries, Adelaide L., Kenneth G. Hamilton, Minnie J. Smith, and Douglas L. Rights, eds. *Records of the Moravians of North Carolina*. 11 vols. Raleigh: North Carolina Historical Commission, 1922–1969.

Glass, Brent D. *The Textile Industry in North Carolina*. Raleigh: North Carolina Division of Archives and History, 1992.

Griffin, Frances, ed. *Three Forks of Muddy Creek*. Winston-Salem: Old Salem, Inc., 1974.

Hanes Corporation. *The Hanes Story*. Winston-Salem: Hanes Corporation, 1965.

Helman, Robert K. *Tobacco and Americans*. New York: McGraw-Hill, 1960.

James, Hunter. *The Quiet People of the Land: A*

Story of the North Carolina Moravians in Revolutionary Times. Chapel Hill: University of North Carolina Press, 1976.

Lawson, John. *A New Voyage to Carolina*. Chapel Hill: University of North Carolina Press, 1967.

Lefler, Hugh T., and Albert R. Newsome. *North Carolina: The History of a Southern State*. Chapel Hill: University of North Carolina Press, 1973.

Linn, Jo White. *The Gray Family and Allied Lines*. Salisbury, N.C.: privately published, 1976.

———. *People Named Hanes*. Salisbury, N.C.: privately published, 1980.

Meads, Manson. *The Miracle on Hawthorne Hill*. Winston-Salem: Wake Forest University, 1986.

Neilson, Robert W., ed. *History of Government, City of Winston-Salem, N.C.* Winston-Salem: 200th Anniversary Committee, 1966.

Newbold, N. C., ed. *Five North Carolina Negro Educators*. Chapel Hill: University of North Carolina Press, 1939.

Norfolk and Western Railway. *The Twin Cities: Souvenir Edition of Headlight—Sights and Scenes Along the Norfolk and Western Railway*. Roanoke, Va.: Stone Printing and Manufacturing Company, c. 1900.

P. H. Hanes Knitting Company. *Historical Sketches of P. H. Hanes Knitting Co.* Winston-Salem: P. H. Hanes Knitting Company, 1934.

Perdue, Theda. *North Carolinians: The Indians of North Carolina*. Raleigh: North Carolina Division of Archives and History, 1985.

Pfohl, J. Kenneth. *Memorabilia of the Salem Congregation, 1931–1961*. Winston-Salem: Goslen Printing Company, 1993.

Powell, William S. *North Carolina: A History*. New York: W. W. Norton, 1977.

———. *North Carolina Through Four Centuries*. Chapel Hill: University of North Carolina Press, 1989.

Ramsey, Robert W. *Carolina Cradle: Settlement of the Northwest Carolina Frontier, 1747–1761*.

Chapel Hill: University of North Carolina Press, 1964.

Raynor, George. *Pioneers and Indians of Back Country North Carolina*. Salisbury, N.C.: Salisbury Printing Company, 1990.

Reynolds, Patrick, and Tom Shachtman. *The Gilded Leaf: Triumph, Tragedy, and Tobacco—Three Generations of the R. J. Reynolds Family and Fortune*. Boston: Little, Brown, 1989.

Rights, Douglas L. *The American Indian in North Carolina*, 2d ed. Winston-Salem: John F. Blair, Publisher, 1988.

Robbins, David P. *A Descriptive Sketch of Winston-Salem, N.C.* Winston, N.C.: Chamber of Commerce, c. 1888.

Robertson, Stewart, Jr. *My Friend Marshall*. Charlotte: Heritage Printers, 1978.

Rogers, Floyd. *Yadkin Passage*. Raleigh: Winston-Salem Journal and the North Carolina Department of Natural Resources and Community Development, 1982.

Rondthaler, Edward. *Appendix to the Memorabilia of Fifty Years, Containing Memorabilia of 1928, 1929, 1930*. Raleigh: Edwards & Broughton Company, 1931.

———. *The Memorabilia of Fifty Years, 1877–1927*. Raleigh: Edwards & Broughton Company, 1928.

Rouse, Parke, Jr. *The Great Wagon Road*. New York: McGraw-Hill, 1973.

Schattschneider, Allen W. *Through Five Hundred Years*. Bethlehem, Pa.: Comenius Press, 1956.

Sensbach, Jon. *African-Americans in Salem*. Winston-Salem: Old Salem, Inc., 1992.

South, Stanley A. *Indians of North Carolina*. Raleigh: North Carolina Division of Archives and History, 1970.

Taylor, Gwynne Stephens. *From Frontier to Factory: An Architectural History of Forsyth County*. Raleigh: North Carolina Division of Archives and History, 1981.

Tilley, Nannie. *The R. J. Reynolds Tobacco Story*. Chapel Hill: University of North Carolina Press, 1985.

Tise, Larry E., et al. *Winston-Salem in History*. 13 vols. Winston-Salem: Historic Winston-Salem, 1976.

Van Noppen, Ina Woestemeyer. *Stoneman's Last Raid*. Raleigh: North Carolina State College Print Shop, 1961.

Wetmore, Ruth Y. *First on the Land: The North Carolina Indians*. Winston-Salem: John F. Blair, Publisher, 1975.

Wilson, Emily Herring. *For the People of North Carolina: The Z. Smith Reynolds Foundation at Half-Century, 1936–1986*. Chapel Hill: University of North Carolina Press, 1988.

Winston Board of Trade. *Facts About Winston-Salem*. 1906. Pamphlet describing business in Winston.

Winston-Salem Business, Inc. *Winston-Salem, North Carolina: A Closer Look*. Winston-Salem, N.C.: 1989.

Winston-Salem Chamber of Commerce. *Winston-Salem, North Carolina*. 1925. Booklet describing the city.

Woodall, J. Ned. *Archaeological Investigations in the Yadkin River Valley*. North Carolina Archaeological Council Publication No. 25. Raleigh: North Carolina Archaeological Council and the North Carolina Division of Archives and History, 1990.

———. *The Donnaha Site: 1973, 1975 Excavations*. North Carolina Archaeological Council Publication No. 22. Raleigh: North Carolina Archaeological Council and the North Carolina Division of Archives and History, 1984.

Woodward, C. Vann. *The Strange Career of Jim Crow*. New York: Oxford University Press, 1974.

Magazine Articles

Africa, Philip. "Slaveholding in the Salem Community, 1771–1851." *North Carolina Historical Review* (July 1977).

Billenger, Robert D. "Behind the Wire: German Prisoners of War at Camp Sutton, 1944–1946." *North Carolina Historical Review* (October 1984).

Foley, Dan. "Death's Moanin' Low." *Real Detective* (October 1932).

Fracaro, Angela. "A Mansion That Lives for Art." *The State* (November 1988).

Howell, Charles D., and Donald C. Dearborn. "The Excavation of an Indian Village on the Yadkin River Near Trading Ford." *Southern Indian Studies* 5 (October 1953).

Jeffrey, Thomas E. "'Our Remarkable Friendship': The Collaboration of Calvin H. Wiley and John C. Cunningham." *North Carolina Historical Review* (January 1990).

Kuykendall, R. L. "The History of Education in Forsyth County." *North Carolina Education* (February 1945).

LeMieux, Liuda. "The Salem Waterworks." *Chronicle of Early American Industries Association* (January 1981).

Lewis, Johanna Miller. "A Social and Architectural History of the Girls' Boarding School Building at Salem, N.C." *North Carolina Historical Review* (April 1989).

———. "Women Artisans in Backcountry North Carolina, 1753–1790." *North Carolina Historical Review* (July 1991).

MacNeill, Ben Dixon. "The Town of a Hundred Millionaires." *North American Review* (August 1930).

McAllister, Donald Steven, and Marcus B. Simpson, Jr. "Alexander Wilson's Southern Tour of 1809: North Carolina Transit and Subscribers to American Ornithology." *North Carolina Historical Review* (October 1986).

Rice, Prudence M., E. Pendleton Banks, and Robert E. Pace. "Contact Zones and Eastern U.S. History: Evidence From a Piedmont Rock Shelter." *Southern Indian Studies* (October 1972).

Rogers, Rhea. "The Clans of Passage." *Wake*

Forest University Magazine 40 (December 1992).

Rouse, Parke, Jr. "The Great Wagon Road." *The State* (June 1, 1972).

Shirley, Michael. "Yeoman Culture and Millworker Protest in Antebellum Salem, North Carolina." *Journal of Southern History* (August 1991).

Smith, Margaret Supplee. "Reynolda: A Rural Vision in an Industrializing South." *North Carolina Historical Review* (July 1988).

Tanja, Kim Johnson. "Morrison's Cafe: A Study of Community and Social Change in Winston-Salem." *North Carolina Folklore Journal* (Winter-Spring 1987).

Thorpe, Daniel B. "The City That Never Was: Count von Zinzendorf's Original Plan for Salem." *North Carolina Historical Review* (January 1984).

Newspapers

Clemmons Courier
Greensboro News & Record
Kernersville Times
People's Press
Salem Gleaner
Twin-City Sentinel
Union Republican
Western Sentinel
Winston-Salem Chronicle
Winston-Salem Journal

Government Reports

City of Winston-Salem. *The General Ordinances and The Charter of the City of Winston-Salem, North Carolina, 1916.* Winston-Salem: 1916.

City-County Planning Board. *Vision 2005: A Comprehensive Plan for Forsyth County, North Carolina.* Winston-Salem: 1988.

Oppermann, Langdon E. "Winston-Salem's African-American Neighborhoods: 1870–1950." Report for the City-County Planning Board. Winston-Salem: 1993.

Town of Winston. *Ordinances and Regulations of the Town of Winston, 1873.*

Town of Winston. *Ordinances of the Town of Winston, 1879.*

U.S. Bureau of the Census. *1980 Census of Population and Housing.* Washington: 1983.

U.S. Bureau of the Census. *1990 Census of Population and Housing.* Washington: 1991.

U.S. Census Office. *Fifth Census, 1830.*

U.S. Census Office. *Sixth Census, 1840.*

U.S. Census Office. *Seventh Census, 1850.*

U.S. Census Office. *Eighth Census, 1860.*

U.S. Census Office. *Ninth Census, 1870.*

U.S. Census Office. *Tenth Census, 1880.*

Winston Board of School Commissioners. *29th Annual Report of the Public Schools of the City of Winston, N.C., 1912–1913.*

Winston Board of School Commissioners. *The Winston Schools, 1894–1895.* Annual report of the board.

Winston-Salem Fire Department. *Winston-Salem Fire Department, 1913–1992.* Dallas: Taylor Publishing Company, 1992.

Unpublished Works

Ad Hoc Committee for St. Philip's Moravian Church. "Preserving St. Philip's." Report to Old Salem, Inc., July 1992.

Bagge, Traugott. "A Memorial." Archives of the Moravian Church, Southern Province, Winston-Salem.

Barnette, Karen L. "Woodland Subsistence-Settlement Patterns in the Great Bend Area, Yadkin River Valley, North Carolina." Master's thesis, Wake Forest University, 1978.

Benzein, Christian Lewis, John Daniel Koehler, and Frederic William Marshall. "The Brethren's Address to President Washington."

Original text of the speech made to President George Washington on his visit to Salem, June 1, 1791. Archives of the Moravian Church, Southern Province, Winston-Salem.

Blum, Edward. "Last Years of the War: Stoneman's Raid in N.C." Archives of the Moravian Church, Southern Province, Winston-Salem.

Casstevens, Frances H. "The Great Philadelphia Wagon Road." Research paper for the Yadkin County Historical Society, 1986.

Cross, Jerry L. "The John Kelly Tavern." Research report for the North Carolina Division of Archives and History, 1992.

Eaton, Clement. "Winston-Salem in the First Quarter of the 20th Century: A Recollection." Southern Historical Collection, University of North Carolina at Chapel Hill, 1976.

Fries, Adelaide. "Winston-Salem." Archives of the Moravian Church, Southern Province, Winston-Salem, 1895.

Fries, Francis L. "Woolen mill diary, 1840–42." North Carolina Baptist Collection, Z. Smith Reynolds Library, Wake Forest University.

Fries, John Christian William, and Johanna Nissen. Letters to their son, Francis Levin Fries, 1827–1832. Archives of the Moravian Church, Southern Province, Winston-Salem.

Glenn, Joanne. "The Winston-Salem Riot of 1918." Master's thesis, University of North Carolina at Chapel Hill, 1979.

Gray, Thomas A. "Graylyn, A Norman Revival Estate in North Carolina." Master's thesis, University of Delaware, 1974.

Hancock, Beverlye H. "Skeletal Analysis of the Donnaha Site, Yadkin County, North Carolina." Master's thesis, Wake Forest University, 1987.

"The Industrial Development of Wachovia up to the Beginning of the Civil War." Archives of the Moravian Church, Southern Province, Winston-Salem.

Jones family papers. Personal letters and diaries of Dr. Beverly and Julia Conrad Jones, 1860—1865. Southern Historical Collection, University of North Carolina at Chapel Hill.

Lehman, O. J. "Reminiscences, 1857—1904." Archives of the Moravian Church, Southern Province, Winston-Salem.

Leinbach, Johann Heinrich. Diary. Archives of Old Salem, Inc., Winston-Salem.

Lineback, Julius A. "The 26th Regimental Band: Being a History of the Military Band Attached to the 26th Regiment, N.C. Troops, 1862—1865." Southern Historical Collection, University of North Carolina at Chapel Hill, 1904.

Marshall, Frederic William. "Historical Account of the Beginning and Progress of the Settlement of the Brethren in Wachovia, 1753–1775." Archives of the Moravian Church, Southern Province, Winston-Salem.

Martin, Nancy Stockton. "Changing Times." North Carolina Room, Winston-Salem/Forsyth County Public Library, c. 1975.

McCuiston, Margaret Blair. Recollections of the last reunion of the 26th North Carolina Regiment in a letter to Archie K. Davis, May 29, 1975. Southern Historical Collection, University of North Carolina at Chapel Hill.

Meyer, Rod. "The 1752–1771 Great Wagon Road Through Forsyth County." Manuscript of a speech given April 16, 1992. In author's possession.

Mikell, Gregory A. "The Donnaha Site: Late Woodland Period Subsistence and Ecology." Master's thesis, Wake Forest University, 1987.

Miller, Bertha. "Blacks in Winston-Salem, N.C., 1895–1920: Community Development in an Era of Benevolent Paternalism." Ph.D. diss., Duke University, 1981.

Neilson, Robert W. "The Story of the Water Supply System in the Town of Salem, N.C.,

1778–1913." Private research paper. Archives of the Moravian Church, Southern Province, Winston-Salem.

Rapport, Leonard. "People in Tobacco." Unpublished manuscript for the Federal Writers Project. Southern Historical Collection, University of North Carolina at Chapel Hill, c. 1945.

Reese, Nora Lee Rogers. "The Moravian Attitude Toward the Negro and Slavery." Research paper. Old Salem, Inc., 1965.

Reichel. Travel diary from Lititz, Pa., to Salem, N.C., May 22 to June 15, 1780. Archives of the Moravian Church, Southern Province, Winston-Salem.

Reynolds, G. Galloway. "The Shallow Ford: A National Historic Site." Private research paper. Lewisville, N.C., 1989. In author's possession.

Rice, William. Untitled research paper on black history in Winston-Salem. North Carolina Room, Winston-Salem/Forsyth County Library, 1991.

Roberson, Houston. "A History of the Kate Bitting Reynolds Memorial Hospital." Master's thesis, Wake Forest University, 1983.

Shaffner family papers. Personal letters and diaries of John Francis and Carolyn Fries Shaffner, 1861–1866. Southern Historical Collection, University of North Carolina at Chapel Hill.

Shirley, James Martin. "From Congregation Town to Industrial City: Industrialization, Class and Culture in 19th Century Winston and Salem, North Carolina." Ph.D. diss., Emory University, 1986.

Snider, J. R. Untitled history of the Winston-Salem Police Department. Winston-Salem, 1993. In author's possession.

Tobacco Workers International Union letter to members, July 17, 1944. Myron Howard Ross Collection, Southern Historical Collection, University of North Carolina at Chapel Hill.

Wall, Carolyn. "Urban Idealism: Winston-Salem's Search for the Good City." Master's thesis, Wake Forest University, 1974.

Washington, George. "The Reply to the Brethren." Original text of the speech Washington made in Salem on June 1, 1791. Archives of the Moravian Church, Southern Province, Winston-Salem.

Wilson, Jack Hubert, Jr. "A Study of the Late Prehistoric, Protohistoric, and Historic Indians of the Carolina and Virginia Piedmont." Ph.D. diss., University of North Carolina at Chapel Hill, 1983.

Index